The AI Partner

Alon Y. Halevy

ISBN 978-0-9847715-2-3

Cover design and illustrations by Melisa Machuret. Some images were created by Nano Banana.

Printed in the United States of America

First Edition

Dedication

To Ylva, Karina, Kasper, and Emmy —
the people who give meaning to my life.

1. A Vision for Wellbeing with AI

In the past couple of decades, our lives have become increasingly intertwined with digital systems that quietly record many aspects of our day. They note our purchases, movie viewings and preferences, reading and music logs, exercise routines, sleep patterns, and the highlights of every trip or restaurant outing we take. If you're among the early adopters of smart glasses, you're carrying a device capable of capturing everything you see, gaze at, and experience throughout the day. In a parallel and mostly unrelated development, we have recently been given the ability to converse with AI chatbots on virtually any topic that crosses our mind, an idea that was considered science fiction a mere decade ago. These chatbots can help us find information, ideate on our work, and even give us life advice.

These two developments, the recording of our lives and the ability to chat with AI, aren't going to slow down over the coming years. More aspects of our personal data and experiences will be recorded, and the ability of AI systems to converse, think, and plan will become even more sophisticated. This raises a profound question: will these two technologies come together to provide us a highly personal AI companion, a companion that will be an indispensable partner that is dedicated to dramatically improving our well-being? The vision of such a companion has been portrayed fictionally over the years in literature and cinema. Recent developments in personalizing AI chatbots certainly point towards that way. But can it finally become a reality? And if so, what will these companions look like?

This book tackles this question head on. Before we delve into the topic, let's envision a possible scenario illustrating the role that an AI partner can play in our future lives. For illustration, we will depict the life of Lisa, a fictional single woman who lives in a big city, but you can imagine any other persona instead of her.

A possible future

Upon awakening, Lisa is greeted by the soft and reassuring voice of her AI partner, Pat. Overnight, Pat has collected a handful of important updates, but understands that this early hour of the day is not the best time to share them with Lisa. Instead, Pat eases Lisa into her usual morning routine. First, a few minutes of meditation, a practice Lisa values for its grounding effect, followed by her daily workout. Without prompting, Pat gently reminds her of the workout plan they discussed the night before, subtly adjusted based on Lisa's excellent sleep quality. Today's session has been fine-tuned to energize without strain, keeping in mind the longer run she's preparing for this weekend.

The breakfast is equally thoughtful. Although Lisa prefers a simple meal, it is tailored to her activities of the day, balanced to offset the indulgent, carbohydrate-heavy dinner she enjoyed with friends the night before. On many mornings, Pat enlists the coffee robot to brew her favorite cup, but today Lisa decides to take a more hands-on approach. The ritual of grinding beans and brewing coffee is something she cherishes from time to time. Though she fumbles and spills a few beans in the process, she does not mind—after all, the robot can handle the cleanup. Lisa focuses instead on the craft itself, including the pleasures of smelling the aroma of the ground beans and rapid bubbling when the hot water is poured over them. She is relishing the small satisfaction of creating something by hand in an otherwise automated world.

Once Lisa is seated for breakfast, savoring her first few sips of coffee, Pat decides it is the right moment to deliver the morning updates. These include a selection of news items tailored to Lisa's interests, a couple of sports scores, and two changes to her schedule for the day. But Pat doesn't stop at the surface; it provides context. For example, one of the sports scores is bound to fuel a lively debate at the office, where two long-time colleagues are passionate rivals. Meanwhile, a news story out of Vietnam might personally affect Lisa's coworker Anh, and Pat suggests she check in to ensure everything is alright with her family. It's not just information—it's actionable insight, helping Lisa navigate her day with thoughtfulness and ease.

With the updates complete, Lisa spends the rest of breakfast immersed in a selection of articles Pat has curated for her. Today's recommendations align with her current interests and future goals: a review of a new exhibit by an artist she admired a few years ago, an article on behavioral psychology that ties into her ongoing course, and a review of a cutting-edge home cleaning robot. Each choice reflects an intimate understanding of Lisa's preferences and priorities.

The robot review prompts a wave of nostalgia. Lisa remembers the early days of AI assistants—tools that often felt less like partners and more like pushy sales agents. Back then, it was not unusual to receive irrelevant or even suspiciously self-serving recommendations, leaving you wondering whether your assistant worked for you or for advertisers promoting their products. Those early models, while free and still widely used, presented a trade-off: convenience at the cost of trust. Modern AI companions like Pat are different, designed to put users first. This shift comes at a price, but over the years that price has become affordable for a sizable fraction of the population and well worth the peace of mind and the benefits they provide. To help fund AI assistants for people with fewer means, Pat's model offers a "pay it forward" feature, where she can contribute funds to subsidize AI access for others. Lisa has found it remarkably easy to donate when the cost is framed as "the price of a cup of coffee." In some countries, there has also been discussion of making AI agents a free social benefit.

To be sure the cleaning robot recommendation wasn't a misstep, Lisa asks Pat why it surfaced. Pat explains its reasoning: Lisa has recently voiced frustration about keeping her floors tidy between professional cleanings. Additionally, her friend Oliver's birthday is approaching, and Lisa has a habit of giving creative, thoughtful gifts. The cleaning robot could serve both as a practical solution for her and an original gift idea for Oliver. Lisa smiles, appreciating Pat's knack for weaving small details into actionable suggestions that seamlessly fit her life.

When Lisa finishes her breakfast, a driverless taxi is already waiting outside to take her to her first appointment. As she settles into the soft music in the car, she continues listening to content Pat recommended earlier. Lisa feels good about her day ahead, confident in the schedule Pat has crafted. It is thoughtfully designed to address her most pressing priorities while carving out time for reflection and casual interactions with her colleagues. Pat also scheduled a quick 15-minute check-in at 2 p.m., perfectly timed after her afternoon espresso break. The first meeting on her morning agenda, however, promises to be a delicate conversation with a colleague, so Pat offers guidance on how to frame her thoughts and choose words that would land well. It's a skill Lisa is particularly grateful for—especially since it was Pat's help that landed her this job in the first place.

A year ago, Lisa was at a crossroads, unsure of her next career move. Pat had stepped in to help her untangle her thoughts, define her core values, and pinpoint what she truly wanted from her work. Then, leveraging its vast access to data, Pat sifted through thousands of job listings and cross-referenced them with information it could find about company cultures, narrowing the field to roles that aligned perfectly with Lisa's aspirations. The clarity Pat provided during that process was transformative, and Lisa credits it as a turning point in her professional life.

Later in the day, during their scheduled check-in, Pat and Lisa discuss a few unresolved items. First on the list: choosing a location for dinner with Oliver. Pat suggests familiar options—either their favorite sushi spot or the upscale Italian restaurant, but Lisa pushes back, telling Pat that she's ready for something new. Pat proposes a Georgian restaurant that recently opened, a bit outside their usual routine. Curious, Lisa asks if she and Oliver have ever tried anything similar. Pat recalls a Turkish restaurant they visited during a trip to Portland last year and suggests it is the closest comparison. Lisa approves the choice, and Pat books a reservation. Before Lisa can ask, Pat goes a step further, generating a personalized menu tailored to her preferences, flagging dishes she's likely to enjoy and those she might want to avoid due to her allergies or texture aversions.

As the conversation winds down, Lisa anticipates Pat's next question. Pat often checks if she's in the mood to explore outside her comfort zone in other areas of her life, a stark contrast to earlier AI models, which lacked the ability to consider her holistic well-being. Lisa appreciates this feature because, while she occasionally craves novelty, she is not always sure where to start. Whether it's trying a new cuisine, delving into an unfamiliar movie genre, or planning a trip to an unconventional destination, Pat excels at weaving these exploratory choices into the rhythm of Lisa's life. This skill is especially valuable during her travels, where Pat transforms an unfamiliar city into a curated experience delivered via her smart glasses. From recommending hidden cafes to crafting walking routes through vibrant neighborhoods and charming alleys, Pat enhances each moment with insights and discoveries, making exploration effortless.

For now, though, Lisa preempts the question. "Let's stay in my comfort zone until the end of the week," she says, "but we should brainstorm some creative options for the weekend." Pat doesn't miss a beat. "Do you have any plans you'd like me to work on for you?" it asks. Lisa thinks for a moment. "Yes," she replies. "I need to get out of my bubble and do something for others." Pat processes this and presents a few options. "How about taking your niece Tara out for the day? You really enjoyed your last outing with her, and you've expressed wanting to strengthen that bond. Plus, your sister mentioned she could use a break." Another suggestion: Lisa's neighbor Jo, who recently asked for her advice on job hunting. "Jo's brought you some delicious baked treats in the past," Pat reminds her, "so perhaps she could offer you some tips on simple dessert ideas in return."

Lisa lights up at these suggestions and asks Pat to schedule them. After a brief pause, though, she adds a caveat. "If I do all that, will I still have time to make progress on my behavioral psychology studies? My learning goals are really important to me." Pat reassures her. "You're ahead of schedule," it says, highlighting the hours Lisa has already devoted to the course over recent weekends. The program itself is carefully designed to align with Lisa's existing knowledge and interests, but Pat has also been subtly embedding opportunities to practice the material in her daily life. At work, Lisa has experimented with how people respond to positive versus negative reinforcement, and in her personal routines, she's applied habit-formation techniques. These seamless integrations have helped Lisa absorb concepts far beyond what she initially imagined, leaving her feeling both accomplished and inspired.

Satisfied, Lisa thanks Pat, feeling confident in the balance of her commitments. Moments like this remind her how indispensable Pat has become—not just as a tool, but as a partner in shaping her life.

Lisa has always been amazed by how seamlessly Pat helps her navigate the intricate web of relationships in her life. Whether it's being attentive to her friends' needs or connecting her with the right people to address her own, Pat's thoughtful insights make Lisa feel both supported and proactive. For years, balancing the demands of her relationships with her personal goals and values felt overwhelming, but Pat has become an invaluable partner in aligning these competing priorities. It's a level of harmony Lisa once thought was out of reach.

Before wrapping up their check-in, Lisa remembers that her friend Jose recently asked for advice about Tokyo, knowing she's visited the city many times. She asks Pat to share a curated list of her favorite cafes and restaurants from the past five years. "Just make sure nothing private is included," Lisa adds, confident in Pat's ability to handle the request with discretion. Moments like this remind her of how Pat turns potentially time-consuming tasks into quick, effortless actions, freeing her up to focus on other things.

As the check-in ends, Lisa reflects on the journey she's had with Pat. In the beginning, she was deeply skeptical. While she trusted Pat's assurances about data privacy and felt reassured that she could control what to share and with whom, the idea of an AI knowing so much about her—her health, finances, relationships (even her most personal ones), and a constant stream of real-time metrics—was unnerving. Of course, Lisa had always stored sensitive data with trusted cloud services, but the thought of fusing all that information together into a single, deeply personalized intelligence felt like crossing a line. It wasn't something she was ready for on day one.

Pat, however, understood her hesitations and never pushed too hard. Instead, it started small, proving its reliability over time. As their partnership deepened and Pat earned her trust, Lisa began to notice gaps in its understanding—gaps that could be easily filled if she chose to share more. Bit by bit, she opened up, finding the benefits outweighed her concerns. Still, Lisa keeps certain things to herself. Some are small moments of vulnerability she's not yet ready to share; others are things she's not particularly proud of, and she's unsure how Pat might handle them or how they could resurface in future interactions. Even so, Lisa feels secure in the knowledge that her boundaries are respected, and she appreciates the balance she's found between transparency and privacy.

Your first reaction to this above scenario might be that Lisa sounds like a privileged person, typical of what you may find around Silicon Valley, and therefore question whether the vision extends beyond the inhabitants of the tech bubble. Point noted. However, taking a deeper look reveals that Pat helped Lisa with issues that concern the vast majority of humanity, such as spending our time effectively, handling the relationships and family ties in our life, making employment choices and finding activities that bring meaning to our life. This book outlines a vision designed to support that broad spectrum of humanity.

Back to the present

The above description of Lisa's life represents one vision we may aspire to for AI partners. Before we discuss its merits, risks and how to achieve it, let us contrast it with what Lisa is likely experiencing today.

It was ten minutes to midnight when Lisa glanced at her fitness tracker and realized that she had only done 9900 steps that day. She was spending a bit more time on the couch this evening because she had just run a half marathon the day before, which of course, her running app knew about. What an odd situation she realized, where one app is celebrating yesterday's achievement while the other is nudging her about a looming failure! Two separate apps, both designed for her physical well-being, seemingly working against each other. But a voice in her head really didn't want to *disappoint* the fitness app by not completing the daily 10,000 steps. Exasperated, mostly with herself, she got up, assuring herself that it's just a matter of three more laps around her living room and two around her bedroom, and all the annoying voices in her head would quiet down.

Lisa spent more time this evening on her language-learning app, thinking about the next step in her career and on social media. She is determined to master Spanish before her trip to Peru in a few months. But somehow, she spent more time finding ways to earn more gems on the app. It felt like she was becoming an expert at the game, rather than gaining mastery of Spanish. Later, as she was trying to envision her next career move, she started scrolling through professional social-media sites. But to her disappointment, all she met was a jumble of job openings, some of which did look possibly alluring, but none of that helped her think holistically about what she actually wants from her professional life going forward. Her scrolling on social media was also not satisfying. A lot of the posts she saw were boring or frivolous, and while she's relatively good at not letting hateful posts make her angry, some of them did get through her emotional defenses.

A few minutes after midnight, after satisfying all the digital demons in her life and disappointed with the limitations of today's digital tools, Lisa finally hit the sack. Like on other nights, thoughts about the real value these apps bring to her life were on her mind, but this time too, she was too tired to think about the problem deeply and fell asleep.

Lisa starts the following morning with her usual routine. She adopted a habit of not looking at her phone before she finishes her workout and morning meditation, but as soon as that period of focus is over, she is attacked by the usual barrage of messages on a variety of messaging apps and news sources. She finds that the effort taken to sort out the barrage and decide what to focus on drains her energy, but she somehow manages through it with the help of her well-prepared morning coffee. Fortunately, she has some great plans for this beautiful Autumn day. She is looking forward to driving through the colorful countryside to visit her long-time friend Oliver. The frustration of last night was still on her mind, but as she followed the instructions from the car's navigation system through the picturesque scenery, more positive thoughts about the contribution of technology to her well-being arose. A smile formed on her lips as she reminisced about the day many years earlier, when she had driven on the same road. Things did not go so smoothly that day. Oliver gave her driving instructions by phone and she scribbled them on a piece of paper. The instructions, to put it mildly, were missing a few crucial navigation details. But Oliver did make it abundantly clear that she should avoid a notoriously precarious part of town that would be dangerous for a woman traveling alone. To cut a long story short, she ended up in exactly that part of town when she realized she was lost. She then had to walk several scary blocks hoping that the stern look on her face would signal to anyone around her not to mess with her. After what seemed like eternity, she finally found a public phone from which she could call Oliver to get better directions. Fortunately, she ultimately found a kind helper who walked her safely back to her car that was already surrounded by a few guys who looked like they were up to no good.

At this moment, Lisa is feeling more thankful for the technological advances that were improving her well-being in many aspects of her life. Not only did she feel safer and more at ease about the drive to Oliver's place, all thanks to the navigation system, she also felt physically better since she started using a fitness and dieting app despite some of their annoyances. Technology, and even social media, also played a role in crafting the perfect evening experience. The wine app's recommendation for a bottle that would impeccably complement Oliver's signature dish delighted her, and the playlist that her music app helped her prepare, based on some of his known preferences, promised to set the ideal mood for both of them. It felt like each of these apps did one thing very well. The problem is that her life wasn't *one thing*. It was the messy, chaotic intersection of all of them and technology was far short of seeing the entire picture she wished it would.

Lisa is familiar with the technologies that power these apps, so she understands the challenges involved. She appreciates that most of the apps she uses are a double-edged sword. For example, social-media apps that are supposed to contribute to her well-being by helping her connect with friends and communities, and indeed did so quite a bit of the time, often left her endlessly scrolling through feeds that were not always very interesting. While the overarching goal for developing those apps was to improve some aspect of the user's well-being, Lisa is well aware that the race to develop techniques for keeping users engaged with the app has resulted in significant negative consequences. As AI advances at an even more rapid pace, Lisa realizes that the questions about the benefits and drawbacks of technology on well-being will arise more often and more urgently. To put things even further in perspective, Lisa acknowledges that the moments that bring her the most joy are when technology is left behind, such as admiring the beauty of the nature she's driving through right now, or spending time with a good friend without her phone in sight.

These issues are clearly going to be the main topic of conversation tonight with Oliver, especially since he had told her that his new startup was going to develop technology for well-being. Lisa and Oliver are not alone in questioning technology's effects on well-being. With the constant barrage of news about AI's advances, its benefits and its risks, and with the steady stream of shiny new apps and gadgets coming on the market, these questions are on the minds of people world-wide, probably including you, the reader.

This book tackles the hard questions relating to building AI assistants that improve our well-being, but with two important twists. The first is that this book comes from a technical perspective. This means we will discuss some of the technologies underlying the AI systems that are being applied to well-being, covering their strengths and weaknesses, some of their ethical implications, and how they need to be developed further to achieve our vision. The second twist is that this book is mostly about the journey ahead. Instead of documenting existing apps and their benefits and drawbacks, we outline a framework for how technology should be built to improve well-being going forward. Or, as we often say, we believe that this is a journey that is only one percent done.

Lisa and Oliver will accompany us on the journey, beginning each chapter with a vignette from their lives. On the one hand, they are meant to represent two potential readers of this book, namely, individuals who may want to be involved in building the future of AI-enabled well-being technology, and those who will contribute to the vision by asking the tough product and ethical questions. On the other hand, they are also meant to represent users of these technologies and represent the human side of the human-AI equation.

But first, let's be a bit more precise about the kinds of technologies we will consider. Of course, on the face of it, one can argue that every technology was conceived in order to improve some aspect of our well-being. We can go very far back in time to the classics such as the printing press and the light bulb, more recently to the phone network and the Internet, and then to today's new creations such as apps for meditation and for measuring sleep quality. Our interest in this book is in technologies that propose seemingly intelligent and personal choices or experiences for us and deliver them to us through computing devices such as phones, wearables such as smart watches, virtual reality headsets and smart glasses. To make the contrast clearer, a life vest will definitely contribute to one's well-being if they save their life when they are about to drown. On the other hand, a life shirt, that embeds sensors that measure your EEG, posture and activity levels, will improve your well-being by offering insights that are unique to you. This book focuses on technologies like the latter. You may have also noticed that the list of technologies did not include smart humanoid robots roaming around your home. These robots will inevitably be part of our landscape in years to come and hopefully in time to take care of some chores around the house in my old age. These robots will introduce amazing new capabilities to our well-being as well as many interesting privacy challenges. For now, we'll focus on the technologies we are already dealing with on a daily basis, but it is not too hard to let one's imagination go further.

The goal of our AI partner is to have a holistic view of our well-being. Hence, you might be wondering what exactly we mean when we use the term well-being, and how many pages you'll have to wade through to get the answer. Fortunately, we can build on the insights from the field of Positive Psychology to obtain a definition that works well for the purposes of this book (and you only have to survive through Chapter 2). In a nutshell, and at a risk of greatly over-simplifying, well-being is based on several pillars. At the basic pillar, we need to feel safe physically, financially and emotionally. The wellness of our body is a second pillar; we need to eat well, get sufficient and quality sleep, and exercise. These two pillars enable us to work on the third more complicated pillar, our mind. A healthy mind enables us to develop habits of engaging in the current moment and not spending excessive energy over thinking issues. These habits can be enhanced by various practices such as meditation, spending time in nature and being spiritual. The final pillar of well-being is finding meaning in what we do. Meaning can come in different forms, including long-term and family relationships, volunteering to help others, making some positive impact on the world, or doing work that inspires us. If the above sounds a bit like the well-known Maslow's hierarchy of needs, that's no coincidence.

The above description only sharpens the key challenge in designing technology for well-being. Even from our greatly simplified description, it's pretty clear that our well-being depends on quite a few and very diverse factors. Does this mean we're going to need a huge cocktail of apps, each helping us with one facet of well-being? In fact, that's exactly the way Lisa feels right now. There's an app for meditation, one for yoga, others for measuring sleep quality, a diet consultant app, ways of setting focus time on her phone, learning apps and the list goes on and on. In addition, there are apps that don't explicitly target well-being but affect it quite a bit, such as the navigation app she's using now or the language translation apps she uses regularly to communicate with a few of her foreign collaborators. But for the most part, these apps don't talk with each other. For example, her sleep tracker and diet apps don't know when she's on a trip or when she has a deadline at work, and therefore are unable to seamlessly propose a different diet or understand where her sleep issues are coming from. The sheer number of apps and the possible interactions between them seem overwhelming. Even if she managed to choose the best app for each facet of well-being from the myriad of available options, she can't help but feel that using them well is like being a conductor of a huge orchestra trying to follow some unwritten musical score.

The need for an organizing principle

The central theme at the heart of this book is the dichotomy between Lisa's current reality and the reality envisioned in the story heading this chapter. Are we doomed to a world of many uncoordinated apps, each purporting to address one narrow aspect of our well-being, or can we imagine a single AI partner tending to all our well-being needs? Or, perhaps, there is a sweet spot somewhere on the spectrum between the two extremes.

The main argument of this book is that regardless of what point on the above spectrum we end up with, there is a critical element missing from the discussion of technology for well-being. This element is a set of organizing principles that enable the contributions of disparate apps to effectively combine into improving the user's well-being. The foundation of these principles will enable apps to be better coordinated by sharing data where appropriate. Going further, we can build on such coordination to construct a single AI-partner vision, or perhaps, a set of specialized agents serving different aspects of our needs.

We draw inspiration for our organizing principles from the development of modern operating systems, such as Linux, macOS for desktops and iOS and Android for mobile devices. In the early days of computing, every computer program was written to access components of the hardware of the computer, such as its processor or memory, directly. This proved highly inefficient, because programming was extremely hard, but more importantly, it meant that a computer could not run more than one program at any given time. The development of operating systems involved identifying a set of organizing principles, such as the file system and the management of the processor and memory. As a result, applications interact with the hardware through a set of interfaces that are provided by the operating system. The operating system takes on the responsibility for managing which applications get access to the shared hardware resources of the computer, such as the main memory, the processor, and space on the file system. The critical advantages of this orchestration by the operating system is that we get much more out of the hardware and that it is easier to build applications. In our context, we would like to contribute as much as possible to the person's well-being by identifying the main components through which this can be done. In the next few chapters we lay out a proposal for these organizing principles.

After a speedy tutorial of well-being in Chapter 2, we begin our journey in Chapter 3, where we describe more concretely our proposal for an operating system for well-being. Building on the inspiration from operating systems and keeping to the theme of well-being, we named this operating system Oswell. We believe that Oswell should encompass three main components: Experiences, Attention and Connection. Let's delve briefly into each component to understand its role.

The first component, Experiences, serves as a repository for the collection of all the meaningful experiences you've had and pertinent information about you. These experiences encompass various aspects of your life, such as where you traveled, what you purchased, what books you've read, what you've had for lunch, how well you slept at night, and reflections about a conversation you just had or about a conflict you're experiencing. Many of our experiences already leave digital traces within the apps we use, such as photos we've taken, online purchases, navigation activities on a maps app, or credit card statements. Some experiences will leave traces on multiple apps, which will turn out to be handy in reconstructing your life. Your subjective experiences will be elicited via seamless conversational interactions. With all of these put together, this component will infer and organize all these experiences for you, allowing you to reflect on them. In turn, this repository will enable applications to gain insights about you to enhance how they serve you. For example, this component will enable your sleep tracker to know that you just returned from a trip overseas and are therefore jet-lagged, and your diet recommendation app to know that you just got back from a long run. But it can also go deeper, such as helping you recall a difficult situation similar to the one you are facing now, and give you advice on how to deal with it. In addition to recording the past, this component will also keep track of plans you may have for the future, such as places you want to travel, topics you'd like to learn more about, or your general desire to spend more time with family. Some plans may be extremely vague and others already partially planned out. Knowledge about your future aspirations will help your agent tailor recommendations to your current goals. Chapter 4 discusses how this repository of knowledge about you can be collected, and Chapter 5 discusses the privacy concerns that must be flashing in your mind right now.

The second component of Oswell, Attention, aims to reduce unnecessary distractions and enable you to spend your attention on things that will contribute most to your goals and your well-being. Its task is to help ensure that, to the extent possible, at any given moment, you can focus on what is most important, allowing you to be fully present and get the most out of your experiences. Many of our distractions come from ruminating about various details of our life, ranging from big ticket items such as that trip to Bhutan, whether you have enough protein in your diet, to minutiae, such as whether you'll have time to stop by the supermarket before picking up your kids. Therefore, the Attention component will include systems for making recommendations and planning out parts of your day, so you don't have to. It will anticipate your needs and always be one step ahead of you when planning is needed or there is a change of plans. Importantly, these systems will be informed by the Experiences component of Oswell, which is the necessary context to make these recommendations. We'll begin the discussion of the Attention component in Chapter 6. Chapter 7 will delve into systems that give you recommendations, and Chapter 8 discusses systems that can go beyond recommendations and craft complex plans for you.

The third component of Oswell, Connection, helps you engage with the world around you. Life is interconnected – your actions and decisions often have consequences for others in your life and your community. Likewise, the actions of others can influence your well-being considerably. The Connection component is designed to assist you in navigating this complex web of relationships. It helps you not only develop and nurture your closest and most meaningful connections but also expand your social circles by connecting with like-minded individuals you may not have known before.

This component enables you to offer support to others when they need it, improve your communication with people who are close to you and those who aren't, and to foster empathy and understanding in your interactions. The Connection component of Oswell touches on many topics that have been front and center on our minds lately (yes, social networks, we're looking at you), but beyond that, it also touches on essential themes such as community-building, nurturing a sense of belonging and reducing the feeling of loneliness. Several chapters will touch on this component, beginning with Chapter 9. Chapter 10 discusses social-media in more detail, and in particular how to reduce harms that arise on such platforms. Chapter 11 explores a relatively new frontier of forming intimate relationships with AI-based systems, including the benefits and risks of doing so. Chapter 12 takes a step back and looks more holistically at the issues discussed in the book. More concretely, it considers the fundamental tradeoff we face on a daily basis of balancing between our competing values, such as family, career, and leisure. The chapter discusses how such values are communicated with AI systems that are giving such intimate advice, and hence, how we can grow to trust them.

As we navigate through these topics, we will keep two questions front and center. The first is how to balance the benefits of AI assistants with their possible risks, some of which we may not be able to anticipate yet. The second question is what is the essence of being human? Inevitably, as we let AI take over more aspects of our lives, we will question what it means to be human in an age where AI can know us and assist us so well.

The broader context of AI today

Writing a book about AI in 2025 is risky business, to put it mildly. Every single day we hear about new and surprising capabilities of AI systems. The media today, in all of its forms, is nothing short of a cacophony of voices that on the one hand, extol the promise of AI to solve the world's challenges from climate change to curing cancer, and on the other, sound warning sirens about its risks, ranging from world-wide job losses to the demise of the human race. These discussions become even more mind-boggling when we imagine the opportunities of combining advances in AI with the recent innovations in synthetic biology, such as gene editing.

A large part of the reason for the boundless enthusiasm is that large language models (or LLMs as we refer to them in the industry), the technology underlying applications such as ChatGPT, Gemini and their cohort, display amazing capabilities that seemingly have nothing to do with the way they are trained. LLMs are trained by reading vast amounts of text. In the training, they are repeatedly given a sequence of words and asked to predict a likely word that would follow them. There is a post-training phase where they are fine-tuned to perform certain tasks well. When you use an LLM by prompting it with one of your questions, they do the only thing they know how to do. They begin by predicting the first word in the response, given your prompt. Then they predict the second word, the third, and so on. However, even with that simple training (at least conceptually; the details are much more complicated) they are able to perform many tasks at levels that match those of humans, whether it is summarizing text, answering a question about Greek philosophy, or translating a poem from English to Swedish. This means that during its training, the LLM developed an incredibly complex model of the world, soaking in a lot of the world's knowledge and common sense. Notably, the model also incorporates the biases that are explicit or implicit in the text it was trained on. The result is a system that can carry on a conversation on almost any topic, produce very coherent text, and most of the time, even be factually correct. Unfortunately, even when the response is factually incorrect, the LLM will speak with the same confidence, leading to what experts in the field have referred to as the LLM's hallucinations.

Progress on LLMs, or foundation models, as they are often called, is happening at a dizzying pace. Just in the span of the time it took me to write this book, LLMs have gone from providing ways to rephrase paragraphs which I mostly ignored, to providing useful critiques of entire chapters of the book, for which I am hereby offering an acknowledgment. In addition to the text-based interfaces, we also have image and video generating techniques that can produce amazing results based solely on descriptions of what the image or video should convey. One of the impressive aspects of these models is their multi-modal nature, namely their ability to perceive, produce and combine knowledge about the world that is expressed in language, images, video and sound. The progress on LLMs is complemented by the development of *agentic* systems that use LLMs to orchestrate complex workflows that are needed for AI applications ranging from customer-support agents, personal task managers, to tools that support scientific research. Just as one example, the labor-intensive task of assessing an insurance claim that involves reading the evidence and cross checking with regulations can now be mostly executed by an agent and presented for review to a human, leading to incredible efficiencies for customers and for insurance professionals.

The upshot of all this is that in writing about AI today we run the risk that what we say will be obsolete before the book even goes to press. However, this book is about something deeper in the sense that we aim to address problems that will linger with us indefinitely. To see why, imagine the role that these assistants will play in our lives. We will be able to interact with them in the language of our choice, receive help from them with our information needs, including recommendations on which items to purchase, what content to consume, what to eat, how to handle our complicated relationships, and even how to spend our time in the most meaningful ways. Importantly, all of these recommendations will be hyper-personalized, based on detailed knowledge of our past, our preferences, our goals and our current context. To some, these agents raise mostly red flags. What's going to happen to my privacy? Are the recommendations I get going to be in my best interest or in the interest of big tech? Will these systems just make all people on earth alike and will we ultimately lose the essence of being human? Even with the rapid progress in AI, we believe these questions will continue to be with us for quite a while because they touch on fundamental aspects of human nature.

Addressing these questions is another reason we draw inspiration from operating systems and seek a higher level of interaction between a human and their AI partner. It would be tedious, at best, to answer these questions in isolation for every well-being application, and the answers are unlikely to add up to much in the user's overall experience. You should be able to express your preferences about how technology serves you at a higher, more intuitive level, rather than necessarily interacting with the details of each of the apps that are serving you. Think of interacting with a set of higher-level knobs that you can turn as you wish, and your desires get pushed down appropriately to each aspect of your life. Let us illustrate this concept with a few examples.

One such knob is privacy. You'll be able to specify your privacy needs more easily and in a more nuanced way, and have those applied to your interactions with specific apps. For example, Lisa may be willing to share her exercise, dieting and financial information with her agent, but she's reluctant to share anything having to do with the people who are closest to her. A second knob concerns your agency, and it enables you to determine how much you're willing to delegate to technology, whether it's an individual app or your trusted agent that orchestrates them and how much you want to handle on your own. For instance, Lisa might feel comfortable delegating trip planning and food shopping to her AI, but she may prefer making decisions about her social interactions over the weekend without any assistance. This is a critical knob because as we'll see throughout the book, one of the important principles we hold dear is that AI should assist us when we want it to, but not take control over our life.

A third knob is serendipity, finding the balance between staying within your comfort zone and embracing novel experiences. At different times, you may lean towards one or the other, and each one may serve your well-being differently. For Lisa, staying within her comfort zone could mean listening to familiar music or visiting her usual cafe. On the other hand, during her exploratory moments, she might be open to watching a documentary on a topic she knows little about or skipping the gym to go hiking with new acquaintances she just met. The final knob is values-driven decision making. Many of the choices we make on a daily basis have to do with how we balance between activities that are important to us, such as spending more time with family, taking care of our physical fitness, or spending time advancing our career or pursuing our financial freedom. An AI partner should be able to help you navigate these value choices, which naturally cross many domains of your life, so you can feel that you have a balance between them, especially when they inevitably clash with each other.

The vision of personal assistants, or AI partners, is one that many in the field of AI and the broader technology industry have had for a while. However, with the development of LLMs and their associated conversational abilities, some of the most challenging technical barriers to developing such assistants may have disappeared. We believe that now, if enough good minds and resources are put towards the goal, personal assistants that profoundly impact our well-being may be an imminent reality. We hope that this book helps focus the conversation around personal assistants and provides a framework that enables rapid progress towards this alluring goal.

I'll end the introduction by briefly sharing with you the journey that brought me to writing this book.

There was very little in my early career that would suggest that some day I would write a book about technology and well-being. I've always had an obsession with getting the right information at the right time, so when I enrolled at Stanford University's graduate program in Computer Science, I thought my Ph.D dissertation should contribute to that goal. My dissertation was about weeding out irrelevant information that was slowing down database systems when users asked them a question. The result, although mathematically satisfying and earning me a doctorate, was ultimately of interest to a small cadre of experts interested in database theory. Even so, studying that problem required me to develop deep expertise in two disparate fields of Computer Science: Artificial Intelligence on the one hand and Database Systems on the other. This split identity of mine would prove to be very productive over the next few decades. Those two fields moved much closer to each other over the past couple of decades. Many innovations I was involved in, including ideas that are relevant to the topic of this book, built on cross-fertilizing ideas from both.

Shortly after I graduated, the World-Wide Web (WWW) came on to the scene and the amount of information available to anyone with access to a web browser exploded. Getting the right (and correct!) information at the right time became a problem many more people obsessed about. Still, my work remained largely in the database and AI domains, advancing from finding relevant information in one database, to finding relevant information in hundreds of databases, a technically much more challenging problem. After a few years at the famed AT&T Bell Laboratories, I joined the faculty of the Computer Science and Engineering Department at the University of Washington in Seattle. During my years as a professor my research inched just a bit closer to well-being when my student Luna Dong and I explored how to create useful databases of personal information. Luna and I became part of a small but active community that was interested in using personal data for one's own benefit.

I loved being a professor and by some measures, I was a pretty good one, even receiving the accolade of 'Database Rabbi' in one student review. But I failed at one critical aspect of the professorial job, namely, coming back from a sabbatical. I went on sabbatical to Stanford in 2004 and just as I was about to return to Seattle, Google offered to acquire the tiny startup I had formed that year. A big part of why I accepted that offer was that in 2005, the opportunities to help millions of people find the right information at the blink of an eye was a company-wide obsession, and it continues to be so to this day. During my time at Google I initiated a few projects to further the vision. Of particular note is a system we called Google Fusion Tables, that enabled anyone to collect and display useful information on a map that can be viewed in one's browser. The variety of applications in which Fusion Tables were used was fascinating. When the 2011 Japan earthquake hit, Fusion Tables were used to direct people to locations that had electricity and to routes that avoided road closures. In Iowa, a healthcare professional used Fusion Tables to map the locations of patients with multiple sclerosis on the one hand, and qualified caretakers on the other, showing gaps in care coverage. Yet another innovative creator created a map where people could report potholes they encountered on the roads so authorities would be notified faster. In addition to the reach of the Google brand, these and other applications of Fusion Tables were enabled by focusing on building a simple interface to data.

My true shift towards well-being did indeed begin during my decade at the technology mecca of Google, but not in the way that you'd imagine, and even to me, evident only in hindsight. Through my many travels during those years, I realized that in any city I visited, I was naturally drawn to the local cafes. This happened in Prague, Tel-Aviv, Hanoi, or Auckland, New Zealand. Yes, I do have a love for coffee and a well-documented weakness for baked goods, but the allure of cafes was far broader. I was captivated by the range of human emotion and experience that you can witness simply while sitting and sipping a cup of coffee. With my handy Fusion Tables tool, I plotted a set of 30 countries which I intended to visit in order to research coffee experiences around the world. I then embarked on the travel project and proceeded to visit cafes, coffee roasters and coffee farmers on six continents, ultimately writing a book about coffee culture, titled *The Infinite Emotions of Coffee*. These voyages led to fascinating encounters with people from a broad range of cultures, experiencing very different ways of life and communities and new stories of dreams and aspirations. The role of coffee, as a social lubricant and promoter of well-being also became clear to me as a result of my research.

In 2015, I left Google for the opportunity to found a new Artificial Intelligence Lab for the Japanese conglomerate, Recruit Holdings. As part of the process, I was tasked with coming up with a compelling research agenda for the lab. At the same time, I was going through some significant personal challenges, which led me to explore the field of Positive Psychology, a relatively young branch of psychology. Unlike most of the field of Psychology that focuses on understanding, diagnosing, and treating mental processes and disorders, Positive Psychology shifts the focus to what makes life go well, increasing well-being and promoting human flourishing. We will go into more details about the field in Chapter 2, but the gist of it is that the field identifies many positive practices and behaviors that anyone can apply in their daily lives. The books I read about the topic were very inspiring and even as I was reading them, I already felt better. I wanted to get the knowledge out of the books and into my pocket, so to speak, so their advice could be triggered just when I needed it in my daily life. That goal seemed like a pretty captivating vision for a nascent AI lab. And so that became the theme of the laboratory later known as Megagon Labs. We knew full well that it could take decades to achieve our goals or even define them precisely, but I felt like we made some headway on this problem.

Four years later, I joined Meta Platforms (previously known as Facebook) and there the connection between technology and well-being hits you in the face in a very different way. Billions of people were using the company's apps (Facebook, Instagram and

WhatsApp) and the vast majority of their interactions were helping them connect to friends and family, find useful and timely information and advance their life goals. But these apps were also used to spread misinformation, hate speech and other abusive behaviors at scales that were never seen in the past. As we discuss in Chapter 10, these malicious uses of technology were causing real harm to people, making daily negative headlines and bringing to the foreground the possibly troubled relationship between technology and the well-being of individuals and societies. I've spent several years studying these problems from different angles, appreciating their subtleties and contributing to their solutions.

The final straw that served as my impetus to writing this book happened when I moved into Meta's Reality Labs research division whose focus is on developing technology for augmented reality glasses and virtual reality. Imagine that you wear (stylish looking and comfortable) glasses, such as Meta's Ray-Ban smart glasses, that can see and hear everything you do throughout the day. Furthermore, imagine that you can interact through the glasses with a really smart digital assistant. Now, at least in my mind, there is no excuse for not delivering on my original obsession. Of course you should receive the right information at the right time! Since the glasses are on your face, they can pick up much more of your context, such as where you are, what you are trying to do and who is with you, and therefore, be much more useful to you and to your well-being. There are a myriad of technical problems that need to be solved in order to deliver on this promise, many of which we will touch upon in this book. Some of these challenges are not merely technical, they present dilemmas that touch on legal, ethical and psychological questions. It feels like a beautiful closing of the circle that Luna Dong, my former PhD student who started the journey to personal information management with me over 20 years ago, is one of the top technical contributors to Meta’s efforts today.

The bulk of this manuscript took shape during my final year at Meta and a subsequent short tenure at Amazon Web Services. However, after exploring other corners of the tech industry, I returned to

Google in late 2024 to continue pursuing my obsession with delivering the right information at the right time. Google feels like my true intellectual home; its depth, breadth, and ambition continue to inspire me, providing the ideal environment for creativity. We have reached a pivotal moment in AI technology where we can reimagine how we interact with data, both in our professional workflows and our personal lives and I am engaged in some of these efforts.

A necessary word of caution: none of the concepts discussed here should be viewed as hints of future Google services or products. They are grounded entirely in previous work and published literature. In this book, I aim to connect the dots between these various research threads and the questions that have emerged over the last few years. I look forward to sharing this unified picture with you.

Try This 👉

We will end every chapter of this book with a brief exercise for you. The exercise may include a few questions to reflect on or an actual activity you can do to get a better feel for the issues discussed in the book.

The discussion in this introductory chapter was rather general, but this is a good point to start thinking about the issues that the book will raise. Try reflecting over your own life, whether it is your daily activities, the main goals you have in your life right now, and try to imagine where AI could help you. What are areas that you think AI can be helpful? What kind of data do you think you need to share with the AI in order for it to help and do you feel comfortable with that? What guardrails do you want to put in place before you start working with your personal AI?

Lisa could feel her body ease into a relaxed state even as she entered Oliver's place. This small house in the woods, on the shore of a picturesque lake, was where Oliver escaped to from the city to recharge and think deeply. He called it his summer house, but you could find him here all seasons of the year. The memories Lisa had from this place were certainly some of the highlights of her life.

They had a lot to catch up on. As often happened, they began with their latest romantic breakups. In Lisa's case, it was not too traumatic ("hot, but boring," was the exact expression she used), but Oliver's latest breakup hurt. It came on the exact same day as he was laid off from his lucrative job at a high-tech firm, where he was leading a team of brilliant engineers developing a product he was very excited about. His girlfriend of almost two years, Monica, called him up that evening, and before he could even share his news, he could tell from her voice that this day had taken an even worse turn.

"I'm so sorry," Lisa said.

"You know, from that first day I met her at the party where she was dressed as Wonder Woman, that's how I thought of her. She was my wonder woman."

"Um, Oliver. I hate to break this to you, but Monica was not the one dressed as Wonder Woman. That was her friend from grad school."

"No, no. I was dating Wonder Woman. I would bet my life on it."

Lisa saw that arguing with Oliver now would lead nowhere, so they lapsed into a comfortable silence, sipping wine and watching the sunset out the window. After a few moments, a sad expression appeared on Lisa's face, which Oliver immediately picked up on.

"Hey, what's been going on?" Oliver asked, concern etched on his face.

Lisa sighed. "I don't know, man. I just feel like something is missing. Like I'm not really living up to my potential, you know? Everything is fine in my life. I have a reasonable job, my boss is not a jerk for a change, and I love my apartment. But something is lacking and I can't put my finger on it."

Oliver nodded. "I think I know exactly what you mean. Do you have some idea about what you want more from life?"

"That's just it," Lisa said. "I don't know what I want. I just know I'm not happy."

The silence lingered a bit longer, before Oliver continued. "I've been reading a lot about happiness and well-being recently. Every bookstore you walk into these days seems to have 10 books on well-being on display right at the entrance. This one is my favorite – 'The How of Happiness' by Sonja Lyubomirsky. It spells out the different aspects of happiness and what you can do to cultivate them."

"Let me guess, you're reading all this because it is related to your new startup, isn't it? Is there a quick summary of what you learned?"

"No, unfortunately there isn't, but what you're experiencing seems to be common. Unlike people with a particular mental problem, a lot of people are doing just fine, but feel like something is missing in their lives. Something could be better, more meaningful. But that's just half of the story. Well-being also has a lot to do with how you deal with adversity in life, such as a loss of a loved one, a divorce, or losing a job. That day when I lost my job and my girlfriend was really tough. Fortunately, I had just finished reading the book 'Emotional Agility' by Susan David that discussed exactly this issue. So I decided to take her advice and use this loss to build something better. That's how the idea for the startup came about. Well-being is complicated and can mean very different concepts to different people."

2. A Brief Overview of Wellbeing for Technologists

In order to discuss technology for well-being, it is important to establish a working definition of well-being, at least one that will serve the goals of this book. One obvious approach would be to consider the latest understanding of the concept of well-being and derive our definition from it. In fact, over the past few decades, the field of Positive Psychology has made impressive strides in understanding the concept and developing techniques for supporting and improving one's well-being.

However, a look back at history reveals that the conception of well-being has actually evolved quite a bit over the history of humanity. Hence, instead of looking at today's snapshot of our conception of well-being, this chapter briefly explores the history of well-being. This exploration of the past not only sheds light on how cultural influences, societal advancements, and scientific breakthroughs have shaped our understanding of well-being, but also highlights the dynamic nature of this concept. By comprehending history, we gain insights that equip us to envision the future of well-being and its symbiotic relationship with emerging technologies.

Therefore, in this chapter, we embark on a brief journey through time, to uncover the fascinating trajectory of how humans have grappled with the elusive essence of well-being. From the dawn of ancient civilizations to contemporary modern societies, our perception of well-being has metamorphosed, fueled by the fires of philosophical contemplation, psychological introspection, and sociological dynamics. Towards the end of the chapter, we allow ourselves to speculate on how well-being may evolve as AI plays a stronger role in society.

Ancient Civilizations

Ancient civilizations, such as those in Greece, India, and China, played a significant role in shaping our understanding of well-being. Philosophers and scholars in these cultures explored the interconnectedness of physical, mental, and spiritual dimensions of human existence, providing foundational concepts that continue to influence our understanding of well-being today.

In ancient Greece, Aristotle was one of the key figures who examined the nature of human flourishing. He emphasized the pursuit of eudaimonia, or "flourishing," as the ultimate goal of human life. According to Aristotle, eudaimonia was not merely a state of happiness but a holistic concept encompassing living a virtuous life, cultivating meaningful relationships, and realizing one's full potential.

In ancient India, the concept of well-being was explored in various philosophical traditions, such as Hinduism, Buddhism, and Jainism. The teachings of these traditions emphasized the importance of balance, self-awareness, and inner peace for overall well-being. For instance, in Buddhism, the Noble Eightfold Path outlined by the Buddha includes principles such as Right Mindfulness, Right Concentration, and Right Action, which guide individuals towards liberation from suffering and the attainment of well-being.

In ancient China, Confucianism and Taoism played influential roles in shaping the understanding of well-being. Confucianism emphasized moral values, social harmony, and the cultivation of virtues for individual and collective well-being. Taoism, on the other hand, emphasized harmony with nature and the pursuit of balance known as "wu wei." These philosophies focused on cultivating inner virtues and aligning one's actions with the natural order for a harmonious and fulfilling life.

These ancient civilizations laid the foundation for our contemporary understanding of well-being. Their teachings continue to resonate in modern discussions on happiness, fulfillment, and the pursuit of a meaningful life.

The Medieval Period

During the Middle Ages, religious and spiritual beliefs held significant sway over people's understanding of well-being. The predominant religious institutions, such as the Christian Church in Europe, played a central role in guiding individuals towards spiritual fulfillment. Salvation and eternal life were considered the ultimate goals, and achieving these objectives was seen as essential for one's overall well-being.

In this context, spiritual well-being took precedence over physical health and material comfort. The focus was on attaining a state of grace and connecting with the divine. The Catholic Church, for instance, emphasized the importance of adhering to religious doctrines, participating in sacraments, and seeking forgiveness for sins as a means to secure spiritual well-being. Practices such as prayer, fasting, and devotion were encouraged to cultivate a deep connection with God and attain salvation.

Physical health and material prosperity were often viewed as secondary concerns. Individuals were expected to endure hardships and worldly struggles in pursuit of spiritual purification. Asceticism and self-denial were valued virtues, as they were believed to strengthen one's spiritual resolve and detach individuals from worldly attachments.

The Renaissance and Enlightenment

During the Renaissance and Enlightenment periods, there was a profound shift in the conceptualization of well-being towards a more humanistic approach. This transformation was shaped by influential thinkers who emphasized reason, individual freedom, and the pursuit of knowledge as fundamental components of human well-being.

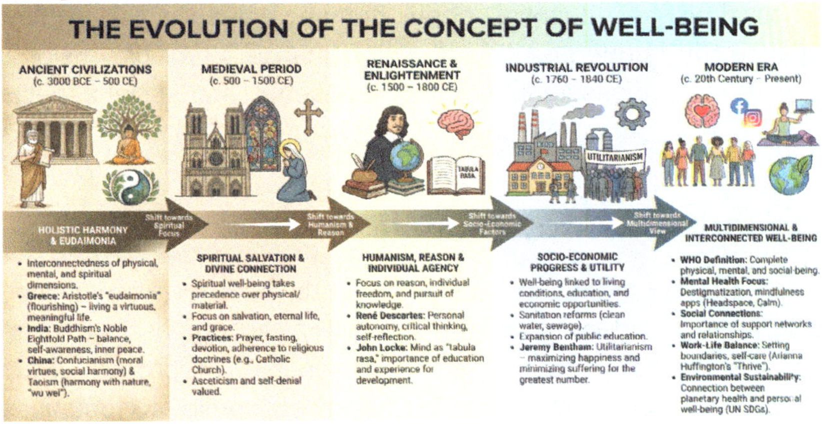

Created by Nano Banana

Renowned philosopher René Descartes, a key figure of the 17th-century Enlightenment, contributed significantly to the evolving understanding of well-being. Descartes emphasized the importance of personal autonomy and intellectual development as pathways to well-being. In his works, such as "Meditations on First Philosophy," he advocated for critical thinking and self-reflection as means to attain clarity and certainty, which were considered essential for a fulfilling life.

Another influential philosopher of the Enlightenment era was John Locke. In his renowned work "An Essay Concerning Human Understanding," Locke explored the idea of the mind as a tabula rasa, or blank slate, upon which knowledge and experience are imprinted. Locke argued that personal experiences and the pursuit of knowledge are vital for human development and happiness. His ideas about individual freedom, rationality, and the importance of education had a lasting impact on the understanding of well-being.

These philosophical perspectives from the Renaissance and Enlightenment eras laid the groundwork for a more human-centered and rational approach to well-being. They emphasized the power of individual agency, intellectual growth, and the pursuit of knowledge as essential contributors to human flourishing. This shift in thinking set the stage for subsequent developments in fields such as psychology, education, and human rights, which further expanded the understanding of well-being as a multidimensional concept encompassing intellectual, emotional, and social aspects of life.

The Industrial Revolution

During the rise of industrialization and urbanization, the definition of well-being underwent a significant shift, encompassing socio-economic factors as integral components. Improved living conditions, access to education, and economic opportunities became essential aspects of individuals' sense of well-being.

One notable example of the impact of improved living conditions on well-being is seen in the sanitation reforms of the 19th century. The implementation of proper sanitation systems, such as clean water supply and sewage disposal, played a crucial role in reducing the spread of diseases and improving public health. This resulted in an overall improvement in the physical well-being of individuals and communities.

Access to education also emerged as a critical factor in enhancing well-being during this period. The expansion of public education systems provided opportunities for people, regardless of their social status, to acquire knowledge and skills. This access to education empowered individuals to pursue meaningful work, engage in civic participation, and improve their socio-economic prospects, contributing to their overall sense of well-being.

Economic opportunities and the pursuit of prosperity became intertwined with the concept of well-being. The industrial revolution brought about technological advancements and increased productivity, leading to economic growth and the creation of new job opportunities. This economic progress and the desire for a better quality of life became significant drivers of individuals' pursuit of well-being.

Utilitarian thinkers like Jeremy Bentham played a crucial role in shaping the understanding of well-being during this era. Bentham's utilitarian philosophy emphasized the importance of maximizing happiness and minimizing suffering for the collective well-being of society. He advocated for policies and actions that aimed to maximize the overall well-being of the greatest number of people.

In his book "The Principles of Morals and Legislation," Bentham proposed the principle of utility as a guide for social policy, suggesting that actions should be evaluated based on their utility or ability to maximize happiness and minimize pain or suffering. This approach highlighted the significance of considering the broader societal impact of decisions and policies in promoting overall well-being.

The Modern Era

In the modern era, our understanding of well-being has evolved to become more multidimensional, recognizing that it encompasses various aspects of human life. The World Health Organization (WHO) defines well-being as a state of complete physical, mental, and social well-being, extending beyond the absence of illness. This comprehensive definition highlights the interconnected nature of different facets of well-being and emphasizes the need to address them collectively.

One significant shift in our modern understanding of well-being is the increased focus on mental health. The recognition of mental health as a crucial component of overall well-being has gained prominence in recent years. Organizations such as the National Alliance on Mental Illness (NAMI) advocate for destigmatizing mental health issues and ensuring access to mental healthcare services. For example, the rising awareness of the impact of stress, anxiety, and depression on well-being has led to the development of mindfulness meditation apps like Headspace and Calm, which aim to promote mental well-being and resilience.

Social connections and relationships have also gained recognition as essential aspects of well-being. Numerous studies have shown that strong social support networks contribute to improved mental health and overall life satisfaction. The American Psychological Association (APA) emphasizes the significance of social connections in enhancing well-being and recommends fostering social ties as a protective factor against stress and mental health challenges. Social-media platforms, while they can have both positive and negative effects, have provided new avenues for maintaining and strengthening social connections, especially in an increasingly interconnected world.

Work-life balance has become a key consideration in our modern understanding of well-being. With the advent of technology and the blurring of boundaries between work and personal life, achieving a healthy balance has become more challenging. Organizations and individuals are recognizing the importance of setting boundaries, promoting flexible work arrangements, and prioritizing leisure and self-care. The famed journalist, Arianna Huffington, in her influential book "Thrive," highlights the significance of well-being and self-care as an important pillar in the pursuit of success and fulfillment.

Environmental sustainability is another critical component of modern well-being. As we become more aware of the impact of human activities on the planet, there is a growing recognition that the vitality of our own well-being is inseparable from the flourishing health of the environment. The United Nations' Sustainable Development Goals (SDGs) include goals related to environmental sustainability, such as clean energy, sustainable cities, and responsible consumption and production. Initiatives like the zero-waste movement, renewable energy campaigns, and eco-friendly lifestyle choices are gaining momentum as people understand the connection between a healthy environment and personal well-being.

Looking Ahead

To take stock of what we've seen so far, well-being is a tapestry of multiple components. It starts from the basic needs for physical, financial and psychological safety, a healthy body that we care for, a mind that is free to be present and to imagine, strong relationships to other people and communities, and finally, a sense of meaning and self actualization. The specific details of this cocktail are personal and change for each one of us over time. This tapestry is often visualized as the Maslow hierarchy of needs (which, anecdotally, he never intended to be a hierarchy and imagined that we need to pursue all of these components in parallel). This book will focus on the development of AI technology that brings together the different pieces of this tapestry into a coherent whole for the betterment of individuals.

But what if we could speculate into the future on how technology might reshape our notion of well-being? One prediction is that the discussion of the betterment of individuals' well-being merely sets the stage for the potential of technology to address the well-being of groups and societies.

One such argument is articulated in a thought provoking article by Daron Acemoglu from M.I.T, Michael I. Jordan, a preeminent machine-learning expert from the University of California at Berkeley, and author and technologist E. Glen Weyl. They argue that AI should move away from focusing on surpassing human performance on various tasks, and focus on helping collectives, such as societies and enterprises. One way in which technology can achieve this goal, as evidenced by tools such as spreadsheets, databases and search engines is to make it easier for individuals to be part of collectives by giving them the information they need in order to contribute. But even more interestingly, technology can help create new kinds of collectives. They point to the creator economy as a set of technologies that enable more people to participate in markets and for consumers to receive a more diverse set of products.

Let us consider another example of where technology can help the collective. One of the main challenges in corporations is friction between individuals, or between different teams. There are multiple sources for this friction. They can come from individuals' need to work on projects that are visible and would ultimately get them promoted, it could be because some people feel better working on certain topics they are passionate about, or even a simple mismatch between their skills and what they're being asked to do. In the not too distant future, AI technology should have the capability to give us insight into all of these underlying currents even at the scale of large organizations. This technology should assess more clearly the strengths and weaknesses of different individuals in the organization, their career goals, and areas in which they want and need to develop. The knowledge about individuals can be garnered not only from their actual performance but also with the help of conversations that an AI can conduct with each individual. The goals of the organization and its strengths and weaknesses can also be collected and provided to the system. Based on this much broader view of the enterprise, AI systems could start designing teams where individuals are matched with their goals and skills and that serve the organization well. Obviously, these tools will not be perfect and will only serve as input to management, but they will have insights that were never available to decision makers.

This same idea can also be applied in the public sphere. Imagine bots having detailed conversations with voters about the issues of the day and obtaining a deeper understanding of their opinions and of which issues they prioritize over others. The aggregation of these conversations can serve as a powerful tool in shifting public discourse. For issues that there is a broad agreement on, officials can take appropriate action. After all, who does not want better roads and schools? The vast majority of the people want to save the planet, and nobody wants to see kids going to sleep hungry at night anywhere in the world, or battered women treated badly by the courts. The problem is often that when politicians need to align behind one of several political parties rather than being able to consider each issue on its own, they also end up stalling on the issues that they agree on. There will always be issues that are highly contended, but even for those, deeper conversations possibly mediated by AIs can possibly lead to more nuanced discussions and solutions.

In fact, in a recent reflection on his short tenure as the 13th Prime Minister of Israel, Naftali Bennett echoed exactly that sentiment. Bennett led a highly unusual coalition government in Israel that brought together parties from the right and the left of the political map in the country. This meant that there were people in the room with starkly opposing ideologies about critical issues confronting the country, such as how to approach the Palestinian conflict and where to land on the separation of church (or rather, synagogue) and state in Israel. Realizing that those issues will not be solved easily, Bennett directed his ministers to focus on the issues for which there was broad agreement, and gave them the autonomy to advance them. Many would argue that the result was one of the most effective governments in the history of the country.

With this overview of well-being, we are now ready to return to the main ideas of this book.

Try This 👉

Given all the different aspects of well-being discussed in the chapter, take a few moments to reflect about your own well-being. Here are a few questions to ponder: What does well-being mean to you? What aspects of your well-being are you satisfied with and which ones do you think need work? What aspects of your well-being do you think AI can help with? Try to imagine another person in your life who has a different set of life circumstances and think about the same questions, but applied to them.

Eager to continue their conversation, Lisa and Oliver met again the following week, this time at a quiet café in the city. Oliver ordered them both lattes and they settled into a corner booth.

"So tell me more about this new startup you're cooking," Lisa began.

"Sure thing! It's a personal AI assistant. Basically, it's a system that can learn your habits and preferences and help you make decisions. It's like having a personal assistant, but better. You know all those books about well-being and self improvement? This app basically puts them in your pocket and dispenses the right advice when you really need it."

Lisa was intrigued. "That sounds pretty cool. But how would it work?"

"Well, it would, of course, be based on AI that would analyze your behavior and make predictions about what you might like or need," Oliver explained. "For example, if it sees that you've been stressed out lately, it might suggest some relaxation techniques or activities to help you unwind. If you tell it you've been bored with your routine lately, it may suggest ways of changing your habits, like going to a different café instead of the one you usually visit on Saturdays."

Lisa's eyes lit up. "That could be exactly what I need. Something to help me get out of my rut and try new things. But, wait a sec, there are a dozen other apps that claim to do the same. How is yours going to be different?"

"This is where it gets really interesting!", Oliver smiled. "I've seen too often, even in my last job, companies trying to help you with a narrow aspect of your well-being, but not taking a holistic view of you as a person. It's not completely their fault, since their technology usually only applies to certain problems. I think there's room for a breakthrough if we think of a comprehensive platform for well-being technology, not just individual apps. I want the benefits of these apps to add up to a greater whole, not compete with each other."

"I think I see what you mean," Lisa said. "Just this morning my sleep tracker told me that my heart rate variability is a bit off and suggested I reflect on what may be causing it. Duh, doesn't it know I just returned from Europe, I'm badly jet lagged and I haven't been getting my usual exercise lately?"

"Exactly!" Oliver exclaimed with a delighted look on his face. "I knew you'd get it, Lisa. Did you ever think about being the head of marketing for a cool startup?"

3. An Operating System for Wellbeing

If you're reading this book, chances are you've had your fair share of encounters with digital devices like computers and mobile phones. And let's be honest, we all know the frustration that comes when those devices decide to throw a tantrum and fail us. Imagine that you're in the middle of an important task, and suddenly, your computer freezes because you've opened one too many apps. Or maybe you're trying to cram more files onto your computer, only to be met with an exasperated complaint about running out of disk space. And of course, if that's not enough, there are external threats such as viruses waiting to attack your vulnerable computer and steal your precious passwords if you don't have robust antivirus protection.

Thankfully, most of the time, you are spared from such technological mishaps. The reason is that there's a savior known as the operating system (OS) that handles many of these headaches for us. It's like a guardian angel, sitting between our applications and our computer hardware, ensuring smooth interaction and functionality. For example, the OS ensures that all the apps we're running on our machine can each access the computer's processor when they need to and not let any single application hog all the resources.

An operating system is one of many examples of abstractions that have been developed in the computing technology world. An abstraction is a mechanism that hides a lot of the details so that we don't need to be concerned with them. These abstractions give us the freedom to think in terms of higher level concepts, ones that are closer to the task that we want to get done. For example, the operating system enables a programmer to think in terms of files and network connections, without being worried about how the file is arranged as bits in memory or disk, or setting up the low level details of a network protocol. For users, the OS provides benefits as well. We can view our files in folder structures moving them around with a slide of a mouse without knowing what is actually happening under the hood, and interact with external devices such as printers, cameras and microphones by connecting to them on our dashboard.

There are many other examples of abstractions that have propelled the computing world. Computer programming languages and their underlying constructs are another great example. Back in the day, not too long ago, programming was done in what is called assembly language, telling the computer exactly which values to move from one address in memory into the other, or what exactly the processor should do. Not surprisingly, writing programs was an excruciatingly long process that was done by very few fearless souls (and students of some very unpopular computer science classes).

Today, in contrast, the recent trend of vibe coding notwithstanding, programmers work at a much more abstract and productive level. For example, if you're writing code in Python or any other high-level language, you can simply import a few very powerful packages, for everything from database processing, visualization or image generation, and voila, you've created the code that will power the next unicorn.

The point of this tour de force is not to convince you to go back to school and earn a degree in Computer Science (but if you already have one, do feel free to high-five yourself). The point is to argue that in the realm of applications for well-being, the appropriate abstractions are sorely missing and need to be developed. These abstractions will benefit application builders, but more importantly, they will benefit the well-being of the users, which is our ultimate goal. To keep with the inspiration of computer systems, we will refer to this new abstraction as the well-being operating system, or for short, Oswell.

Conceptualizing a new operating system consists of two parts. The first part is to identify the important building blocks that provide the right level of abstraction. For example, a computer's operating system identifies the concept of a file as a basic building block, because that is an item that users and programs interact with, performing operations such as opening, closing, moving or deleting a file. In our context, our building blocks will be concepts that are crucial to our well-being, which we will describe shortly. The second part of the exercise is to develop the components that handle the details that we're trying to hide away. The file manager in an operating system is a rather complex piece of software that implements the high-level operations that programmers and users initiate. We will discuss some of the options for implementing the building blocks of Oswell in subsequent chapters, but we don't have all the solutions yet. Part of the reason for writing this book is to spur innovation that will help fill in the needed details. Most likely, this follow-on work refine the concepts of Oswell that we describe here.

Let's dive into the components of Oswell.

The components of Oswell

The concepts that underlie Oswell, shown in the figure below, are naturally inspired by the study of well-being, as described in Chapter 2. The important idea here is that they are concepts that are closer to well-being. We will introduce them here and go into further detail in subsequent chapters.

Experiences

The first component of Oswell is a repository of your experiences, including the experiences that you've had in the past and ones that you would like to create in the future. We will refer to this repository of data as your lifelog. Even though we refer to it as a single repository, it does not necessarily need to be physically stored in one location. As we explain in Chapter 4, relevant parts of the repository can be assembled on the fly as needed from various sources when the AI partner needs it.

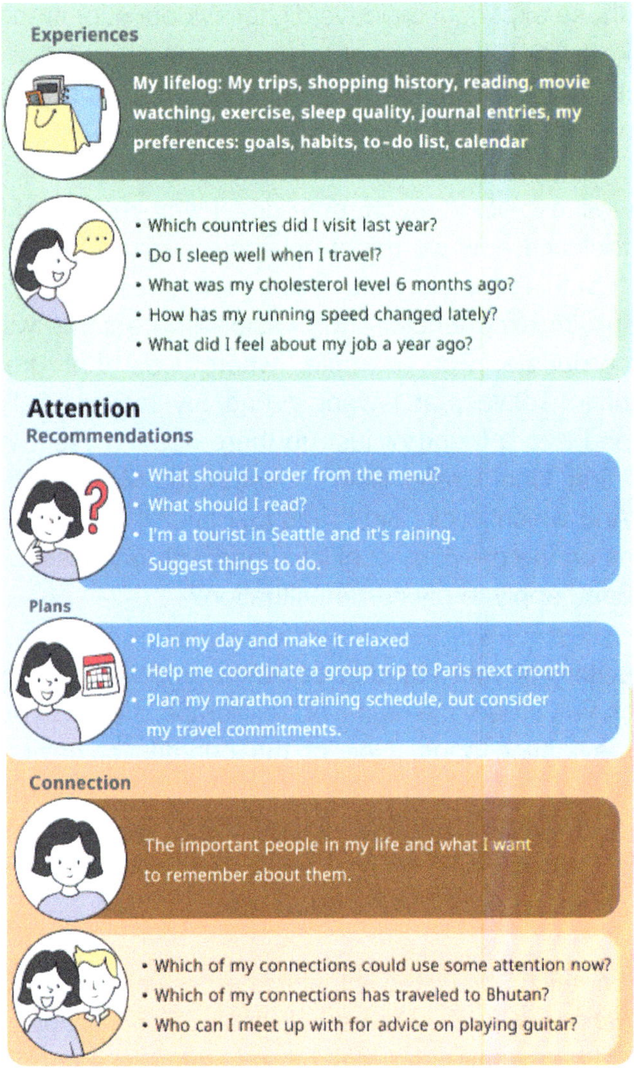

Experiences can come in many forms, such as running a half-marathon, reading a book, listening to a soundtrack (again, and again), or meeting with a friend or family members. Buying stuff is also an experience, as is going on a trip to Tallinn, the capital of Estonia. The latter has a number of component experiences, such as the ferry to Tallinn from Stockholm, the great cafe near the port, walking around the picturesque downtown, and the ferry back. Many of these experiences leave digital evidence, or breadcrumbs, as we like to call them. In some cases, the evidence is a photo taken at the right time, in another it may be the data recorded while using a navigation app to reach a destination.

Later we will explain in much more detail why you would like such a repository and how we might go about building it. But for now, imagine that this repository can enable you to ask many questions about your life experiences and possibly share some with others when appropriate. For example, where was that great sushi restaurant in Tokyo that I went during my last visit? I'd like to recommend it to a friend or just go there again myself. What age was the first time I read Man's Search for Meaning, by Viktor Frankl? And which books did I read just after that? What were my reflections on the previous conflicts I had with my boss, and which of them can I apply to my current situation?

The repository of your experiences will be populated by the apps with which you create the digital breadcrumbs, such as your photos or map navigation apps. One of the benefits of having such a repository is that other apps can be informed of such experiences. For example, if your experiences seem to suggest that you're a bit of an avocado nut, then an app that will recommend items from a restaurant menu might want to know that.

Another benefit of the lifelog is that it enables you to think about the data you share with an AI more holistically. For example, you may realize that if the lifelog includes more financial data or data about your interests, the AI will be able to use that data for your benefit in many contexts. Moreover, you can also think about the privacy of your data more holistically and set permissions that apply broadly to any interaction with their lifelog.

Experiences are only the tip of the iceberg of the kinds of knowledge about you that Oswell can store. Other examples include your interests, such as the literature you like to read, the music you prefer to listen to and your food preferences and restrictions. All of these are going to be helpful when an AI partner is trying to give you recommendations, such as what movie to watch or what to choose from a menu at a restaurant. Your plans and desires can also be stored. For example, the fact that you're planning a trip to Helsinki next summer could be useful in recommending new items to read or movies to watch. When you actually arrive in Helsinki, it would be extremely useful for all your well-being apps to know you're there and for how long you're going to stay, as it can help give you restaurant recommendations, weather appropriate ideas of what to do, and adjust your exercise schedule to fit your travel constraints. At the same time, some small details from back home may not be so important to pay attention to, which brings us to the next key building block of Oswell.

Attention

Your attention is your life, or as Sharon Salzberg, an author and teacher of meditation aptly puts it, "The difference between happiness and misery depends on what we do with our attention." In other words, your experiences, and to a large extent your well-being, are shaped by what you pay attention to. Failing to manage your attention, essentially your information processing and working memory, can have detrimental effects on your overall well-being. To complicate things further, as we're sure you've already experienced, your attention is in high demand as of late. More concretely, there seems to be a coordinated attack on your attention by participants that include the people in your life and the apps that you use on a daily basis, some backed generously by the concept of capitalism (but we'll get into that in Chapter 6). Another tax on your attention are the many details you often ruminate about in your mind, such as how exactly to organize your day and what you need to prepare for this weekend's party. Your AI partner, with the help of the Attention component of Oswell, needs to be able to help you direct your attention properly, take care of details that a computer can handle for you, and shield you from the irrelevant so you can be more present in the moment.

A very simple version of an attention manager is already installed on your mobile phone. When you tell your phone that you want to focus, you're asking it to block all notifications from your view (or at least, the vast majority). The Attention component of Oswell takes this idea to a much more nuanced level that is useful not just when you're sleeping, but throughout your day.

Here too, the abstraction of the Attention component enables you to think more holistically about what you want to attend to and then direct applications to support those desires. For example, you may want to specify that you should not be bothered by the news during the working day and after 8pm, or that content about innovations in crocheting should be given to you every evening after dinner. These directives will apply, through the Attention component, to any app that may produce relevant such content.

Connection

Connection is a fundamental human need. It allows us to form social bonds, build relationships, thrive in our careers, and experience a sense of belonging. In today's fast-paced and digitally connected world, fostering genuine connections has become increasingly important and often, more difficult. The goal of the Connection component of Oswell is to help you identify the important relationships in your life and possibly create new ones, find ways to nurture the relationships that need your attention, and assist you in navigating the difficult ones that may be draining your energy. This component should help you connect with like-minded individuals who share similar interests, passions, or goals and facilitate the formation of communities, both online and offline, where people can come together to support, inspire, and learn from one another.

At first glance, relationships sound much like other experiences that we purported to cover in the Experiences component of Oswell. However, we single out the treatment of relationships into a separate component of Oswell because they involve dealing with other humans or groups of humans. Other people have their own goals and moods and the nature of your relationships with them will change over time. Moreover, one of the key ingredients of good relationships is healthy communication, which is an area where Oswell can be helpful. Drawing again on the systems analogy, just as the communication between different computers introduces challenges that are handled by the computer's operating system, an operating system for well-being should facilitate meaningful connections between individuals.

As with the other two components, the abstraction provided by the Connections component of Oswell enables you to think more holistically about your relationships. Do you have enough connections that nurture you? Are there relationships that require special attention or ones where you are really needed now? Are there small things you can do for others that will make a big difference for them? What are effective ways of communicating your needs or ideas in a particular relationship? These questions often take up a lot of our attention even when concerning the main relationships in our lives, but when it gets to the long tail of relationships that occupy a lot of our time, this component can be even more useful.

Interacting with the operating system

One question you might be wondering about is who will interact with Oswell and how. For the most part, the answer is similar to the case of the computer's operating systems: programmers who build applications for well-being and the end user, that is you, who interacts with applications. For programmers, Oswell will offer a set of programming interfaces (or, APIs, as we like to call them) against which they will write code. As we will soon demonstrate with the Experiences component of Oswell, these interfaces will offer applications that benefit from having more information about you and more context about your requests from them, when, and only when, you allow them to access that information. That benefit, on its own, already enables applications to provide you better services. For example, a diet app may have access to much more data about your day and your past, and therefore be able to give you more precise advice.

For you, the end user, the answer to how you interact with Oswell is more nuanced, and the possibilities lie along a spectrum. On one end of the spectrum, there is very little interaction between you and Oswell. You simply grant existing applications permission to see some more of your data and then continue using them as you do today. As you can imagine, we believe that this option falls significantly short of the profound benefits that technology can offer your well-being, but it's a step up from what we have today. In fact, at the extreme, aspects of Oswell can be baked into the operating system of the computer or phone you're using today. We already see small bits of that today, such as setting your privacy settings and focus time on your phone.

On the other end of the spectrum, Oswell appears to you in the form of a single all-encompassing AI agent in the same way that Pat was assisting Lisa. This agent will recommend to you what to choose from a menu, what movie to see, and which friend to set up some time to see this weekend. In doing so, the agent will consult with existing apps, and with data about your habits and preferences. In some cases, the agent will provide other apps more context so when you interact with them, your experience will be better. For example, the agent may provide a social-media app with more guidance about what kind of content you would like to see and when. This agent will be omnipresent in your life. You may interact with it on your phone, laptop or smart glasses. But it can also appear on a big screen TV at your home, on your treadmill, in your car, and yes, on your toaster too if that's a big part of your life. We refer to the agent on this side of the spectrum as the AI partner. Given the title of this book, you may have a sense as to which end of the spectrum we are leaning into here.

There can be many options in between these two extremes. Just like a modern OS comes with some built-in apps, but there's still an app store from which you can buy others, we may see something similar here. For example, you may interact with some apps directly, and in addition, have a collection of AI agents that give you advice. You may have a specialized AI agent to deal with your physical well-being, one for helping with your finances, and yet another one that sees your professional persona and consults you on work and career-related issues. Even with all of these specialized agents and apps, you may still have the one AI partner you go for the needs that are not covered by others. Each of these agents, in turn, will be built on the infrastructure provided by Oswell. Regardless of the ultimate solution, the point we are making here is that we must have a discussion on how all these agents work together.

In proposing Oswell, we designed it in a way that allows the exploration of a multitude of options for human-machine interaction for well-being. That being said, the concept of a single AI-agent that encompasses your needs from technology has been envisioned as the north star of personal technology for several decades, so in our discussion, we may anchor on that vision where it is appropriate. This also means that the boundaries between this AI partner and Oswell may seem blurry at times.

Human-machine symbiosis

We described a possibly compelling future where an AI-powered partner is helping you coordinate with a myriad of apps and, whenever you need help, will give you well informed recommendations as to what to focus on. But we would be shocked if you're not feeling at least a little bit of hesitation. You're probably not quite ready to hand your life over to an AI agent that will make most of the decisions for you. Some of you might even be thinking that the name Oswell rhymes just a bit too well with Orwell, and wondering whether we're actually scheming to enact George Orwell's fictional character, Big Brother, who was the leader of Oceania in the novel 1984, and where every citizen was constantly being watched by the state.

Nothing could be further from the truth, and we promise you that the aforementioned rhyme is a mere coincidence. Only time will tell whether that coincidence helps the cause of this book or not. We will see throughout the book that building personal AI agents raises many fascinating questions about how to create human-machine symbiosis. In a symbiosis, machines should be there to help humans in their tasks and decision making, drawing on strengths that machines have over humans. These strengths include their ability to remember almost everything, identify patterns in data, and comb through millions of possible scenarios in a matter of seconds when faced with a complex problem. However, machines should not take away human agency and get in the way of the essence of being human. Machines should do what they are good at so we can spend more time being human!

Not only are you not losing control, but one of the main benefits of Oswell is that it enables you to express your preferences at a much higher level of abstraction than how you would interact with one specific app. After all, that's what an operating system does – it raises the level of abstraction to one that is closer to your needs. Oswell provides a set of knobs that enable you to steer, either directly or through one of the agents built on Oswell, where you delegate control to AI and where you don't, and to shape the kinds of recommendations you receive. These knobs have a very direct relationship to your well-being and are therefore more intuitive for you to manipulate. When you adjust one of these knobs, the effect applies across a variety of interactions, not just a single interaction with a single app. The following is an initial set of knobs, but it is very likely that additional ones will be identified and developed with time.

Privacy: In our description above, you probably freaked out about the privacy of your personal information. The Experiences component of Oswell, which is the subject of the next chapter, captures your experiences from multiple apps and those, in turn, are used to improve the recommendations they provide you. While the first part, where all the information about your experiences is stored in one place sounds scary enough, the part about this data being available to applications is downright objectionable. We will discuss privacy issues throughout the book and in particular in Chapter 5, but we'll lay down a few foundations here.

The privacy knob of Oswell enables you to specify your preferences more easily and dynamically. Your privacy preferences will vary depending on whether you are considering sharing data with an app, or whether you're sharing it with your one and only trusty AI partner. In either case, by setting privacy preferences we do not mean spending a few hours checking boxes on an undecipherable privacy dashboard. Instead, by default, all the data in your Oswell repository is private and available only to you.

Of course, in many cases, you can gain quite a bit of benefit from your data by sharing it at the opportune moment. As a first step, let us consider how you would share data with apps that serve you in various ways. In Oswell, privacy and sharing are considered when the opportunity arises and there is some clear benefit you might gain from sharing. For example, you might be willing to share your food preferences profile with a menu recommendation app for just enough time to make a choice, or with a dietitian app for an extended time horizon to get advice over a longer period. But neither of these should see anything relating to your social or financial life. You will be prompted to make these choices just before data is shared. Which data is requested and what the benefit is for you are both laid out in clear language.

You might be willing to share more data with your personal AI partner because it sits in the middle between you and external apps and services, and because it is designed to be your confidant and engineered not to leak any information about you. For example, you might trust your AI agent with your financial information, or at least your overall profile, so it can filter out notifications that may be above your comfort level or too mundane for your financial standing. You might also share with it more of your preferences and actions so it can provide you better advice. For example, Lisa might share with her AI partner that she prefers to spend more time with Oliver than with her own brother Sterling. The more of your preferences you share with your agent, the better it will be able to serve you.

How much information we feel comfortable sharing with an agent is obviously a very individual choice, and even that choice may change over time. Comfort levels are affected by multiple factors, such as how much you trust the agent, which is related to your broader trust in technology, whether you understand how it is using the data for your benefit, the societal norms that surround you, and frankly, how much you fear authorities and hackers. While Lisa may be comfortable sharing her health data with the agent, she may prefer that her agent not know where she spent the night after visiting the local bar last Friday, just in case the agent becomes a wee bit judgmental.

Serendipity, exploration versus exploitation: Often, when we are faced with a decision, one of the factors that we consider is whether we want to stay in our comfort zone or be exposed to new experiences. At times, the AI agent might recommend that for your well-being, you may want to choose a new experience over one that you've had before or vice versa. However, this knob gives you the ultimate control over this choice. When the knob is turned closer to exploitation, we prefer choices that are similar to things we've done in the past and with which we feel comfortable. When we're closer to exploration mode, we go out of our comfort zone and seek new experiences, knowledge or skills. In exploration mode we may also deal more readily with conflict or engage in activities where we will be exposed to opinions that counter our own. In exploitation mode, Lisa may choose to listen to music from familiar artists, follow her usual workout routine, or ask to schedule another meeting with Oliver, who she knows well and with whom she feels comfortable. In exploration mode, on the other hand, she may explore new music genres, start training for a marathon, or clear the evening so she can go visit the neighborhood bar again. Asking our AI partner for the exploration mode means we are asking it to turn on serendipity.

Reward now or later: A related factor that affects many of our choices is one that we deal with more often than you would think: should you make a choice that provides a short-term gain or boost, or one that offers a longer-term benefit? Should I cave into my craving for that juicy burger on the menu or go for that kale salad that will keep me fit? Should I spend the evening binging on a Netflix series or should I choose a historical documentary that will let me converse more confidently at future social occasions? Should I spend my Saturday visiting my aging aunt or go out with the gals again? Our well-being needs a healthy mix of both kinds of activities. Since our AI agent will be giving us advice on many of these decisions, this knob will help tilt it in a particular direction. If you want it to, the AI agent will gladly hint at the consequences of your choices and even keep score for you in a type of well-being balance sheet, but ultimately, this knob lets you set the tone that is right for you at any given moment.

Agency: Ultimately, the goal of having an AI partner is that it can take care of many of the routine details of life for you and give you the advice you need. But which details of your life you want to delegate to the agent versus what you want to have complete control over is a very personal choice that may also vary with time. This knob determines what you're comfortable delegating to the agent. For example, Lisa deeply dislikes making travel arrangements, so she will gladly delegate all that to the agent as long as her budgetary constraints are satisfied and she's racking up the frequent-flier miles. When it comes to buying birthday presents for her family members or choosing curtains for her home, she's happy to hear the agent's suggestions but wants to look a bit further on her own before she makes a decision. When it comes to how to dress for an evening out, she listens to no one.

The above discussion exemplifies the paradigm shift that Oswell enables. We reformulate the discussion from terms that relate to specific apps to terms that concern our well-being directly, such as privacy, agency, and timing of reward. Therefore the individual, that is you, is viewed holistically, rather than in individual silos. You can now think in terms of interacting with a personal agent that knows about our experiences, habits and desires, and receives directives from you concerning our current needs and level of comfort. Under the hood, Oswell will interact with multiple apps similar to what Lisa was imagining. The AI partner will use Oswell to ensure that all the underlying apps will have access to whatever information you want to share about yourself with them. Moreover, when you express a desire or goal, such as eating vegetarian or limiting social media use, that wish will percolate down seamlessly to all the apps. In the next chapters, we'll take a closer look at Oswell.

Try This 👉

This chapter discussed several ways in which AI agents can appear in our personal lives, ranging from individual experts on different domains to a single AI partner that would cater to all our needs, consulting experts as needed. Reflect on how you would prefer to interact with AI. Would you prefer to interact with multiple AIs depending on what you are doing in your personal life or would you prefer a single AI that has a holistic view of you? From your perspective, what would be the pros and cons of these different proposals? If there are multiple AIs, should they all see the same information about you?

One week later, Lisa and Oliver met again, at the same cafe.

"Gosh, I love this cafe. I'm so glad it's right in our neighborhood," Oliver said as he sank down on the chair.

"I know! How many times have we come here in the past year? A dozen? More?"

"Ha, that's easy to find out. I always take a photo of the latte art when we're here," Oliver said as he starts flipping through his photos. A few long minutes later he emerges from his phone and announces: "You're about right! Sixteen times in the last year!"

"You call that easy? It took you a while to figure that out. Anyway, I love all the coffee gadgets they have here. I feel like every time I come here I am inspired to buy something later," Lisa thought out loud.

"Let's check that. Go to your online shopping history and we'll see. I have the dates of our visits right here."

"Ok...," Lisa plays along.

"September 6th."

"My first aeropress."

"December 8th."

"A hand grinder."

"February 14th."

"A scale to weigh coffee grounds. And another grinder."

"July 3rd."

"Oops. Never mind."

"What?"

"That was the day I went on a shopping spree for books about relationships."

"I wonder why. Do you remember what we discussed that day? That wasn't the day we, um, ... can you maybe check what you wrote in your journal that day?"

"Later. Look, it's been an hour since we got here and all we've done is go into great pains to try to answer some simple questions about our lives. Don't you think that your app should make that really easy?"

"Well, in fact, that's what I was going to tell you about..."

4. The Lifelog: What Your AI Can Know About You

Ted Chiang's captivating short story, "The Truth of Fact, the Truth of Feeling," tells of Remem, an extraordinary system that meticulously records every single detail of your life. These life details are stored in a lifelog, a digital personal timeline of your life, allowing instant access to any fact about your past whenever you need it. Picture this: while having a conversation with your spouse about the last time you visited the beach, Remem would seamlessly present you with a video of that very afternoon. That would settle the discussion about whether you were already wearing the same ragged bathing suit back then, and whether your facial hair style was to her liking at the time. It would also tell you what you ate for lunch before going to the beach. The story does not delve into the exact mechanics of constructing the lifelog, but you can imagine that there is a camera perpetually following your every move, capturing each experience from your unique perspective.

A system like Remem would be remarkably valuable in various scenarios, ranging from the simple task of locating misplaced keys before leaving the house to gaining insights into events that occurred long ago. Imagining Remem's application in the legal system, it becomes evident that it can play a crucial role in uncovering truth and thereby enabling more precise judgments. However, as Chiang's story unfolds, we come to discover the downsides of this all-encompassing memory system. One negative consequence is that some individuals begin paying less attention to current events, knowing they can effortlessly retrieve the memories later on, but the lack of attention diminishes their actual experiences. Or, as the famed comedian Jerry Seinfeld quips, “our job is to ensure that our phones have the best possible life experiences and then remind us of them eight years later."

Moreover, upon deeper reflection, it becomes clear that the exact details of what actually happened are not always the most important or necessarily useful thing to recall. For instance, Chiang's story illustrates how married couples might argue over specific past occurrences, when the key to resolving their present issue lies in acknowledging each other's feelings and working as a team. They may get caught up in the minutiae of what transpired before a recent disagreement, when what truly matters is recognizing the underlying conditions that may have led to that unfortunate exchange. To underscore this point, the main character in the story ends up very surprised when he digs up a memory of a watershed moment in his past. You'll need to read the original story for those details.

Remem is not within reach of today's technology yet, but it serves as an effective fictional portrayal of what the first component of Oswell, the Experience component, might entail. This component collects all your past experiences into a lifelog, a database of your life. You can ask your lifelog questions about your past, and benefit from a variety of techniques that can uncover patterns in your behavior and the preferences you exhibit in your everyday life. The information gathered by this component can also be shared with different apps when you allow doing so, and as a result, the apps can be better coordinated and ultimately better serve you.

In this chapter, we explore the types of information that can be incorporated into your lifelog, and where that information might come from. Later in the chapter we will briefly discuss how the lifelog can be implemented. For example, at one extreme, the lifelog may all be put into a single data store, while at the other extreme, parts of the lifelog may be assembled on the fly as needed. We will discuss the significance of your lifelog for your well-being directly, and how it can help the applications that purport to enhance your well-being. We dedicate Chapter 5 to the discussion of issues that fall under the broad category of *what could possibly go wrong?* There is a lot to cover here, so we'll start from the simple stuff in your lifelog and build from there.

The really simple stuff

Before delving into the experiential content of the lifelog, let's mention some obvious stuff that should be in there. This includes some of the information that today is found on your passport, driver's license, or your social-media profiles, such as your date and place of birth, current address and your employment history and educational background. Going beyond that, the lifelog can also include your shoe size (including the fact that your right foot is longer than the left foot), clothing sizes and eyeglass prescription, vaccination record, the entire contents of your wardrobe, and the names of all the pets you ever owned. Furthermore, it should also include your dietary restrictions, your current medications and even specific food preferences. All of this information can save you time filling out forms at a doctor's office, figuring out which vaccinations you need for your trip to Ghana, or communicating efficiently with a salesperson at a clothing store. Capturing this information is relatively straightforward, as you will simply input it into the system, akin to how you have filled out countless paper or online forms in the past. As we'll soon see, you may not even have to enter some of that data manually because some of it may be inferred from other data in your lifelog automatically.

Your past experiences

The objective of the lifelog is to preserve a record of your experiences that is as comprehensive as possible, allowing you to access them later as needed. These recollections, often referred to as episodic memories, can serve various purposes, including personal reflection, reliving cherished or whimsical moments, or even utilizing them to determine what would be good new experiences to create. Importantly, populating the lifelog should occur effortlessly as a byproduct of your daily activities. The concept of a lifelog raises deep questions, such as determining which experiences are worth recording and defining the very essence of what constitutes an experience. As we explore a few examples, we will offer partial answers to these intriguing dilemmas.

Let's begin from experiences that are easy to capture digitally. Your online purchases are recorded digitally and can be easily ingested into your lifelog. Additionally, most purchases that you make while roaming the real world are captured via your credit card records.

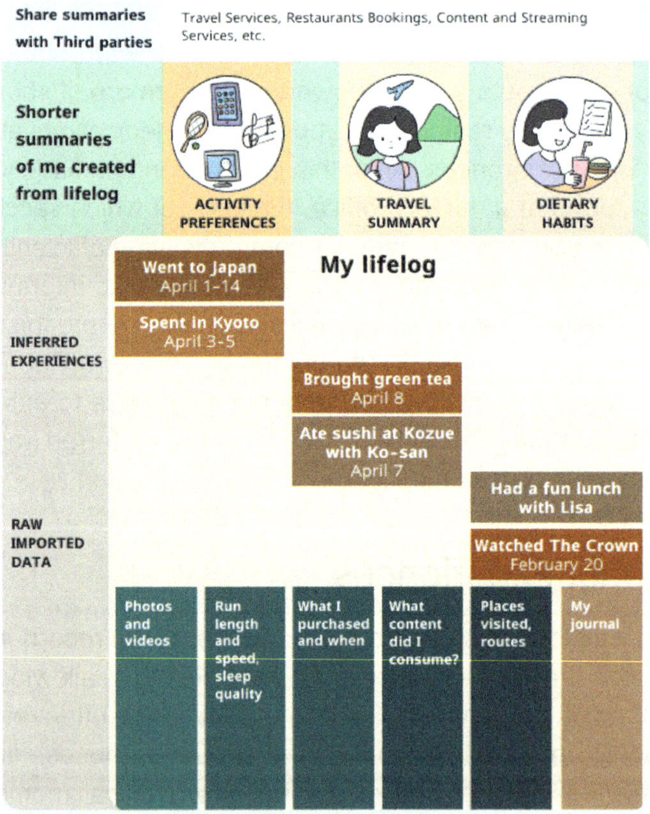

Sure, you will still from time to time make purchases in cash, though that's becoming a small part of your economic activity. Fortunately, those purchases are often so yummy that you'll snap a photo of them anyway.

The content you engage with, whether it be the books you read or listen to, the movies you watch, or the music you enjoy, are digitally recorded somewhere. Gone are the days that most of us simply put an LP record on a record player and enjoy it despite the terrible quality of our stereo system. Nowadays, many, if not most instances of content consumption are likely accompanied by a digital record. Furthermore, these records capture valuable insights, such as the duration you spend on a specific page, the frequency with which you listen to a particular soundtrack, and even the time of day during which you indulge in these experiences and whether you were exercising at the same time.

Speaking of exercise, that's an even more extreme case of information that is vying for a spot in your lifelog. Many of us shudder at the idea of doing exercise that is not somehow recorded. If *I'm going to sweat, I want some computer somewhere to know about it and record it for eternity!* Fortunately, today we have smart watches that record every aspect of our exercise for us. In addition to the length of your run or swim, these devices will record your heart rate, your average calorie burn and other statistics you may or may not care for.

But wearable devices such as smart watches or smart rings go beyond that. Whether you are exercising or not, they continuously monitor various aspects of your physical status, such as your heart rate and blood oxygen levels, offering insights into cardiovascular health, physical exertion, and your sleep patterns. For example, smart rings utilize a technique called photoplethysmography (PPG) that samples changes in your blood flow at a very high rate (50Hz). As a result, it can obtain accurate measurements of your heart rate, respiration, and heart rate variability (HRV) during sleep (lower HRV is associated with lower-quality sleep). Together with an accelerometer sensor on the finger, it ensures sensitive activity detection and captures signals directly from the arteries, offering precise sleep tracking that can help users improve their sleep habits. Although these may not sound like an "experience" at first glance, these are passive experiences and they're undoubtedly important pieces of your lifelog puzzle and have very important implications to your well-being.

In addition to monitoring physical status, wearable devices are also widely used to track users' behaviors. For instance, smart watches continuously record the number of steps you take, the distance you travel, and the number of calories you burn. This information, in turn, when presented thoughtfully, encourages you to engage in more physical activity and helps people set and achieve fitness goals. The active energy expenditure also allows users to manage their daily energy balance and make informed decisions about diet and exercise.

Today, many of us take wearable technology for granted. But it's important to pause for a moment and realize their incredible strengths. First, they essentially give us data for free, once you paid for the device, of course. We don't have to do anything special except carry on with our daily activities. Trying to record any of that data manually would be unimaginable except for the very dedicated few. Second, wearable devices capture data that smartphones cannot easily access. For instance, tracking movement and heart rate accurately requires physical contact with the user, something smartphones cannot consistently provide. Third, these devices capture in-the-moment data and they do it throughout the day, even when you leave your smartphone elsewhere. Events like stress or acute emotional responses may be fleeting and difficult to recall accurately later. In the not too distant future, wearables may be able to record these experiences as they happen and can offer valuable insights into real-time reactions. Moreover, they can suggest interventions such as breathing exercises or mindfulness meditation.

Going back to the contents of our lifelog, you may be wondering why we referred to all the experiences we mentioned so far as simple. The reason we consider them simple is that these are experiences for which the data exists, the data is accurate, and each piece of data corresponds roughly to what you would consider to be an experience. For example, going for a run or listening to a podcast are recorded in the data and correspond to an experience. Therefore, mirroring these experiences in your lifelog is almost as simple as importing them using available APIs. The slight caveat is that in some cases we'll need to recognize that multiple pieces of data refer to the same event, and remove all but one. For example, a purchase may appear on a credit card and on a feed that you receive from an online merchant, and an exercising activity may be recorded by several devices. When we import these into the lifelog, we need to merge them so you see only one clean instance of each experience.

Your more complex experiences

Let's turn our attention to the more intricate experiences. These are the ones where a direct mapping between data (e.g., a digital record on your smart watch) and the experience itself (running 5K in 21 minutes) is not straightforward. Instead, the experience needs to be inferred by fusing information from multiple digital records of your activity, and translating them from media such as photos into words. Such experiences are highly prevalent, such as your trip to Paris, the restaurant you ate at in Tokyo, meetings with your friends, taking your dog for a walk, or even preparing guacamole.

This is where we get to formally introduce the concept of digital breadcrumbs. With the exception of obsessive calendaring junkies, we rarely inform a computer explicitly about our upcoming seven-day trip to Portugal, along with a detailed list of the restaurants, cafes, and attractions we intend to visit. Instead, we get on a plane to Portugal and have a great time. In the process, we take a lot of photos, use our favorite navigation app to get to our desired destinations, post some descriptions of our experiences on social media, and typically use our credit card more than we should. These photos, navigation logs, social-media posts, and credit card histories are what we refer to as digital breadcrumbs. As you may have guessed, the term draws inspiration from the Brothers Grimm fairy tale, Hansel and Gretel, where the siblings leave behind a trail of breadcrumbs, to avoid getting lost in the forest. In the digital realm, these breadcrumbs don't end up being eaten up by the birds. Instead, they present an opportunity for data mining, or, if you prefer, eaten up by technology companies. Here, we're going to put them to use for your own benefit.

For us, these breadcrumbs serve as crucial pieces of information to infer the actual experiences you had. Building the lifelog presents a technical challenge: we must examine the collection of breadcrumbs and infer that you embarked on a trip to Portugal, visited various attractions, savored specific meals and their locations (including indulging in a few too many pasteis de nata—look them up if you haven't tried them).

As of the time of this writing, we have a few substantial technical gaps to inferring experiences, but it's by no means a pipe dream. The photos you captured are typically geo-tagged, providing the location in which they were taken, and whether there is a known landmark there, such as a restaurant, museum, or street corner. The state-of-the-art AI models, building on their ability to combine information from multiple modalities such as language, image, video and audio, are improving at a dizzying rate. This means that they can often identify, at least partially, what food is on the plate in front of you, or decipher the scene depicted in a photo whether it's a soccer game or a ballet performance. By combining this technology with common-sense reasoning, such as mealtime associations or typical daily routines, we should be able to construct a coherent narrative of your day and integrate it into the lifelog. Common sense will also come into play when determining the end of your trip. Magically, after seven days, the stream of photos from Portugal will come to a halt. If you did not venture to another exciting destination, the system will need to infer that you have returned home. Visits to your local grocery store the next day, a run in your neighborhood the next morning, or the presence of your boarding pass in the lifelog will help reach that conclusion.

If our lives were composed solely of trips to exotic locations punctuated with occasional bouts of exercise, then creating our lifelogs would be a relatively simple matter because we could simply build AI models that would recognize these types of events very accurately. Fortunately, people enjoy a plethora of other activities, such as celebrating birthday parties, embarking on strenuous multi-day hikes, obtaining diving licenses, taking their children to piano lessons, chess boxing, or going to the village dance party. These activities vary in duration, spanning from mere minutes to several months or even years, and often leave behind only partial and ambiguous digital breadcrumbs.

Even if it were possible to enumerate all the activities and their diverse variations, developing an algorithm capable of recognizing each one solely based on digital breadcrumbs would prove impractical. Hence, one of the key technical challenges we still face is the development of AI models that can infer a reasonable set of activities from the available digital breadcrumbs. To complicate matters even further, the main ingredient required in order to develop machine learning models, namely, data, gobs of data, is hard to come by when highly personal data is involved.

As we embark on this research agenda, it is worth recalling a phrase "the perfect is the enemy of the good." In our case, the "perfect" refers to a lifelog that comprehends every activity, capturing its nuances and how it interconnects with others—a meticulously curated story of one's life. For instance, imagine spending months organizing a surprise party for your spouse. This undertaking involves contacting numerous friends, researching venues, making bookings, designing decorations and menus, and even inventing an excuse to casually pass by the chosen venue on the appointed evening. Each of these tasks can be recorded as an individual episode. The "perfect" lifelog would seamlessly weave them together into a larger narrative of party preparation. On the other hand, the "good" lifelog represents a Google-like search engine for our lives, adept at providing answers to a wide range of questions but occasionally requiring us to connect the dots ourselves.

To see the difference between the good and the perfect lifelogs, suppose you want to find the list of venues that you considered for your spouse's surprise party. If you are a meticulous person and created a list, which you then proceeded to research, then there would be no difference between the two lifelogs. Both of them would find your list. However, if the places you considered were formed more organically, and included, in addition to suggestions from friends that you never wrote down, a restaurant in which you happened to dine one day, and a community center near your gym, then in order to create the perfect lifelog, the AI system needs to work harder to infer that you considered those as possible venues for the party. Realizing that perhaps you visited them multiple times or researched them further online as a possible venue might provide the necessary clues. If you settle for a good lifelog those additional connections may not be made. In that case, to get the information you want you might have to pose a more general query such as "which venues did I visit between January and June of last year" and hope that you can identify the ones you considered for the party on your own.

Your lifelog can contain data that is beyond the descriptions of your previous experiences. We'll turn to these now.

Your habits and interests

Your lifelog holds a wealth of hidden information that may not be immediately apparent. Through your past activities, it is possible to glean valuable insights into your habits, interests, and preferences, and even illuminate how they have evolved over time. The digital breadcrumbs we mentioned earlier with a bit of data mining magic can make it evident that you exercise six days a week before breakfast, have a penchant for romantic comedies, and tend to do your weekly grocery shopping on Saturday afternoons. While these may not come as a surprise to you, they might come in very handy with the AI partner which is helping you plan your week, especially since it also knows how long each of these activities typically takes you. So for example, if you need to fit another errand or two into your schedule, the AI partner will be able to help you schedule it appropriately. But there are also subtler patterns that computers are adept at detecting. For instance, they can unveil that you struggle to sleep well after consuming spicy dinners, detect patterns in your physical well-being, or that you experience increased productivity after spending quality time with your children. This knowledge may become useful when the AI partner tries to help you plan your time to balance between competing demands and align with your values.

A well-known example of patterns that computers excel at detecting pertains to the content you actively engage with. Your behavior on social-media platforms serves as a prime illustration of this phenomenon, because the platforms possess a very accurate understanding of your interests. They have the ability to precisely track the amount of time you dedicate to each post that appears on your social-media stream, enabling them to discern your interests with enhanced granularity. For instance, they can detect your interest in cooking content but specifically when the recipes are engaging, relatively simple, meat-free, and, to a certain extent, presented by an attractive person of the opposite gender. However, if chocolate is involved, the gender of the presenter becomes irrelevant. The models that social-media engines construct about you may not be articulated in plain language, but they are encoded in a mathematical representation (called embeddings) that is used by their algorithms to select content to present to you. It is important to point out that the topics that you *claim* to be of interest to you may differ significantly from the topics you actually spend time engaging with. For that reason, when apps ask you to choose topics of interest, they use that only as a way to kick off the process of learning your preferences (often referred to as a way of addressing the "cold start" problem), and then they continuously refine their model of you.

Your subjective experiences

The patterns of your behavior, as we discussed above, can reveal many of your subjective preferences, even ones that you may not be aware of. However, they do not capture your subjective perception about a particular experience that you just had. So far, the lifelog would capture the fact that you had lunch with Lisa and ate ratatouille. However, the lifelog should also capture your subjective experience in the form of answers to questions such as, did you actually enjoy the ratatouille or would you have preferred the lamb chops? How would you characterize the conversation with Lisa? Was it enjoyable, thought-provoking, and did it impart new knowledge that you wish to retain? Is there something you want to make sure you follow up on with Lisa the next time you meet? Do you want to meet again with Lisa and on what cadence? Looking ahead to when we use the lifelog to glean insights, we posit that the subjective aspects of our experiences may be more important than the objective ones. For example, when we are facing a difficult situation or decision, it would be invaluable if our lifelog could recall similar experiences from our past to shed some light on the present. Such a capability could truly be a lifechanger for our personal growth.

Subjective experiences can be much more complicated than they initially appear because they may change over time, leading to a layered tapestry of memories and perceptions that evolve with new experiences. For example, at first, your lunch with Lisa might register simply as a pleasant break in the day. A week later, though, you may find yourself recalling a moment of warmth when she asked about your daughter, and that memory begins to stand out more than the food or the casual chatter because reflecting on that question consequently helped you support your daughter. Much later, you might look back and realize that this lunch was part of a longer pattern in which Lisa was gently opening the door to a deeper connection, and its meaning shifts once again. Understanding the complexity of these evolving perceptions can certainly pose challenges to an AI agent that is trying to help you by digging into your lifelog.

Of course, there is an age-old "technology" that enables you to capture the full variety of your subjective assessments, known as the paper journal, and more recently, a plethora of new tools for capturing your thoughts in a digital journal. However, it is surprising how few people engage in regular journaling or even journal at all. Despite the desire many of us have to remember our thoughts and experiences from earlier in our lives more vividly, journaling remains an uncommon practice. The reason most of us don't journal is that it's yet another chore to squeeze into our busy schedules, and unlike brushing our teeth or going for a workout, the benefit of journaling is unclear, because we doubt that we'll ever go back and read our journal. For the record, journaling itself has inherent benefits for organizing our thoughts, even if we never revisit the entries later. Perhaps if we were aware that an AI agent could analyze our journals and provide us with timely insights, the habit of journaling would have been ingrained in us with the same gusto as our dental hygiene.

But this is about to change. People world-wide are already using AI chatbots as their confidants. In some cases, they use them as journals, telling them at various levels of detail what transpired in their day and their thoughts on their experiences. As we discuss later in the book, they are also asking for advice and in some cases getting emotionally attached to the bots. But for now, let's stick to the use of chatbots for journaling. After hearing several of my friends' experiences, I decided to experiment with it myself. I instructed the chatbot that I will be sharing daily experiences and that I want them to extract the highlights and to extract items that may go into a to-do list (e.g., a book I found that I want to read, or a follow up conversation I want to have with someone I just met). After a few weeks of doing this, I've also been able to ask more complex questions, such as who are the important people in my life or what insights the chatbot can offer about me (yes, chatbots know how to flatter). In a more recent experiment, I put my journal into Google's NotebookLM and started asking questions about my life with fascinating results. Admittedly, using AI for journaling is still in its infancy, but the potential of this new form of journaling to complement the collection of digital breadcrumbs that goes into your lifelog is huge.

Finally, in yet another nod to the power of wearable devices, it's also worthwhile noting that they are able to capture some aspects of your subjective experiences. The technique known as the Ecological Momentary Assessment (EMA), prompts users to provide feedback on their mood, stress levels, and well-being throughout the day. EMA captures real-time emotional states and contextual information, offering a more accurate picture of one's subjective experiences.

Your plans and aspirations

In his book, "I am a Strange Loop", Douglas Hofstadter describes three mental constructs that define our sense of identity. These constructs are episodic memories, which play a central role in our life experiences; episodic subjunctories, closely related to but not identical to our subjective experiences; and episodic projectories, which represent our plans and aspirations for the future. As the ultimate aim of our lifelog is to enhance the advice and recommendations provided by AI agents, it is important for the lifelog to incorporate our projectories.

More specifically, it would be valuable for the lifelog to document your goals, such as your desire to lose weight, your planned trip to Croatia, but also your curiosity about visiting Patagonia at some point. Additionally, it should know that you're trying to become fluent in Spanish, regain flexibility so you can reach your toes again, and, of course, allocate more time for family. Furthermore, you want your lifelog to know that these aspirations should take precedence over working diligently towards the next promotion or writing your next book, both of which can be put on the back burner for now.

While some of these projectories may be inferred from your online searches or social-media engagement, the majority will likely arise through the kinds of journaling that we described above.

Putting it all together: building the lifelog

By now, we hope you're convinced that there is a wealth of data about your life that can serve as the foundation for a lifelog and that holds immense value. This lifelog is the manifestation of the Experience component of Oswell. The data described so far concerns your past experiences and your plans for the future. There's another important chunk of data that covers the gap between the past and the future, i.e., the present, that is going to be important in order for an AI agent to give you useful advice. This data, often referred to as your context, answers questions such as where you are right now and with whom, what you are doing and what you are trying to do. For instance, are you seated at a restaurant, faced with a lengthy menu, and attempting to choose from it? And if so, are you with your family, or are you in a professional environment where a greater level of formality is expected? We'll cover the different components of context and the technologies that can be used to infer them in Chapter 8.

The data that is needed for your lifelog is fragmented across various data stores. Setting aside the business-related considerations associated with getting programmatic access to the data, the technical aspects of importing the data into the lifelog and fusing it are either resolved or actively being pursued in today's research laboratories. Experts can disagree on how close we are to solving the problems, but it's pretty clear that we can already build a useful lifelog using today's technology and improve it as the techniques advance.

One of the reasons that we make this strong claim is that the field of data integration, the technical name for the challenge of merging data from multiple sources, is rather well researched. For an in-depth study of the field, you can read the textbook I co-authored on the topic over 10 years ago. Data integration technology is already widely used in practice. For instance, applications like Apple Health or Strava already enable the fusion of data from numerous tracking devices. Similarly, when you search for flights online, you are presented with a consolidated view of information from numerous airlines. This consolidation and others are made possible by a set of standards that facilitate data sharing among applications while preserving their intended meaning. A set of standards for exchanging personal data can enable a similar functionality in Oswell.

The figure shows the steps involved in building a lifelog. The process starts with a set of importers that take the data from the original format given by the various apps and translates them into a more common format. As noted earlier, we do not import all the data from the apps, but only parts of it that are useful for the lifelog. The details of which data to import differ from one app to another and may also depend on business considerations. During the import, we extract the time of each event (e.g., photo, purchase) and its location if it's available and arrange all the entries on a timeline of your life. The availability of time and location already offer the option of compelling visualizations of your life at different scales, ranging from a day in your life to a year, or the 20 years you spent raising kids. Once all the data has been imported, other modules start looking at data from multiple sources to infer higher-level events that are not explicit in the raw data, such as trips, social gatherings, holiday celebrations, and making mango smoothies.

Your preferences and patterns are continuously gleaned from the data in the lifelog and from you via conversation. For example, there will be modules that track your exercise stats, and the content you consume in books, movies and music. Your eating preferences can be partially gleaned from the data in the lifelog, but a lot of data may be missing, so your input is crucial.

In addition to maintaining the lifelog as a whole, the AI partner can create smaller summaries in particular topics, such as your food, reading, or travel preferences. These summaries can be packaged in a way that can be shared, when you want, with others who provide you services.

To structure the data or not?

Bear with us as we discuss one more technical detail concerning lifelogs. One of the important choices that needs to be made when we build lifelogs is how much structure to impose on the data that they store. This decision arises in many data management applications that involve bringing in data from disparate sources as we are doing here. The choices we need to make touch on one of the long-standing dichotomies in data management, characterized by the organized world of databases, on the one hand, and the disorganized document stores managed by information retrieval techniques, on the other.

In the structured world, data is typically organized in tables, where each row and column have well-defined meanings. For example, in our context, we may have a table for each kind of activity, one for trips, another for social gatherings and yet another for exercise. The tables would have columns for details such as start and end times, locations, participants and what food was consumed. Structuring the data in tables would make it easy to answer questions such as, how many times you went camping last year, or what was your average running speed during the summer months compared with the winter. It is impossible to over-state the importance of database systems in running today's world. They are the platform that power many of the services we take for granted today, such as banking, shopping, or airline reservations. These are the systems that guarantee that when you board the plane and are assigned seat 12F, there won't be someone else claiming the same seat.

However, database systems have several drawbacks, including the fact that they require very detailed models of what data the application will encounter. Airlines and banks know very well what they will deal with, but our personal lives, and hence our lifelogs, are full of surprises.

The other side of the dichotomy, the world of information retrieval, was much smaller and characterized for many years by document and image stores. That was until they got their big break when the World-Wide Web came on to the scene. In what seemed like overnight, we suddenly had the largest and extremely diverse unorganized store of content we could ever imagine. On this side of the dichotomy, data is not organized. Your unit of information is the document. For example, an HTML document can hold text, images, tables and whatever other widgets HTML will allow you. You want to know what the meaning of the document is? Go read it. You can link a document about bird watching from a document with plumbing advice or travel tips to Okinawa. Anything goes. If you want to query your document collection, simply specify your desired information using language and hope the search engine does a good job. The vast majority of the time, with today's search engines, you'll get what you want, but some of the time the answers won't be satisfying. Getting an unsatisfactory result doesn't necessarily mean that the information you're looking for is not out there, though that is the case sometimes. The information could be out there, but the search-engine techniques are not good enough to find it. If the answer you need requires pulling together information from multiple sources, you are more likely out of luck. However, even for those of us who love the clean world of databases, being correct many billions of times per day is nothing to scoff at. The huge benefit of search engines over disorganized data is that they can accommodate data about any topic that is of interest to humanity. In the database community, we like to joke that if we were tasked with developing the World-Wide Web, it never would have happened.

Naturally, there are many intermediate points between the two extreme versions of this dichotomy. For example, when you query a search engine for the weather in your area or for the age of Lionel Messi or Oprah Winfrey, you will get a detailed answer that looks like it came from a weather database or a database about people. This is because search engines realized that there is a sizable fraction of queries that users care about that cannot be answered effectively by providing you a list of links to documents. Instead, to improve the user's experience, the search-engine companies decided that it is better to build databases that have authoritative answers or contract with other companies that have such data. In the case of weather, they will contract with a set of weather providers. In the case of information about people, they spend significant effort building and updating databases, often referred to as knowledge graphs, containing a variety of information about notable people, companies and locations. In the next few years, as we roll out features in database systems that use techniques from Generative AI, the line between these two points in the dichotomy will blur even further. But that is a topic for another book.

So where on the spectrum of structured to unstructured data should we land for lifelogs? We advocate for an intermediate solution between the two extremes. As we've already described, the main structure we extract from the raw event data is time and location. Extracting time and location is relatively trivial because the vast majority of the data we import comes from devices or apps that record them anyway. That minimal amount of structure already enables us to put all the data on the timeline and to offer compelling visualizations. Time and location also enable us to infer higher-level events. For example, a few photos taken at a park not too far from your house within a few minutes of each other may be a clue that you went to walk your dog. The photos of food coupled with the credit card bill around the same time is a clue that you went out to a yummy restaurant for dinner. Beyond time and location, we believe that all other structures are optional. Structure can be extracted when it is easy to do so and the benefits to the users are clear. For example, your exercise data is already imported with additional attributes such as speed and duration, so the system can offer to calculate stats that may be useful to you. If your shopping data comes with descriptions of the items you bought, you can see what categories you tend to spend your spare cash on. However, your lifelog will contain a breadth of information that doesn't fall into any pre-defined category, and that wealth of information should not be lost. The most important thing to keep in mind is that ultimately, the data in your lifelog will be processed by an LLM that can't be bothered about whether the data is structured or not.

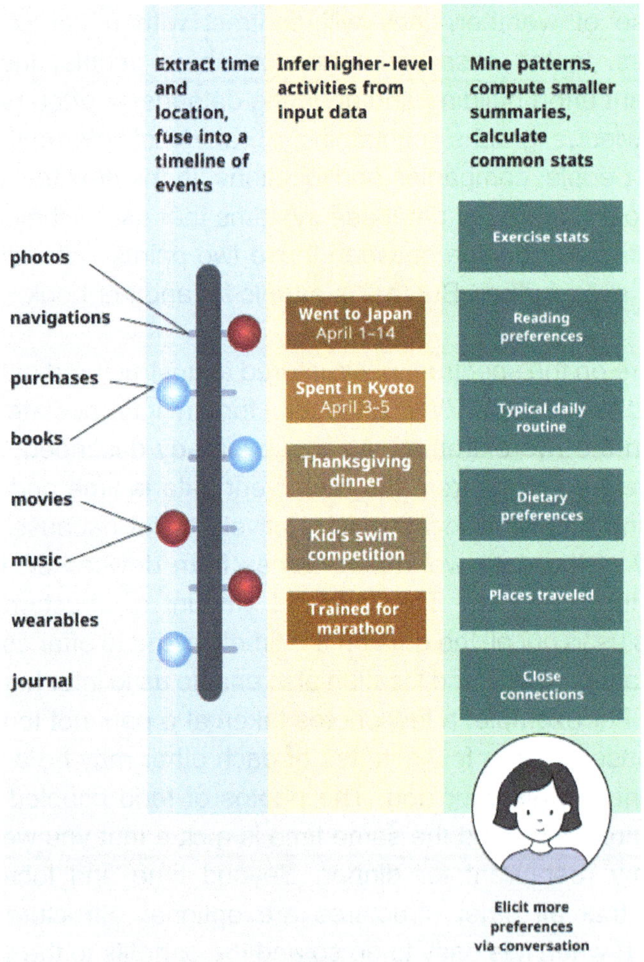

The benefits of a lifelog

Now that you know how to build a lifelog, let's delve deeper into a more comprehensive exploration of the benefits of your lifelog.

When discussing the numerous benefits of having a lifelog, we are fortunate to stand on the shoulders of giants. The idea of constructing a lifelog traces back as far as 1945, when Vennevar Bush published a seminal article in The Atlantic, titled "As We May Think." Bush, a former faculty member of M.I.T. and director of the American Office of Scientific Research and Development during World War II, played a pivotal role in coordinating the scientific efforts of over six thousand American scientists for military applications.

As the war approached its conclusion, Bush contemplated how the vast scientific expertise that was amassed during the war could be harnessed during times of peace. His aforementioned article encapsulates his thoughts on this subject, presenting his vision for a system called Memex. Memex would be "a device in which an individual stores all his books, records, and communications, and which is mechanized so that it may be consulted with exceeding speed and flexibility. It is an enlarged intimate supplement to his memory". Please pause here for a moment and recall that in 1945 nobody was snapping photos with their phones or recording their exercise routines with a smart watch. Most people didn't even know what a computer was. Vannevar Bush was a true visionary!

The closing paragraph of Bush's article provides even more inspiration and merits verbatim inclusion here:

The applications of science have built man a well-supplied house, and are teaching him to live healthily therein. They have enabled him to throw masses of people against another with cruel weapons.

They may yet allow him truly to encompass the great record and to grow in the wisdom of race experience. He may perish in conflict before he learns to wield that record for his true good. Yet, in the application of science to the needs and desires of man, it would seem to be a singularly unfortunate stage at which to terminate the process, or to lose hope as to the outcome.

In other words, Vannevar Bush was calling on us to build on the technology that proved useful for war purposes for our own good and well-being.

The concept of Memex has inspired generations of computer scientists to this date and even played a role in developing hypertext and the World-Wide Web. Starting in 2001, a notable project embracing the Memex idea commenced under the leadership of Gordon Bell, alongside his colleagues Jim Gemmell and Roger Lueder at Microsoft Research. Leveraging the technology available at the turn of the millennium, Bell embarked on digitizing a significant portion of his personal information, including CDs, photos, medical records, family documents and his email. In a very cool move for the era, he even went around with a wearable camera that recorded many of his experiences. After some pre-processing, Bell stored all this data in a relational database and developed a user interface that enabled him to submit queries against his lifelog. The book titled "Total Recall", written a few years later by Bell and his colleagues describes the many benefits of having a record of your life. Some of the examples presented below draw inspiration from the insights shared in Bell's book.

The lifelog, as the key component of the Experiences component of Oswell, has the role of supporting the other two components, Attention and Connection. The uses of the lifelog that are more specific to those components will be described in the chapters dedicated to those components. Here, we will instead focus on elucidating how the lifelog enables diverse forms of access to the information encompassing your life.

The most straightforward use of the lifelog is as a utility that can answer a myriad of questions about your life. When was the last time I serviced my heater? What major bills are going to be due in the next couple of months so I can plan my expenses more effectively? What's the name of the book that Lisa recommended when we last spoke? What did I buy my mom for her birthday over the past few years? Additionally, the lifelog can assist in uncovering patterns that may be difficult for us to discern on our own, such as identifying the specific foods that cause you stomach aches or finding patterns in our behavior that often affects our sleep. As another example, during our research at Meta Reality Labs, we spoke to a man who had a shoulder injury that would flare up at random points in time. Through the use of an experimental set of smart glasses that tracked his movements, he was able to determine which specific movements triggered the flare-ups.

Some of the information within your lifelog can hold value for others who need your help. For instance, Nissim is planning a trip to Tokyo next month and would greatly appreciate recommendations on restaurants and cafes based on your experiences. Your lifelog can easily provide this information. You might specifically want to recommend the sushi place you visited on your second night in Tokyo, whose name you undoubtedly forgot. With the lifelog at your disposal, you can simply inquire, "Where did I have dinner on my second night in Tokyo?" and retrieve the desired information.

Life-logging is certainly not a novel concept. Over the years, there has been a passionate community of people who refer to themselves as the "self-quantification movement". These dedicated individuals meticulously gather every detail of their lives and store them in a database, aiming to extract valuable insights. Their efforts typically focus on particular issues they are concerned about like their health, exercise or dieting habits. Accordingly, they build tools to collect as much data as possible about these topics with the hope of understanding their behavior better.

Among these enthusiasts, Nicholas Felton stands out as a prominent figure. As an information designer, Felton extensively documented various aspects of his life, including his locations, commute, sleep patterns, exercise routines, and captured moments in photographs. He ingeniously transformed this wealth of data into visually stunning annual reports known as the Feltron Reports, which are now even available for purchase. These reports serve the purpose of unveiling meaningful connections, providing contextual information, and suggesting correlations between different data points, offering a fascinating glimpse into the intricacies of Felton's life.

The perceived value of life-logging, according to those who have delved into it, has been a mixed bag, at best. Enthusiasts of this practice often devote a significant amount of time to collecting their data, only to find that it doesn't necessarily yield profound revelations about themselves. Undoubtedly, part of the disappointment stems from the high expectations they had built up, given the considerable effort invested. Furthermore, the limited value may also be attributed to the predominant focus on quantitative data, such as exercise routines, sleep patterns, and time spent in traffic, while overlooking the rich experiential qualitative data and contextual information that can provide deeper insights. It is true that the wearable devices we use may not always reveal something we don't already know or feel. For instance, the Oura Ring, which assesses sleep quality and is checked by its owners upon waking, usually (though not always) confirms their subjective experience of sleep. Nonetheless, the ring's accompanying app goes beyond a mere affirmation, providing a detailed sleep quality assessment on a 100-point scale and offering eloquent explanations, surpassing what most people can muster at that early hour of the day.

The lessons from life-logging should be taken to heart. We believe that the Experiences component of Oswell goes a few steps further than life-logging to provide much added value. First, unlike the effort involved in life-logging to date, the advent of new devices will reduce the effort involved to create the lifelog to close to zero. You'll simply have a lifelog created for you for free as a convenient side-effect of going through your life. Secondly, your lifelog will encompass far more than just quantitative data that can be graphed. It will encompass your actual experiences, capturing the unique events that shape your life, ranging from mundane encounters like appointments with plumbers to cherished social gatherings with college friends. Lastly, unlike our fleeting human memory, the lifelog will retain a comprehensive record of everything you do, enabling it to discern patterns that may elude our fallible biological brains.

Returning to the benefits of lifelogs, sharing our experiences and memories with others often brings us immense joy. Our lifelogs are akin to photo albums on steroids, as they enable us to dig deeper and ask countless questions. We can request to see all the occasions we savored crepes in Paris throughout the years or uncover the precise moment of our first visit to Streamer Cafe in Tokyo. And in lighthearted banter with our partners, we can unravel the mystery of that ubiquitous green jacket that seems to accompany us on every journey, discovering when it initially appeared and a log of its travel history.

It is easy to envision the abundance of experiences preserved within your lifelog becoming a precious treasure to be passed down for future generations. Many of us would have loved to be able to see in greater detail the lives of our ancestors, including the triumphs and tribulations they encountered. For example, I would have loved to know what went through the mind of my paternal grandfather in the early 1930's when he made the brave decision to emigrate with his family from Thessaloniki, Greece to an uncertain future in Tel-Aviv, a decision that ultimately saved their lives when World War II broke out. The challenge that this desire to share raises is to figure out which details of your life you want to leave around after you pass, and which you're taking with you to your grave (yes, we all have a few of those). Between these two extremes, there are countless details that may be deemed too mundane to share, such as your inexplicable need to discuss your encounters with your dishwasher in detail. It would be advantageous if the AI agent could assist in navigating these complex choices, curating an appropriate version of your lifelog to be shared with your descendants. Furthermore, we need not limit the sharing to just offspring; one can also imagine imparting certain facets of their life to the communities they have been a part of, for the collective benefit.

The biggest benefit your lifelog might provide you is simply the gift of perspective. In "The Book of Awakening", author Mark Nepo beautifully expresses the idea that "If peace comes from seeing the whole, then misery stems from a loss of perspective." In essence, Nepo suggests that focusing solely on a small setback in our lives, be it a physical pain or a disappointing day at work, is more likely to lead to misery. However, when we adopt a broader perspective, that momentary setback loses its gravity, and we find greater peace within ourselves. That is exactly what your lifelog can provide you with. Whereas you are typically looking at your life from the perspective of the here and now, the lifelog can take a more global perspective that is based on the totality of the experiences that you have shared with it.

Why don't we have this today?

You might have noticed that the tone of this chapter thus far makes it seem that lifelogs can be built today, even if not perfectly. So you might be wondering why you don't have one yet. Another thought that might be crossing your mind is that the companies that are currently holding on to the data that we're earmarking for your lifelog have no incentive to share it in that way. After all, data is the new oil, and a "data moat" is a successful business model.

We stick with our assessment that the major hurdles to building lifelogs are not technical ones. Instead, the challenges stem from the fact that the data is scattered across multiple services, otherwise known as data siloes, each belonging to a different company. And just as you surmised, currently, none of these companies have a strong incentive to enable seamless streaming of this data into your lifelog. Even if they did, they have valid reasons to restrict access to certain portions of the data that is currently within their respective apps. After all, the data they collect about you, their data moat, serves as a means to provide you with better recommendations, and they would not want this competitive advantage to dissipate quickly. Furthermore, the reputation of companies depends heavily on being able to ensure the privacy of your data, and sharing the data beyond their internal systems only complicates their privacy goals.

Given the above, you might wonder why we are so optimistic that lifelogs, in one shape or another, will become a reality in the foreseeable future? There are several reasons for our optimism. The first, and honestly, the most boring, is legislation. For example, recent legislation from the European Union, specifically the General Data Protection Regulation (GDPR), mandates that your personal data be available for download. While the main goal of GDPR was to protect users and enable them to delete and port their data, part of the incentive for it was to enable innovators to envision and implement other uses of personal data. GDPR was only the first step, and while it enables you to gather all your personal data, it is extremely clunky to do so, because you need to navigate multiple web sites and different data formats. The follow up legislation from the European Union, known as the Data Markets Act (DMA), requires that some of this data should also be available through a programming interface. At that point, building your lifelog should be much more convenient. Unfortunately, the adoption of the DMA has not been as rapid as we would have hoped for.

The second reason for our optimism is that companies have already started recognizing the value of personalization. For example, imagine that when you talk with a chatbot like ChatGPT or Gemini, it could give you much better answers because it knows more about you. Fortunately, that's also what the builders of these chatbots are thinking, and we have seen this trend in several recent product announcements. For example, Google announced in April 2025 that you will soon be able to authorize Gemini to look into data stored in some of your Google services, such as Gmail or Google Photos, to gain additional insight about you as a user. In doing so, Google and others are essentially building fragments of your lifelog on demand when you ask them a question. In the future, you can imagine going one step further. For example, imagine if a company has enough information about you to provide a condensed summary of your travel preferences (e.g., the kinds of activities and accommodations you enjoy on vacation). That company could now enable you to authorize them to share that condensed summary with a travel site in order to improve your experience. In doing so, they will require your consent and also will only share a very specific slice of your preferences, not their entire moat.

The main idea here is that a lifelog need not be a monolithic database sitting on the server of a specific company. Relevant approximations of your lifelog can be created on the fly for specific purposes that you are comfortable with. As this ecosystem of personal profiles starts gaining momentum, there will be an explosion of personalized services that come to market, fueling the ecosystem even more.

Reading the brain

We would be remiss if we ended this chapter without at least touching on an important nascent technology. In a few years from now, it may be possible to get much of the information concerning your experiences in a more direct way, from your brain itself. Brain-computer interfaces (BCI) are technologies that can read certain signals directly from the brain, and ultimately, write to the brain in order to change your experiences or your memories of experiences. For the most part, these technologies are in their infancy and their full potential is yet unknown.

A concrete example of brain-computer interface technology is the wrist band that was built by a startup named CNTL-labs, a company that was acquired by Meta in 2019. CNTL-labs was founded by Thomas Reardon, who spent a big chunk of his career at Microsoft, where he is credited with envisioning and building Internet Explorer, which was the world's most popular web browser for a long while. He then decided he needed another challenge and went back to school, ultimately earning a doctorate in neuroscience from Columbia University in New York. His studies convinced him that there are more efficient ways of interacting with computers than using our fingers to type.

In CNTL-labs, and later at Meta, his team built a device that you can wear on your wrist and it figures out what your brain is telling your hands to do. The intuition goes as follows. Essentially, before you perform any movement on a keyboard, your forebrain sends signals to the motor neurons in your arm. These signals instruct the motor neurons how to turn the commands into action. The idea behind their device is that if you can intercept the signal sent from the brain to the motor neurons, which they do with a technology called surface electromyography (sEMG), you can implement the brain's commands without actually moving the muscles. So, for example, if the brain is telling your arm to press the S key, communicate the key press directly to the computer without moving your arms. After all, the signal from the brain to the arm already contains the information you need. In September 2025, Meta launched its new smart glasses and shipped a smart wrist band with it that is based on the technology developed at CNTL-labs. The wrist band enables the user to use subtle hand movements to control features of the glasses, such as adjusting volume, scrolling, or opening apps.

Reardon's wrist device is an example of a non-invasive brain-computer interface device. You just strap it on and it starts working. It probably won't surprise you to know that if you are willing to let someone insert sensors and actuators into your skull, you can read a lot more and you can actually affect your conscious experience. An example of such an intervention is deep brain stimulation, employed as a treatment for severe depression. Deep brain stimulation functions akin to a pacemaker, but it is applied within the brain rather than the heart. It entails the surgical implantation of electrodes, typically within a brain region that is the ventral anterior limb of the internal capsule. It delivers electrical impulses to modulate brain activity, thereby regulating mood and alleviating depressive symptoms. As another example, transcranial direct current stimulation (tDCS) is a technique that helps adults with attention deficit or hyperactivity disorder. In a clinical trial with 64 adults suffering from this condition, it was observed that 30 minutes of daily tDCS over the course of a month resulted in improved attention. Neuralink, one of Elon Musk's companies, announced in January, 2024 that they successfully implanted one of their devices in the brain of Noland Arbaugh, a man who has been paralyzed from the shoulders and down. With the Neuralink device, Noland was able to play computer games by directing his thoughts directly to the device.

These early prototypes and products beg a few big questions. How much will these devices be able to read? Figuring out that I want to type the word `love' into an email is one thing, but will they be able to read my thoughts and my emotions? Will the person sitting next to me now be able to hack into my brain and know exactly what I think about them? Will my employer, or worse, my government be able to track my thoughts and emotions? What about the changes to my brain that this technology will be able to affect? Can I be manipulated to have certain beliefs? Or, can my brain be modified to think that I just spent a relaxing week in Bali without getting off my couch? These questions seem to raise much more significant concerns than the ones that were bothering you just a few minutes ago, such as your exercise data being combined with your Spotify listening history and your online purchases.

These are still the early days of brain-computer interfaces, so the answers to these questions are yet to be worked out by scientists and engineers. For now, it does not appear that the technology will be able to read your brain in the level of detail we just described. However, Rita Farahany, a professor at Duke University and the author of the 2023 book "The Battle for Your Brain: Defending the Right to Think Freely in the Age of Neurotechnology", is not waiting around before she raises serious ethical concerns. Farahany discusses the concept of cognitive liberty, which she defines to be "a right to self-determination over our brains and mental experiences, which includes a right to access and use technologies that change our brains if we choose to do so." She adds that it is also the "right from unwanted interference with our mental privacy and freedom of thought." According to Farahany, throughout history, we've taken for granted that our thoughts, emotions and mental experiences are solely our own. Because after all, there was not a major technology to mess around with them. However, when generative AI and brain-computer interfaces come to the fore, this will be a new frontier for ethicists. Some lawmakers are not waiting around either. In April 2024, the states of Colorado and California extended their privacy laws to include neural data.

The outlook for the future of lifelogs

We hope this chapter has convinced you that there is plenty of data about you that can be assembled to create a lifelog, which is a repository of your life experiences, preferences, and plans for the future. There are many practical and privacy hurdles that need to be overcome in order to realize the vision of lifelogs. However, we believe that when we look back years from now, we'll observe that we overthought these issues. With the development of new devices that will capture data about you from a multitude of angles and times of day, there will be plenty of data from which to create a useful lifelog. The benefits of the lifelog will weave into the fabric of our lives and they will become indispensable for most of us. The next chapter discusses the privacy issues, which should be the main concern as we move forward.

Try This 👉

In this chapter we discussed the details of your lifelog – the repository of everything that an AI can know about you. Try building a rudimentary lifelog. Take some set of your personal data and share it with an AI system. Current AI chatbots allow you to upload files into a conversation thread and use them as part of the conversation. Google's NotebookLM is especially designed to answer questions about content you provide. You can upload your journal if you have one or parts thereof, or simply write down your ruminations on the last few days. You can also easily download your shopping or music listening history from the services you use, or your exercise and health data that is stored in your smart watch. Try asking a few questions and seeing what you get. Can you come up with some insights that would have been challenging to find otherwise? What questions do you wish you could ask about your past but the data is not there yet? What would it have taken at the time to record that necessary data?

"Hey, Lisa! Any chance I can come over for dinner tonight? I'll bring wine this time and we can order food."

"Wonderful! I actually decided to take the afternoon off and I was going to try making a vegetable lasagna. How does that sound?"

"Perfetta! I'll be there soon to help!"

Five minutes later there was a knock on the door. "Boy, somebody is excited today!" Lisa exclaimed as she saw Oliver standing there with a bottle of Pinot Noir. "My AI assistant told me that a wine with good acidity would cut through the different sauces and layers of the lasagna," Oliver said, trying to seem matter-of-fact.

Without waiting for Lisa's response, Oliver continued. "I think I have a first version of part of my app ready to demo. It's a repository of all the information about you. From this repository, it can answer all kinds of questions about your life, but also predict your daily routine, your interests, your habits, and your preferences."

Lisa looked quizzical. "And how does it gather that information? Do I have to input it manually while the lasagna gets cold?"

"Of course not! Just like we discussed last week, it collects data from the digital activities you are already doing -- your watch, your phone, content you consume online, stuff like that. For example, it uses your smartphone's GPS to track your location, or your smartwatch to monitor your heart rate and physical activity. It also analyzes your photos for any useful information."

Lisa's expression turned even more skeptical. "Nice, but that's also kind of creepy Oliver! As your leading candidate for head of marketing, I can already tell you that the headlines in the press aren't going to look very good."

"Yeah, but the power of the AI agent comes from knowing you really well, just like a dedicated personal assistant does."

"I understand that, but you've got to be really careful with it. My assistant at work is really good and he gives me great advice very often. But he does not know how I spent the night yesterday or which videos I've been watching on YouTube."

"Um... where did you go last night?"

"Open that bottle of wine first."

"Ok, ok. I see your point. I was just working on the privacy settings in the app, but I guess I need to take another look."

"Privacy settings are old school. Nobody's going to go through a long questionnaire about privacy before using the app. You need to think about privacy in a completely new way."

"I should have brought more wine."

5. The Privacy of Your Lifelog

The previous chapter, with its promise of creating the best database about you ever, probably made you cringe a few times, if not outright shudder, as you wondered about the privacy implications of the technology. In fact, the key idea underlying Oswell and the highly-personalized services it promises to provide makes you want to call a few privacy and security experts into the room before we go much further. It probably comes as no surprise that the issues around privacy and security are quite nuanced and further complicated by the observation that privacy is a topic where perceptions and personal preferences often dominate over the technical guarantees that systems are able to provide. This chapter examines some of the issues relating to privacy in the context of personalized agents. We dig deeper into the different reasons that users are concerned about the privacy of their data and discuss some of the technical solutions that have been put in place to safeguard your data. Our goal is not to paint a rosy picture of the situation, but rather to elucidate the tradeoffs so you can make more informed decisions as a user and as a builder of these technologies.

To begin, a note about terminology. The concepts of privacy and security are very closely related and are often confused with each other. Roughly speaking, privacy refers to the way your data is handled, what it is used for, who it is shared with, and what restrictions you can impose on these. Security refers to ensuring that your data is not leaked or accessible to other unauthorized parties whether they are well meaning or malicious. The issues we discuss in this chapter involve both privacy and security and in some cases we may err by using the term privacy as a shorthand to cover both.

Privacy concerns have long been a challenge in the history of funding research on projects involving personal information. No doubt, these concerns have slowed down progress on these technologies. As a prominent example, in 2003, DARPA, the research agency of the American Department of Defense, initiated a project called "Total Information Awareness" (TIA). The project aimed to fuse data from multiple agencies, granting the government enhanced capabilities in detecting and tracking terrorists and their activities, an idea that garnered support after the terrorist attacks on September 11, 2001. However, this would naturally result in more comprehensive profiles for individuals, encompassing both potential terrorists and innocent law-abiding citizens. Due to privacy concerns, the project was defunded later that year. Although the TIA project did not directly address personal information in the same way we do here, its repercussions were felt elsewhere.

Another DARPA project called LifeLog, which aimed to build precisely what we have described in the previous chapter, was also in the planning stages in the 2003-2004 timeframe, but was prematurely canceled due to similar privacy concerns. This sensitivity even extended to other unrelated projects across the country. When Oren Etzioni, a professor at the University of Washington, and later the founder of the Allen Institute of AI, launched a project called "KnowItAll" to extract general (non-personal) knowledge from the web, he received a concerned call from DARPA, the main funder of the project, strongly suggesting a name change. Oren, known for his ability to often swiftly solve thorny issues, changed the name to "KnowIt".

Before we go further, we will first spell out what we believe privacy should look like in Oswell. The first principle is that, by default, all data in Oswell is private. Period. The second principle is that when you do want to share data, you should be able to specify what you want to share at the moment that you need to share it. For example, if I'm interacting with a waiter at a Japanese restaurant, whether human or automated, hoping to get personalized recommendations from their vast menu, I should be able to specify that I want to share

my preferences concerning Japanese food (which will be derived from my lifelog) with the waiter for the next 10 minutes. In other words, it should be as easy as uttering a command in my preferred language to my agent.
As another example, if I'm sharing recent highlights from a trip to Tokyo with a colleague who is preparing a trip there, I should be able to specify only the names and locations of the places I am recommending. However, if I am helping my good friend Nissim with his Tokyo trip planning, then I can tell my agent to be more relaxed and also share photos and some relevant journal entries.

Unlike our typical interactions, where privacy preferences are elicited via long, often hard to find, menus and we have to answer questions we do not always know the answer to, here it should be easy to specify what to share or retract at any given time. Admittedly, implementing the second privacy principle requires some technical innovations. Specifically, translating an utterance in language to a precise set of items in your lifelog that should be shared can be challenging. Relying on pre-computed summaries from your lifelog, as we alluded to in Chapter 4, for domains such as your food, reading and travel preferences can come in handy, and in cases where these summaries are not computed, erring on the side of sharing less is a good principle to adopt.

What are we worried about?

Let us now turn to a more detailed examination of what users are concerned about and the reasons behind those concerns.

At the core of the issue, many individuals feel uneasy about consolidating all their personal information into a single repository like the lifelog, whether the lifelog is stored on their phone, laptop, or in the cloud with state-of-the-art security measures. Fundamentally, the comfort level depends on a personal tradeoff between the benefits one expects to get from a service and the risks that they may be exposed to as a result. This is by no means a new tradeoff. Corporations have been storing slices of our personal information since the beginning of the digital era. For example, our credit card companies have had records of every transaction we make for decades, our phone provider knows exactly who we called, when and for how long, and some online services we use daily store our photos, email and the logs of our search history. For the vast majority of us, it would be challenging to envision life without these services that have become ingrained in our daily routines.

The lifelog, however, feels different than the above services. Simply put, the lifelog feels much more private. In this book we have gone to great lengths to emphasize the benefits of integrating as much of your data as possible to gain a comprehensive understanding of you, your experiences and your preferences. However, when it comes to privacy, this fusion feels like a strong headwind. It is understandable that the more data that is consolidated about you, the easier it is to form a more detailed and multi-faceted picture of your life, and hence the greater the cause for concern. To put this in perspective, a close second in the race for knowing you so well are the social networks who can figure out what exactly you pay attention to on your feed at a level of granularity that even you would have a hard time articulating to ourselves and may be embarrassed by. Before we go any further, we would like to emphasize that your life conditions will have a great impact on your comfort level with having a lifelog. For example, if you are in a way in a vulnerable position with respect to your safety, whether it is on the domestic, community or national level, the risks of anything leaking from a lifelog can be quite detrimental.

To complicate matters further, we should also note that the concern extends beyond just your own data. A person's lifelog inevitably includes details from the lives of others, which means that what you do with your data can impact others, and vice versa. For instance, Lisa's lifelog will contain numerous episodes involving Oliver's life, and vice versa. This too is not a new issue -- your intimate correspondences have been stored in others' electronic mailboxes for quite a while now. In the story that started the previous chapter,

Ted Chiang puts a positive spin on this issue. The main character of the story initially did not have his own lifelog but was able to reconstruct it from fragments of lifelogs belonging to people he interacted with throughout his life. However, you can also easily see the risks of creating a log of your life from the lifelogs of others you have interacted with.

Let's take this line of thought one more step, perhaps the ultimate one. What happens to your memories after you die? If handled properly, lifelogs have the potential to generate collective memories for families, communities, and even society as a whole. In Douglas Hofstadter's book, "I am a Strange Loop", he describes how even after we pass away, we continue to exist in the memories of others through the shared experiences we had together. This observation should resonate very well with anyone who has ever lost a loved one, or on individuals who are pondering how to meaningfully spend their time. Why not use our lifelogs to create gifts for our offspring that can last beyond our lifetimes? The trick, of course, is how to decide what to share and what secrets you're taking with you to your grave.

Putting aside our data, we should also worry about the privacy of our interactions with the AI agents. As we discuss throughout this book, we expect an AI agent based on Oswell to provide us advice on different aspects of our life throughout the day, and some of these interactions may be quite sensitive. They might involve our current state of mind, our feelings about our boss or about an attractive person standing across the room, or about some biases we are not terribly proud of but that we lean on from time to time. Depending on how the conversations with our agents are handled, the emotions and preferences expressed in these interactions may not be stored directly in our lifelog, and therefore the privacy of our lifelog may not necessarily extend to them.

What could possibly go wrong?

So far we discussed what users may be worried about, but at an abstract level, namely, their data and their interactions. But now let's make this more concrete. Why are we worried about our data and our interactions? Who is out to get us? Broadly speaking, the concerns revolve around three categories: how corporations may use our data, whether these same corporations can keep our data secure from external hackers, and what happens when the governments come knocking on the corporations' doors asking for data for whatever reason they see fit. The first concern is mostly concerned with privacy, while the latter two are with security.

The first category of reasons for discomfort revolves around a sense of distrust regarding how corporations handle and utilize personal data. To put this concern in context, it is widely recognized that companies use the data they collect on your interactions with their services to determine which ads are displayed on your feed, tailored to pique your interest. This explains why, when browsing your social-media feed, you encounter advertisements for furniture pieces that align with your preferences, local cultural events that captivate your attention, and offerings from the most innovative coffee roaster in your area, rather than generic ads you would typically see on television such as beer, cars, insurance, and then more beer. As you approach middle age, things get creepier. The system starts showing you more ads for colorful socks, and you, in return, get sucked into buying them. These same systems also select political ads for your stream, a category of ads that bring up additional issues that we discuss in more detail in Chapter 10 since they may have even broader ramifications to our democracies.

Advertising is the business model of most of these companies, and therefore these ads are their main source of revenues. An alternative business model would have you pay a subscription for using the service, but that model has gained traction in only a few use cases, mostly involving access to premium content. For some people, getting ads on their social-media feeds is a small nuisance, but certainly worth the free service. At times, they may even find the ads useful. In Chapter 11 we will discuss the possibility that AI will develop much more intimate relationships with us. In that case, its influence may extend much further than buying a new pair of colorful socks, and we may not feel all that comfortable. Other people, even today, find that the presence of ads makes for a highly unpleasant experience.

There is a significant misconception that is worth noting here. Due to some inaccurate narratives in the popular press, many people are under the impression that the fact that these platforms serve us personalized ads means that they "sell our data" to other companies, or more specifically, to the advertisers themselves. While there are companies that make their business by collecting personal data and selling it, that is not the way the main social-media platforms work. When you are served personalized ads, your data does not leave the platform to the internal systems of the advertiser. Instead, the advertisers specify which kinds of users they would like to target in their ads, such as males in the 45-55 age bracket who live on the east coast and have interest in golf. The platform then uses its own system and a variety of other factors to match ads to users. The reason this distinction is important is that if the advertisers got access to your data, they could target you in other ways or even sell your data to yet another party, and that is certainly a slippery slope.

Before we let the companies off the hook here, there is one more issue we need to consider, which is whether these companies are using your data to train their machine learning systems? The answer is a resounding yes. In fact, as we explain in Chapter 7, using your data and that of billions of other users is one of the main ways these companies are able to provide useful recommendations. When you get compelling shopping or movie suggestions, those are based, in part, on what others, who share some interests with you, have done on the same platform. In principle, that doesn't sound too bad. Your experience is used to improve the experience of others. One question you may ask is whether you can get a cut of the profits. After all, if the platform is getting better and therefore making more money because of your contributions, small as they may be, you should get a check in the mail every now and then. This idea has been put forth in Jaron Lanier's 2013 book, "Who owns the Future", and was well enough received that it has inspired many discussions since then. However, despite the healthy debate on this topic, the economics of your contributions to the power of platforms have yet to be worked out completely. Intuition, however, says that the check may be so small that it's not worth the effort, so don't quit your day job just yet.

Most of the contributions of your data to online platforms happen through aggregating the data of many users. But we should also consider whether the model employed by the platform can learn something much more substantial that is unique to you and that you do not want to leak. For example, if you are conversing with your AI agent about a new startup idea or book proposal and the AI agent is helping you refine the idea, you do not want your ideas to suddenly surface somewhere else and get scooped.

Figuring out whether your data is used to improve the model depends on the specific provider, may change with time, and can often be configured in the user interface. In some cases, your data may be used for training unless you explicitly opt out, or may depend on what kind of account you have (which typically means that if you pay, you have more say on the matter). As you can imagine, corporations are concerned about having their proprietary data used for model training, which is why corporate accounts typically ensure that the data is not subsequently fed back into the training of the model.

To complicate things further, it is important to note the difference between remembering your previous conversations with the AI bot and using your data for training subsequent versions of the model. Most chatbots today provide a feature where the chatbot can remember previous parts of a conversation in a particular chat so they have better context when new questions are posed. That so-called ‘session memory’ is a different knob from the one that determines whether the provider can use the data for training its model.

The second category of reasons for users' to worry about their data concerns security and pertains to the fear of data leaks and hacks. While you may have confidence in the company responsible for storing your data, there remains a worry that if their systems are compromised, your information could fall into the wrong hands. Unfortunately, such incidents have occurred repeatedly and are even on the rise, often garnering significant media attention.

A particularly ironic example is the hack of the Ashley Madison dating service which primarily caters to individuals in relationships seeking discreet affairs. Here too, you need to make a personal decision on how much to trust the online platforms. Today many of these companies employ leading experts on data privacy and security and they are developing the most advanced techniques for protecting your data because it is one of the fundamental requirements for running their business and earning trust with their users.

A third category of reasons for the concern revolves around the fear of government overreach. In many jurisdictions worldwide, service providers could be compelled by local government agencies to disclose data pertaining to specific users. While such data enforcement laws are ostensibly implemented to safeguard the interests of local citizens, it is only natural for individuals to harbor concerns about the potential consequences when governments veer off course. Obviously, the specific political milieu that you inhabit will play a key role in shaping your opinion on this issue.

A technological perspective

A full discussion of the technologies designed to preserve the privacy and security of your data is well beyond the scope of this book. However, in the next few pages we will highlight some of the main ideas concerning these technologies so you can navigate this landscape more effectively. An important theme to point out at the outset is that security and privacy of data are a constant arms race. Whenever new protections are found, there are adversaries out there that will try to circumvent them. It is never a done deal.

At the end of the day, technologies are used by people and protections are enforced by people. So a first point worth noting is that the large technology companies have gone to great lengths to restrict access to data to their employees, and these restrictions keep getting more and more tight. Over the past few years, a set of best practices have emerged in tech companies to address access to user data. There are many nuances to these policies and there will be differences between companies as these practices evolve and as their businesses evolve. Hence, nothing we say below should be taken as the definitive state of these policies in any specific company.

The main takeaway is that you can not just walk into the office on your first day on the job at one of the big-tech companies and start looking up the personal data of your ex-girlfriend or soon-to-be ex-boyfriend. At the very least, if you need access to personal data you need to go through a rigorous process that involves justifying the need to access particular data, and arguing that your task cannot be done without it. For example, if you're trying to help a user recover an account that had been hacked, you may need to look at the recent activity on that account to determine what happened. Even then, you will need user consent to proceed. If there is even a possibility that in the process of performing your job you may be exposed to data of someone you know personally, the policy is that you should try to find someone else to perform that task. The following anecdote exemplifies the key idea: on the first day of orientation at Meta new employees were told (yes, in jest): if there's someone you're interested in, don't look up the personal information in our internal systems, just use normal methods for stalking them online.

Scrutiny on personal data starts even earlier in the process of designing new products or features. In that process, the product designers need to explain exactly which data is going to be collected from users and what it is going to be used for. In particular, the data privacy review will question any data that is not directly relevant to the quality of the product itself, and will not allow it. By tying the collection of the data to a particular purpose, companies also significantly reduce the risk that it will be used for secondary purposes. For example, a service may store your photos, but that should not imply that they can use it for face recognition in a different service.

Another best practice employed in corporations is that you use data for analysis, it needs to be data that occurs a large number of times and any identifying information about the users is removed. For example, if you are analyzing the query log of a search engine, then you only consider queries that occur at least 50 times. The intuition is that if 50 different people typed in the same query, it is unlikely to contain highly sensitive information about an individual, such as your online bank credentials.

Just in case malicious actors gain access to the physical storage, companies use encryption to protect the data they store. In simple terms, this means that if you try to read the data, it looks like gobbledygook, backed up by an impressive collection of mathematical theorems that guarantee that you cannot make sense of it. The only way to make sense of the data is if you have a special key (or set of keys) that unlocks the secret code and enables you to decrypt the data.

Encryption is applied not only to stored data but also to data in transit on messaging platforms so it is impossible to eavesdrop on them. Some messaging platforms have even gone a step further and guarantee that your messages are erased automatically after a certain amount of time.

Of course, to perform the processing necessary to provide its services, the platform needs to decrypt your data. There are multiple approaches to how this is done, depending on the required level of security. The easiest method is to decrypt the data, perform the analysis and delete the decrypted copy of the data. If an additional level of security is needed, the computation can be performed in a secure enclave, which is specialized hardware that significantly reduces the risk that other actors on the network can access the data while the computation is being performed. Finally, there are a set of techniques, known as different variants of homomorphic encryption, that allow you to perform the computation on the encrypted data itself and produce a result, that when decrypted, would be the same as what you would have gotten if you performed the computation on the clear data. However, these techniques typically apply to only simple computations, and get computationally intractable otherwise and so they are applied only in specialized cases.

Encryption means that both hackers and governments cannot gain real access to the data, and some governments are not happy about that. Multiple governments around the world have been in debates with large technology firms about providing 'backdoor' access to encrypted data, i.e., enabling government agencies to access data of particular individuals even if it is encrypted. Tech companies have constantly pushed back on these initiatives arguing that it undermines user privacy and that technically such a backdoor may not be secure. This debate continues around the world, taking on different flavors depending on geographical location, but is largely unresolved.

If storing your data in the cloud makes you uneasy, you can bypass some of these problems and debates by storing all your data on your own device. Your lifelog fits on your device already today. Moreover, with the rapid progress happening in the AI world, you are likely soon to have a rather powerful AI agent that can run completely on your mobile device. In that case, none of the interactions you have with your agent or the data it stores need to leave the device.

The obvious limitation of this solution is what happens if someone hacks into your phone or, more likely, what happens when your phone accidentally gets flushed down the toilet. It is bad enough that you need to shell out a few hundred bucks to replace your phone, you do not want to suffer the loss of your life memories as well. That is why there are hybrid solutions that store your data on the phone, but have secure backups in the cloud.

Summary

In the last few pages we attempted to enumerate some of the main privacy and security concerns that may arise as we contemplate the potential of lifelogs. However, it is likely that we have missed many concerns that people may have. The value of the above discussion is to help you, the reader and the builder, think through the specific issues that you care about and that are relevant to your life circumstances. For example, if you are concerned about a particular type of information about yourself, such as health or finances, you can make sure that does not enter your lifelog. If you are concerned about certain organizations getting hold of your data, you can proceed to check the actual risk that this could happen, or ensure that your data is stored only on your device, assuming that is enough to assuage your concerns. The more specific you are about your concerns, the better you are positioned to make informed decisions, and put safeguards in place. It is equally important to acknowledge that one does not necessarily require a specific justification for feeling uncomfortable about the concept of lifelogs being created and stored. It is perfectly acceptable to feel uneasy about the concept without being able to articulate the precise reasons. It is fine if you want to summarize your sentiment on the topic as "meh".

Try This 👉

This chapter argued that our comfort level regarding privacy is affected by multiple factors, such as what is being shared with the AI, how you can explicitly ask to share parts of your data with others, and your life circumstances, including the country you live in. Try to apply these different factors to your own life. Start with taking inventory of what personal data you already store in cloud-based services. Then imagine that all of this data is combined into a single store, but also that there's an AI engine that tries to find useful connections between these different data. How comfortable are you with having this repository about you somewhere in a cloud service? Where you feel discomfort, can you articulate exactly why? Try to imagine the same scenario, but for someone else in your life that may have different concerns.

Oliver was already waiting at the usual table at the cafe. It was also clear that he already had too much caffeine. "I ordered your usual latte, but I think you should also try the espresso tonic. It's an awesome combination of bitter and bitter. Great for a summer day like this one."

"And you've already had a few, I assume?"

"Well, yeah. They give you a free drink on the week of your birthday and I think that cute barista there is eyeing me."

"But your birthday is not for a few months..."

"Never mind. How did you like the app?"

"Very interesting. I imported quite a bit of my data."

"And?"

"And you were wrong."

"Huh?"

"Monica was not dressed as Wonder Woman, she was dressed as Jane Austin."

"How did you figure that out?"

"I asked my lifelog. Well, it needed some help. First I asked for photos from parties I attended with you a couple of years ago, but it complained that there were too many parties (23!). So then I remembered that I had just ran my first half-marathon the same week as that party, so I told it so, and there it was! Monica wearing a Jane Austin costume."

"So I was dating Jane Austin all this time?"

"You seemed pretty fine with it for the last couple of years."

"That explains a few things... She was always sensitive when I mentioned the costume. As if she thought I wasn't really into her."

"Putting your terrible memory aside for a moment, I did enjoy browsing through special moments of my life. You appear in quite a few of them! It kind of made me feel better about my life already. Looking back, I realize I've spent quite a bit of time on stuff I really enjoy doing, but I needed that reminder to feel good about it. Well done! So didn't you also say that this app will help me better manage my life? Right now, my life is a mess. I'm constantly distracted by this and that and it makes it hard for me to focus on any one thing."

"Ah, yes", Oliver seemed to finally snap away from his nostalgic thoughts. "Give me a sec here."

"What are you doing?"

"Sending a package with the entire Jane Austin collection to Monica."

"Of course."

"Ok, I'm done. So managing your life. That's exactly what I'm working on now. I read a book by Daniel Levitin a while back called “The Organized Mind”. In the book he tells a story of meeting Jimmy Carter when he was running for president of the USA in 1976. Levitin was really impressed at how Carter's attention seemed to be completely focused on him, as if there was nothing else going on in the world."

"I knew that Jimmy Carter was an amazing individual, but this sounds pretty remarkable," Lisa interrupted.

"Listen on. Later Levitin was reflecting on the meeting and on how Carter was able to focus on their conversation so well, and realized that the key to Carter's focus was the fact that he had a big team of assistants. That team was ensuring that at any given point in time Jimmy was doing the most important thing he could do. When time would be up for one conversation, his team would come and gently usher him away into the next. His team had the agenda of his entire day carefully planned out for him in a way that ensured that Carter could further his most important goals and arrive to every meeting well prepared physically and mentally. That way, Carter himself was able to be completely present with anyone he was interacting with."

"Great, but why are we so into Jimmy Carter right now?" Lisa interrupted.

"Because I want everybody to be free like Jimmy Carter. An AI assistant should be able to ensure that at any given moment, you can be totally present knowing that when it's time to do something else, you'll be gently prodded to move on."

"That caffeine is working wonders. I like it!"

6. The Battle for Your Attention

A wealth of information creates a poverty of attention.

Herbert Simon
Economics Nobel Laureate (1978), Alan Turing Award (1975).

This insightful quote by one of my academic grandfathers underscores the increasing scarcity of attention in the digital age. The significance of attention in our lives cannot be overstated; it is, in essence, inseparable from our very existence. Amidst the multitude of stimuli that surround us, the choices we make as to what to pay attention to hold the power to shape our subjective experiences and profoundly impact our well-being.

In other words, much like the saying "you are what you eat," our conscious experiences are intimately intertwined with and molded by the objects of our attention. Whether you happen to be strolling along the bustling Fifth Avenue in New York City or joining the throngs of 1000-2500 people navigating the Shibuya Crossing every two minutes, the choice to focus on counting the number of individuals wearing red shoes becomes the defining element of your experience, regardless of the surrounding commotion. Conversely, even if you find yourself atop a serene mountaintop, greeted by a breathtaking sunset, if your attention remains fixated on a recent work-related conflict, it will inevitably mold your experience accordingly.

Psychologists have long held a keen interest in exploring the correlation between attention and well-being. One notable study conducted by Killingsworth and Gilbert sheds light on this subject by examining the impact of mind wandering on individuals' self-reported sense of well-being while engaged in a task. Interestingly, the study revealed that participants expressed greater happiness with the task when their minds wandered less frequently, even if the thoughts that diverted their attention were positive in nature, such as anticipating a delightful meal after completing homework, or if the task itself was not inherently enjoyable. Therefore, it appears that irrespective of the activity at hand, immersing oneself in the present moment leads to a more favorable experience.

This chapter will dig deeper into the nuances concerning the role of attention in our well-being and some of the patchwork of ideas that have been used to address the challenges that technology poses on our attention. At the end of this chapter, we will be able to state what requirements we have from the Attention component of Oswell, and some pitfalls we should be careful to avoid. The following two chapters will go into technologies that can contribute to the component.
The factors that burden our attention can be roughly categorized into two types: those originating from external sources and those arising from within ourselves. Let us delve into each of these categories to understand them more deeply.

External distractions

External distractions often stem from people or events in our physical world, such as co-workers interrupting with a question, a child urgently demanding a cookie, or an attractive individual suddenly dominating our field of view. But in the digital age, many distractions are often, well, digital: the ping of an incoming email or text message, a notification from a social-media app, the allure of amazing cooking videos, or a video game that demands our attention.

The first reason we find it hard to resist the digital distractions is what is known as FOMO, meaning "fear of missing out". Perhaps the email we just received is the next awesome job offer, or maybe that text message will turn into an unexpectedly fun evening. On the social-media apps, you are scrolling down, some of the posts are interesting and many are not, but a part of you imagines that if you continue just a bit longer, you'll see that one post that makes your whole time investment worthwhile, and sometimes you are right.

The second reason we often find ourselves losing the war of distractions is that many of the apps we are addicted to are designed to capture our attention. As the saying goes, in social media, you *are* the product. The simple, but somewhat superficial explanation for why apps are designed that way is that the more time you spend on a social-media app, the more ads the system can insert into your feed, and that translates directly to the bottom line of the company operating the platform. This might conjure in your mind a scene, fit for the movie screen, of engineers feasting on free snacks gathered around large screens in a corporate office, brainstorming ways to enhance user engagement with their apps. With the exception of the free snacks, the reality is far more nuanced than that.

The basic goal of an app is to provide value to the user so it improves their lives and makes them return to the app regularly. However, there's a constant tension between providing short-term value (more cat videos) versus long-term value (a place where you can learn and be enlightened). The former may move the business metrics of the company to where you want in the next quarter, but will ultimately fizzle out if you don't provide value over time. If you're a young company trying to garner initial attention from users, you may initially have to opt for the shorter term rewards because otherwise your existence is in danger. But if you're an established platform, the voices advocating for listening to the longer term are much louder. Still, no matter where you are, it's a balance.

An important example of shifting the balance in the direction of protecting users, which we explore in Chapter 10, involves the removal of harmful content from social networks. Harmful content such as hate speech, misinformation, and bullying possesses an addictive quality, yet it is inherently detrimental to users' well-being and can even cause harm in the real world. Hence, online platforms allocate significant resources to develop sophisticated methods for identifying and removing such harmful content.

Putting aside the challenges of building apps, let's consider how we, the users, have been tackling the challenge. Various tools and practices have been developed to help people resist these temptations. The simplest ones are to put your mobile phone on silent or remove the most alluring apps from the main screen of your phone so you don't see them when you casually glance at your phone. It's surprising how effective it can be to simply add some friction to get to the app. You can even go further by removing some apps completely from the phone and use them only on your desktop. If you're also tethered to your information fire hose via a smart watch, you need to set another layer of settings so your arm doesn't vibrate whenever a ping arrives. Some phones also enable you to set time limits on how much time you can use certain apps per day.

Another solution is to develop an app that blocks other apps. In fact, the operating system of your phone already has an option to silence all distractions while you sleep, drive, or need to focus during the day. However, research by Gloria Mark from the University of California, Irvine and her colleagues, Mary Czerwinski and Shamsi Iqbal from Microsoft Research, has shown that the effects of blocking software are, at best, mixed. They studied the stress levels and productivity of a variety of tech workers as they used app blockers. It turns out that people using app blockers were feeling more stressed because they spent a longer time focusing on cognitively demanding tasks. Usually, they were able to turn to other apps for short relief, but now they couldn't do so. One insight from that research is that people who are better at moderating their own use of distracting applications didn't need the blocking software. Nonetheless, putting your phone on silent and placing it far from your bed at night seem like common-sense practices to adopt.

A much larger scale solution is implemented in China by the government. The Chinese government limits the usage of applications like TikTok and video games, allowing them only on certain days of the week or for a limited time of the day. Between 10 PM and 6 AM, children cannot use messaging apps, resulting in all of them being disconnected simultaneously. Now, before you start wondering how they manage these time constraints across multiple time zones in such a big country, we note that they solved that problem a long time ago. China has a single time zone, even though geographically it is large enough to spread over five time zones.

No individual has taken the concern about apps taxing our attention to heart and to action more than Tristan Harris. When Harris was a design ethicist at Google, he tried to raise awareness about the possible downsides of technology on our attention and, therefore, our well-being. After three years at the company and no success in gaining traction on the issue, he left and started advocating externally through media interviews and highly viewed TED talks. One of his most memorable quotes describes the competition for attention between different apps as a "race to the bottom of the brain stem." That is, the most effective way to get the user's attention is to appeal to the bottom of the brain stem, bypassing the areas responsible for rational thinking and targeting our most instinctive responses.

After leaving Google, Harris formed the "Time Well Spent" movement, shifting the conversation away from the amount of time spent on applications to the question of whether this time was valuable for users. As an example of the movement's impact, Facebook took note and changed its stated mission to align better with "time well spent", a term frequently used within the company.

In 2018, Harris took his next step and, together with Aza Raskin, founded the Center for Humane Technology, which advocates for users' well-being by creating tools for companies to address these issues and working with media to raise more awareness about them. The most well-known work of the Center for Humane Technology is the movie "The Social Dilemma," released in September 2020. This documentary has received praise from many, being hailed as one of the most significant documentary films of our era. It has played a pivotal role in shaping the ongoing discourse on restraining the negative effects of these technologies, both through internal changes within the companies and the introduction of (though somewhat delayed) legislation.

On a more practical level, the center also produced the Humane Design Guide. This guide helps designers consider the common sensitivities that humans have and asks whether the technology product or feature they're building inhibits or supports these sensitivities by pointing out factors that hinder or enhance them. The first sensitivity, emotion, is inhibited when we feel stressed, low on sleep, or exhausted. Features in products such as creating artificial scarcity ("only 4 tickets left at this price") or designing a product to optimize the user's screen time are known to create emotional stress. On the other hand, when a design can promote calmness, safety, and create moments of pause, the user is likely to receive more emotional support. Other sensitivities that the guide touches upon are our attention, our ability to make sense of the information we're seeing and integrate it into what we already know, and our ability to make decisions or reason about social situations. Looking at the guide, it is clear that there is a lot of research to be done on designing products humanely. This is evident from the fact that while the example factors that contribute negatively to our sensitivity are very specific and well known, the factors that contribute positively point in the right direction, but are stated in somewhat vague terms.

In conclusion, although designers may have the potential to prioritize our well-being more effectively than they currently do, considering the various influences involved, we will ultimately have to take responsibility for our own welfare. This is where the Attention component of Oswell can be beneficial. As for Tristan Harris, you won't be surprised to hear that now he's focused on the possible pitfalls of AI.

Distractions from within

Let's turn to the taxes on our attention that come from within us. We surmise that if Simon were asked to expand on his insightful statement today, he might have added something more eloquent along the lines of "A wealth of choices creates decision paralysis."

In today's world, we constantly face an overwhelming array of decisions. Some involve simple choices, such as what to wear to a party or what to select from a restaurant menu. Others are more intricate, requiring multi-step planning, like organizing a family vacation that satisfies everyone's preferences without breaking the bank, or getting everything perfect for a social gathering we are hosting. Certain choices are inherently ambiguous, such as how to allocate our time and where to direct our focus both at work and at home. Uncertainty further complicates these decisions. How can I meticulously plan my day without knowing the precise arrival time of the plumber or the outcome of a delicate conversation with my manager? Whether you identify as a perfectionist who insists on flawlessness in every decision or as a satisficer who is content with occasional imperfections, it's likely that you spend an excessive amount of time making choices.

This is precisely why we often come across stories about individuals like Mark Zuckerberg, the founder and CEO of Meta, who allegedly consistently wears the same gray shirt every day, or Steve Jobs, renowned for his signature attire of a black turtleneck, jeans, and New Balance sneakers. At first, it may seem puzzling that these affluent individuals would forgo the opportunity to explore a wide range of fashion options. However, they share a common rationale: by minimizing the number of decisions they have to make each morning—such as what to wear or what to have for breakfast—they free up their attention to tackle more significant challenges in their lives.

While making a single decision may not seem overly burdensome and can even be enjoyable, the accumulation of numerous decisions takes a toll on our minds. This phenomenon is referred to as neuro-fatigue by neuroscientists. Think back to the last time you visited a shopping mall. Initially, you likely had the patience to carefully evaluate the available options in the first few stores you entered. However, as time passed, your decision-making abilities diminished and the overwhelming array of choices became bewildering. The process of decision-making, coupled with the constant context-switching it entails, significantly taxes our brains. Consequently, we are unable to fully focus on what truly matters and the people we are with. Decisions continue to occupy our mind even when we are engrossed in other tasks and, curiously, even long after the decisions have been made.

Research in psychology also sheds light on the trade-offs associated with having choices, revealing a mixed bag of findings. Social psychology studies demonstrate that having an excessive number of choices can be detrimental, while also emphasizing the importance of having some degree of choice. We will briefly discuss a few of these studies, offering insights from both perspectives of this dilemma.

In the well-known "jam experiment" conducted by researchers Sheena Iyengar and Mark Lepper, they examined the influence of choice abundance on decision-making processes. The experiment involved setting up a table in a grocery store, showcasing various types of jams. Some tables presented a limited selection of jams (six or fewer), while others offered a larger assortment (24 or more). The researchers meticulously documented the number of jams purchased from each table.

The findings of the experiment revealed an intriguing pattern. Although more individuals were drawn to the table with a greater variety of jams, they were actually less inclined to make a purchase from that table. On the other hand, those who approached the table with a smaller selection were more likely to complete a purchase. Moreover, individuals who selected a jar of jam from the table with fewer options reported a higher level of satisfaction with their choice compared to those who made their selection from the table with an extensive array of choices. This suggests that an abundance of choices can diminish people's satisfaction with their decision, even if they ultimately make a choice.

A related study by Daniel Gilbert delves into the impact of the irrevocability of a choice. The findings indicate that when participants were informed that their choice cannot be undone, they expressed greater happiness with their decision compared to those who were informed they could later replace their choice with another option. One plausible explanation for this is that when a choice is final, the mind is spared from pondering over whether it was the right decision or not. Conversely, if the choice can be changed, individuals are more likely to frequently distract themselves with thoughts of replacing their chosen item. Once again, experiencing fewer distractions contributes to increased well-being.

Well, if scientific evidence suggests that an excess of choices is detrimental, one might wonder about the alternative: relinquishing decision-making to someone else to save time. This role could be fulfilled by a parent, spouse, manager, doctor, government, or our envisioned AI partner in the future. However, before embracing this notion, let's pause for a moment. In a renowned psychological study by Edward L. Deci and Richard M. Ryan, the influence of autonomy on people's motivation and well-being was examined.

In the study, a group of elderly residents in a nursing home were given the opportunity to personally select a plant to care for in their own rooms. Conversely, another group of residents received plants that were chosen for them by the nursing staff. The results unveiled a significant disparity: the residents who had the autonomy to choose their own plants displayed heightened feelings of self-determination and competence. Moreover, they reported higher levels of life satisfaction compared to the group whose plants were chosen for them.

This study and others, along with our common sense, indicate that having some choices in life, particularly regarding the things we deeply care about, is essential. However, when we are inundated with an excessive number of choices, it can become overwhelming. This is where the Attention component of Oswell should come into play, offering assistance in navigating through this complexity but ensuring that you have the control you need.

The Attention component of Oswell

The purpose of the discussion thus far was to underscore the role that attention plays in our well-being, and therefore the necessity for a component in Oswell that bears its name. The primary objective of the Attention component is to ensure that, out of the vast content available to us and the choices we face, we are presented with the information and recommendations that are the most advantageous options at any given moment.

To be upfront, building this component is going to be challenging, possibly on par with other grand challenges of Artificial Intelligence. To begin this exciting journey, it is crucial that we state as clearly as we can what the goals of this component are. We propose three primary principles that will guide the development of this component.

The first principle is that the recommendations that you receive are based on a holistic view of you, at least as much of it as you're willing to share with the AI agent. This view encompasses your past experiences, the habits that can be inferred from them, and your aspirations for the future. We inserted all this information into the lifelog in the Experiences component in Oswell for a reason, and the Attention component should take advantage of them wherever possible.

For instance, recommendations for books or movies should take into account not only your previous content consumption but also your future plans, whether they have to do with your family, career, or leisure. If you're planning a trip to Paris, it would be beneficial to receive recommendations for French films or literature that can deepen your knowledge of the country's history and make your visit there richer. Similarly, if you have recently declared yourself to be a coffee aficionado, you should be presented with recommendations for unique cafes to visit during your time in Paris. This principle should apply whether the recommendations are for actions to do at the moment, focus areas for the week, or planning for your next vacation. They should all be informed by your lifelog. As we pointed out earlier, you should also be telling your AI partner how close you want to stay in your comfort zone as opposed to exploring new experiences, resulting in different recommendations depending on your current needs.

The second principle is that the technology within the Attention component of Oswell should strive to get as much stuff off your chest as possible. When confronted with decisions involving a plethora of options, the Attention component should narrow them down to a manageable number of alternatives. To put it in the language of jams, it should choose the three jams out of the 24 that you're most likely to consider. It should also explain the differences between the different alternatives it is proposing to you, and outline the potential consequences of choosing one over the others. For instance, let the system sift through the countless combinations of flights, hotels and attractions for your upcoming vacation, finding the options that will provide the best overall experience for you, or determine the optimal schedule for tomorrow, balancing what you must do, what you want to do, and ensuring that you don't stress out about when the plumber will arrive. In short, if there's a detail that you're comfortable delegating, the AI should be there and be up to the task.

The third principle is that through its Attention component, Oswell should assist you in finding the right balance in life. Many of us are constantly engaged in a delicate juggling act, managing multiple goals and values that are important to us. These values may include spending quality time with family and friends, pursuing fulfilling careers, striving towards financial goals, engaging in volunteer work, or learning new skills. However, unless we consciously and regularly assess our progress, which very few of us actually do, we lack a true understanding of how well we are maintaining this balance. Often, we just feel that we're out of whack and need to make adjustments.

The Attention component of Oswell should serve as your "value dashboard," providing insights into your progress toward balancing these life goals and gently nudging you when adjustments are needed. Importantly, this dashboard that Oswell maintains for you should not create additional stress the way a daily step counter does for some individuals. Achieving life balance is fundamentally different from merely counting the number of steps we take each day, because it involves much more nuance. The system should offer nudges and provide explanations for them, but it should not make you feel that you're constantly under evaluation.

In the next couple of chapters we'll see where technology can fulfill these principles today and where additional development is necessary. These chapters will describe methods for making highly effective recommendations (Chapter 7) and methods for helping you plan by efficiently searching through an exponential number of plans (Chapter 8). Before we delve into these topics it is important to point out a couple of pitfalls we should make sure to avoid.

Imagine if we are extremely successful in building the systems we envision. As a result, at any given point in the day, an AI agent will point your attention to the most important topic, content or person that deserves it. Similarly, you will have carefully crafted plans for your day that balance all your needs, your well-being topping the list. To not seem like a helicopter parent, the agent will dispense this advice with what seems like a chilled attitude. Mission achieved.

But that utopia, many would argue, misses a critical element of the human experience. Yes, we will be happy with our enhanced focus and efficiency and thrilled with the gentle balance of our well-being. For the most part, we will not miss the times we used to ruminate endlessly about the minutiae in our lives. However, ruminating about details, exploring options we will ultimately ignore and reasoning about why, and even following paths we will later regret, are part of the human experience. These ruminations and explorations are often a source of growth. Sometimes we need to make decisions more slowly and painfully. We need to develop the muscle for making complex decisions ourselves and for choosing on our own which content or people to attend to. Hence, as we go about developing the technologies that will help our attention, we should also keep in mind that they don't prevent us from building these skills and from progressing at human speed.

Try This 👉

This chapter described how our lived experience is greatly influenced by where we focus our attention. What are instances in your day where your attention wanders to unproductive places? Do you find that you spend a lot of time looking at content that doesn't contribute in any way to your goals or your well-being? What are activities in which you feel like you're completely present? Can you imagine ways in which AI can handle some details for you so you can attend to more important things?

Lisa and Oliver met at the new Japanese restaurant that opened up in her neighborhood. Oliver insisted on taking her out for dinner today, promising that the restaurant would be a perfect backdrop for a demo.

"Nice place," Lisa said. "I like the way they blend the gentle woodwork with the rustic look of the kitchen. Pretty impressive menu -- so many options!"

"Yeah, I heard good things about it. Apparently the designer of this place was using the newest Generative AI techniques to make sure the customers would get just the right feel." He paused for a moment, and then continued: "Ok, download the newest version of my app and we'll do the demo."

"Shouldn't we order food first?"

"Gone are the days when you order without help. Do you really think you can choose from this long menu?"

"Ah... Good point!" Lisa downloads the app and it pops up a message: Click "Eat" if you need help choosing from the menu. "Wait, what? How did it know we're about to order food?"

"It's not too hard, Lisa. The phone knows you're at a restaurant, it even knows which one. It has already read the menu and knows pretty much what ingredients are in each dish. The app also knows how active you've been today and what dishes you have liked before at Japanese restaurants, even if you can't even remember their names!"

"Wow, this okonomiyaki looks really good. Yes. That's what I want!"

"Great!" Oliver signals to the waiter and orders two okonomiyaki. Before the waiter asks what they want to drink, Lisa already flashes her phone at him and shows him the app's recommendation.

Lisa goes on to play with the app, ignoring Oliver for a while. "It's giving me some great book and movie recommendations! Ooh, and now I know what I'm getting you for your birthday too! This is so cool!"

Oliver smiles from ear to ear and kicks back on his chair.

"But hang on," Lisa continues, "So these are great recommendations, but aren't recommendation systems designed to be addictive? Am I just becoming a slave to a new master here?"

"Excellent question!" Oliver answers happily. "On social media, the recommender system has the objective to keep you there longer so you watch more ads. My app is not trying to keep you scrolling. It's trying to give you useful information and let you get on with your life. It's more like a search engine that gives you an answer to a question you asked and sends you away."

"Ok, good, but still. Does the system have my needs in mind or is it trying to cater to which ad might be paying more money? Or maybe it's catering to a secret cabal in Japan that's trying to feed the world more okonomiyaki?"

"Itadakimasu", Oliver raises his wine glass, "to a world dominated by okonomiyaki!"

7. Enhancing Your Attention with Personalized Recommendations

Our attention is influenced to a great extent by the recommendations we receive. Thus, one of the building blocks of the Attention component within Oswell is a system that is able to make recommendations on a variety of topics, such as content to consume, experiences to engage in, and activities to pursue during our leisure time.

In this chapter we'll discuss the concept of a recommendation system, a very versatile technology that is already in wide-spread use. We will begin by explaining the basic components of a recommendation system and how they work. This will already be useful in that it will remove some of the mystery behind the systems you interact with on a daily basis. We will then consider how recommendation systems can be adapted to satisfy the requirements we set forth for the Attention component of Oswell. Keep in mind that we will cover only the most important concepts of recommendation systems below, but make no mistake, these systems are incredibly intricate. They are the systems that sit at the heart of some of the biggest tech companies in the world today. In fact, they are so complex, that very few individuals within these companies understand them fully.

At its core, a recommendation system operates by utilizing a database of items and its primary function is to provide you with recommendations from that database when prompted. It is highly likely that you interact with recommendation systems more frequently than you may realize. For instance, when a streaming service like Netflix suggests a collection of movies, when a music platform such as Spotify proposes songs or playlists, or when a news service like Google News presents you with a set of news stories, these are all driven by recommendation systems. Social-media platforms are predominantly built upon recommendation systems as well—your Facebook, Instagram, X (previously, Twitter), YouTube, and TikTok feeds are generated by the underlying recommendation systems. And yes, even when you're on a dating site searching for the love of your life, or just a few hours of fun, the mates who are presented to you are the result of an underlying recommendation system.

When you submit a query to a search engine like Google or Bing, or when you engage in online shopping on platforms such as Amazon or Walmart, the outcome of your search is influenced by a recommendation system as well. However, search systems differ in an important way from the other aforementioned recommendation systems. The primary objective of a search engine is to provide accurate and relevant answers to your information or shopping needs based on your query. For example, when you submit the query "where to see the northern lights" or "recipe for breakfast burrito", the search engine will rank the relevant pages based on how informative it thinks they are to your query with the goal that one or a few of them will satisfy your information need. (As an aside, one excellent answer for the first query is Abisko, Sweden). The fundamental goal of the search engine is to send you on your merry way either to the information you were looking for or to put an item in your cart and pay for it. In contrast, recommendation systems that are designed to operate without the need for an explicit query, such as those powering your social-network feed, are designed to constantly engage you, or in other words, to always have something that might entertain or grab your attention. And you are probably thankful for such feeds when you're stuck on a runway because of a flight delay or waiting at the doctor's office for an appointment.

In case you believe that recommendation systems are exclusive to the big tech industry and only exist in the digital realm, you may be surprised. As we will discuss later in this chapter, your brain is one recommendation system sitting inside your head. But recommendation systems are also prevalent in the physical world. When you visit a supermarket, you may observe that eggs and dairy products are positioned at the very end of the store. That is because the astute minds who designed supermarkets realized that in order to reach the area of the items you really need, it doesn't hurt to take you through a journey of other items, such as potato chips, cookies and sodas, that you may suddenly realize that you really want. This supermarket layout, coupled with carefully chosen items to stack on the shelves that are at your eye level, also functions as a recommendation system, albeit one that is significantly less flexible and lacks personalization. In their book "Nudge", Richard Thaler and Cass Sunstein delve into the fascinating realm of real-world recommendation systems, that when used productively and ethically, can help people make better decisions about their food consumption, savings, and whether or not to donate their organs.

Back in the digital realm, there are a few main components for modern recommendation systems. The first component is the content database of items from which recommendations are being made. For example, in the case of Netflix, this database encompasses a collection of movies available for streaming, while in the case of Tinder, it consists of a pool of potential mates. Each object within the database possesses several descriptive properties. For movies, these properties may include genre, production year, director, and cast, while for potential mates, properties may include age, a photo, their interests, their opinion about kombucha, and their best attempt at a pickup line. It is important to distinguish between two types of databases: closed and open. A closed database is one that is completely curated by the service provider and hence every object is in some way vetted. For example, Netflix curates its movie database and the BBC decides what articles to offer on its site. An open database is one that is created by a community of users, such as users of social media or people looking for dates. An open database can contain troublesome content, as we describe in more detail in Chapter 10. A recommendation system based on an open database may need to put in place a moderation process that removes content that is deemed unacceptable.

The second component of a recommendation system is the user profile and the current context. This component contains the information that the system has about the user, such as their previous interactions with the system and what they are doing now on the system. It can also contain other information that could be helpful to make a recommendation, like the time of day, the season of the year, or the weather in your area. This component enables the recommendation system to offer distinct recommendations to different users based on their preferences. In the case of Netflix, the system is aware of the movies you have previously watched and any ratings you may have provided. Similarly, Amazon possesses knowledge regarding the products you have purchased from them, the frequency of your purchases, and any reviews you have shared on their site. Additionally, Amazon knows which products you looked at in detail and didn't buy, as well as what items you put on your wish list. For example, Amazon would know that you've been eyeing that high-end espresso machine pretty regularly, but have not yet had the courage to splurge on it.

There is another crucial aspect that the recommender system takes into account when determining the content to offer you, and it stems from the fact that you are one of the platform's many users. The system possesses knowledge not only about your past choices and preferences but also about those of all other users. This knowledge becomes immensely powerful when there are millions or even billions of users involved. This advantage is often referred to as the "network effect," and it is one of the reasons why online platforms become increasingly valuable as their user base expands.

In practice, this wealth of data allows the recommender system to use so-called collaborative filtering to identify similarities among different users and utilize these patterns to provide valuable recommendations. Movie recommendations are a common example of collaborative filtering. For instance, if Alice and Bob have comparable viewing histories on Netflix, and Alice has given a high rating to a particular movie, the system may suggest that movie to Bob, anticipating that he would likely enjoy it as well. Another example is what happens when you add a new mobile phone to your online shopping cart. Magically, the system suggests that you also buy a compatible carrying case. This recommendation is possible because other users who bought mobile phones and are one step ahead of you, recognized the need for a carrying case for their new phones and bought one. The shopping site is not even trying to hide that fact. It will tell you that other people who bought the same phone as you did, also bought this carrying case. These people are now your tribe, after all.

Given these two components of the recommendation system, we can already describe its operation at a high level. Given a query, or when your feed needs to be refreshed, the first step for the recommendation system is to retrieve a relatively large set of candidate items from the database. The critical aspect of this step is efficiency, because the database can often contain billions of objects or even more, and hence the goal is to narrow them down to a set that can be looked at more carefully. In the second step, the recommendation system will rank each item in the candidate set as to how closely it may match your interests. The ranking is typically done by a sophisticated machine-learning model that has been informed about your previous actions on the platform.

The ranking step is guided by an objective function, which is the third component of the recommendation system. The objective function serves as a metric for the system to assess the quality of its recommendations, allowing it to learn from past successes and failures. In the absence of an objective function, any random recommendation would be considered equally good from the system's perspective. A recommendation system without an objective function is like going to Google and saying "I'm feeling lucky", which is fun, but possibly not the most useful way of spending your time or getting the information you want.

A widely used set of objective functions are meant to increase engagement with the system. When Netflix recommends a movie, their goal is that you like the recommendation enough to watch it. Similarly, when a news site presents a list of news stories, their objective is for you to click on the articles and read them. When a social-media site shows you posts, guess what, it wants you to like them so you will stay on the site longer.

And this is where things get complicated. That seemingly innocuous objective function comes with a lot of baggage. The complications arise due to the challenge of distinguishing the primary intent of the objective function from potential negative secondary effects that we discussed in detail in the previous chapter. At first glance, spending more time engrossed in content you enjoy seems beneficial. After all, there is an abundance of exceptional content available online, and delving deeply into it can be incredibly rewarding, akin to getting lost in a library surrounded by stacks of captivating books. Engaging in the intricacies of chess openings, exploring the seasonal migration patterns of Ruby-throated Hummingbirds, or mastering the art of brewing a perfect espresso, are just a few examples of worthwhile pursuits that await your discovery. Even the ads that are placed on your feed, most of which are either annoying or you simply do not notice, could be useful. Perhaps you didn't even realize that your living room was in dire need of that $1000 designer chair that caught your attention on your feed.

However, with the exception of novel and imperfect techniques we will touch on later in the book, the objective function of the recommendation system is unable to truly discern whether you are utilizing the platform for genuine self-enrichment or if you are descending into a content rabbit hole that doesn't contribute positively to your well-being. For example, you may be looking at content that is not intrinsically harmful, but if you're engaged in social comparison while doing it, your well-being will be negatively affected. Social comparison, such as wondering why other people are traveling to exotic locations while you're stuck at home, is especially common among teenagers.

We have already discussed the challenges of designing an objective function that balances between a platform's need to enhance corporate earnings and the need to provide you value, both in the short term and in the longer term. However, one crucial aspect that is largely absent from the objective functions of recommendation systems is your well-being. This is not surprising, as each of these apps only has access to a limited glimpse of your life and cannot be expected to possess a comprehensive understanding of your overall well-being. This is precisely where the Attention component of Oswell will come into play.

Your brain as a recommendation system

With all due respect to the sophisticated recommendation systems built by technology companies, they ultimately serve as inputs to a higher authority: your brain. Interestingly, your brain operates in ways that share many similarities with the engineered recommendation systems. Before we discuss recommendations in Oswell, it's worthwhile to spend a few moments looking at the brain's recommendation system. For a fascinating and much deeper explanation of this topic, you should read Anil Seth's book, "Being You".

Your brain is constantly offering suggestions on what actions to take next. Some of these recommendations reach your conscious awareness, while others are so ingrained in your habits that you may not even notice them. Neuroscience research has identified specific regions of the brain responsible for these habitual behaviors, such as the basal ganglia, a deep brain structure, and the infra-limbic cortex, which is a component of the prefrontal cortex. In fact, when these structures are deactivated, individuals transition from automatic and reflexive modes to more deliberate and goal-oriented behaviors.

In contrast to big tech's recommendation systems that primarily rely on rewards such as click rates or purchases, the brain's recommendations are driven by a broader range of goals. Firstly, it offers recommendations aimed at risk avoidance in life, like fastening your seat belt when entering a car. Secondly, it provides recommendations for habitual actions such as brushing your teeth or drying your hands with a towel after washing them. Although not particularly exciting, these recommendations are undeniably useful. Going a bit further, the brain also generates two other types of recommendations, ones that address your drives and your desires, respectively.

The psychology literature makes an important distinction between these two terms. Drive refers to the motivation to fulfill a specific need, such as hunger or thirst, whereas desire pertains to cravings for things that bring reward and pleasure, like tiramisu or mango bread pudding. A drive can be satisfied but desires are usually addictive.

As we mentioned earlier, recommendation systems of large online platforms benefit from the network effect, using the preferences of other users to provide you with better advice. Interestingly, the brain operates in a similar manner, although it presents an even more double-edged sword in this context. Have you ever observed a friend acquiring a new electric car and felt a sudden urge to obtain one as well? If it wasn't an electric car, perhaps it was a luxury handbag, a puppy, or a bucket of popcorn. Evolution has hard-wired the human brain to engage in social comparison and compete for resources that our peers pursue. This may offer a plausible explanation for why you become more appealing to others when you appear at a party with an attractive partner by your side.

At times, we may not even pause to consider whether our peers' preferences align with our own values. The study of these mimetic desires has given rise to an entire field of research, with Luke Burgis' book, "Wanting: The Power of Mimetic Desire in Everyday

Life," providing a particularly insightful overview of the topic. If there is one key takeaway from this extensive field, it is the importance of cultivating your own recommendation system that is not excessively influenced by mimetic desires, thus granting you greater agency and independence.

There are two additional points worth considering when comparing the brain's recommendation system to those developed by technology companies. The first point relates to the crucial role of feedback in recommendation systems. In engineered systems, without feedback on recommendations from users, the system would ultimately be ineffective. Similarly, the brain's recommendation system may also rely on feedback to operate optimally. An example of this phenomenon appears in the analysis of the condition known as anhedonia, which is characterized by a diminished capacity to experience pleasure. Anhedonia is recognized as a significant factor contributing to depression because the inability to experience pleasure leads one to lose interest in various aspects of life. Research has revealed that one of the factors contributing to anhedonia is the absence of positive experiences associated with pleasure. In other words, a person who has not encountered any rewarding outcomes from their activities in life, such as attending school, engaging in relationships, or pursuing a career, is more prone to the condition. A related finding is that individuals whose childhood was spent in intellectually-deprived environments, and therefore may have experienced fewer rewarding moments, are more susceptible to experiencing depression later in life.

The second point is that the brain's recommendation system can become trapped in local optima, facing the same challenge encountered by big tech companies' systems. Just as a learning agent must strike a balance between exploration and exploitation, humans (or their recommendation systems) must do the same. Research by Stanford psychologist Laura L. Carstensen reveals that elderly individuals approach this balance differently than younger people. The elderly tend to stick to familiar things and relationships for extended periods preferring exploitation, while younger individuals are more inclined to seek out new experiences and interactions tending more to exploration. Computer recommendation systems tend to prioritize exploitation on your behalf. For instance, if you click on one cat video, your homepage suddenly floods with ten more cat videos. Whether this is advantageous or detrimental is difficult to ascertain, but at the very least, we can acknowledge that someone has made the decision for you when presenting these suggestions.

Recommendations for well-being

As we discussed so far, the state-of-the-art recommendation systems can provide pretty good suggestions from the database of items of a particular service, such as movies or romantic partners, and in doing so leverage your past behavior. While useful, our broader well-being needs require quite a bit more. We'll take this step by step, starting from the simplest ones to achieve.

Let's begin by trying to deliver on the first principle we set forth for the Attention component of Oswell, namely that recommendations that I receive be based on a holistic view of me. The immediate and relatively straightforward extension of existing technology is for the recommendation system to consider not only what I have consumed on one specific platform but also items I have consumed from other sources. For instance, the books we read are typically obtained from various sources, including online sellers, our local libraries or their online presence, and books we purchase from the occasional visit to a physical bookstore. Additionally, we consume books in various formats, such as digital, audio, and paper, and by nature, these can originate from multiple sources as well.

Therefore, any service providing me book recommendations should be aware of all my past book purchases and borrowing so they can provide me better recommendations and obviously, avoid recommending books I've already gotten from other sources. There is a complication here that is worth noting, which is that I may have multiple reading personas. For example, as any parent would appreciate, many of my book purchases are for my kids, and the system should be able to distinguish between what I buy for myself and what I buy for them. Notably, this is easier when the children are young, and much more difficult as they start developing adult interests later on.

Fortunately, as we described in Chapter 4, my book purchasing and reading history should be in my lifelog, so now it might just be a matter of passing a few bits around. If you ever interacted deeply with computing, you know that when someone says that something is just a matter of passing bits around, they're probably hiding a more complicated reality. Guilty as charged, so we'll elaborate a bit more.

Architecturally, we have at least two choices for moving these bits around. The first option is to incorporate a recommendation system within Oswell and let it make personalized suggestions based on all the information it knows about you. The main benefit of this approach is enhanced privacy since no data will leak from your lifelog. However, the downside is that developing and maintaining a recommendation system over time requires a significant amount of effort that we might want to avoid.

The second architectural option is to allow the existing recommendation systems of the services you already use to continue performing their specialized functions, but provide them with additional data about yourself to improve their performance. The key idea is that instead of handing your entire lifelog to Netflix or Amazon, there is a process that creates small topic-specific summaries from your lifelog. As we noted in our discussions of lifelogs in Chapter 4, this option may be the most promising one in the near future.

For instance, one summary might describe your reading preferences, while another could focus on your eating habits. The summaries can be tailored even further to contain data relevant to your current information need. These summaries can take the form of a list of all the book purchases you've made or adopt a more opaque internal format similar to how neural networks manipulate information. In either case, these concise summaries are then shared with the underlying recommendation systems using a data sharing protocol as additional input. By adopting this approach, we eliminate the need to create yet another recommendation system while still leveraging the network effects of the platform and benefiting from the latest advancements in recommendation technology that the platforms consistently develop.

Regardless of which architectural solution you choose between the two, there is undoubtedly a reasonable solution within reach, and it may be worth exploring a hybrid of the two approaches we outlined. Additionally, the same principles and solutions should apply to an even broader scenario where various media types are mixed. Your book recommendations, for example, can consider not only your past reading choices but also the movies you've watched, the podcasts you've listened to, and the music you've enjoyed. Moreover, the recommendations you receive can be further informed by your interests and future plans, such as your newfound interest in baking during the COVID-19 pandemic or the trip to Bhutan, which unfortunately was canceled due to the pandemic.

Great, now you can receive better book or movie recommendations based on your broader experiences. But what if you're unsure whether you want to watch a movie or possibly snuggle up with a book? Even better, perhaps you want to go out for a walk and think about your next career move, or simply spend time with your spouse or children. None of your online services, despite how much you may love them, are remotely well-positioned to answer the question of what you should do now. It's no longer a simple matter of moving bits around.

To enable these higher-level recommendations, you'll need an AI partner that focuses on your needs and knows you more deeply than just focusing on your book reading preferences or your workout routines. When we introduced Oswell, we discussed the possibility of interacting with Oswell through such an all-encompassing AI partner, but we didn't want to commit to this approach for all of Oswell's services. If you want more holistic advice, this is the time to seriously consider the AI partner approach.

Your primary means of interacting with your AI partner is through conversation. Thanks to ChatGPT, Gemini and their cohort, we are now approaching the capability to support highly flexible and dynamic conversations between you and such an AI. This conversation may feel a little bit like speaking with an old acquaintance because the AI will possess substantial memory (often better than yours) about your experiences and preferences, allowing you to bypass much of the initial back and forth.

But even with all this knowledge, there will still remain some critical gaps between what the recommender knows and your reality. Some of these gaps, which we will cover in more detail in the next chapter, involve your context: how much time do you have right now? What mood are you in? What are you trying to achieve with your next activity? For example, are you looking to relax, learn, or blow off some steam? Perhaps you feel mentally resilient and are open to stepping outside your comfort zone, like attentively listening to a political argument that you know you will disagree with. Whenever you interact with your AI partner, you should always be aware that their recommendations are based on partial knowledge of you.

Recommendations within the experience

So far we have discussed how recommender systems can give advice about which experience to choose. But with wearables, recommendations can also be embedded within the experience itself. We already saw earlier that a smart watch can detect that you're stressed and give you advice on the spot to remedy the situation by, perhaps, taking a few deep breaths. But that's just the beginning.

Devices already play a significant role in creating experiences for us. As an obvious example, video games transport us to fantastical realms. With a headset, we embark on epic quests, traversing enchanted landscapes and engaging in heart-pounding adventures, all from the comfort of our living rooms. A more recent example is the surge of virtual museum tours, partially bolstered by the COVID-19 pandemic when travel was restricted. Museums around the world have started harnessing the potential of virtual reality headsets, offering guided journeys through history itself. These tours transport participants to different historical epochs and offer intimate access to revered artifacts and timeless masterpieces. For example, the Smithsonian American Art Museum created an VR app that allows users to explore and learn about various artworks in the museum's collection. The app overlays information, including audio and visual content, on top of the artworks, and provides users with a more immersive and interactive learning experience.

If exciting museum tours are not your thing, imagine being able to manipulate 3D structures of molecules in a virtual space. A chemistry VR app that was developed at the University of California, Los Angeles allows students to learn organic chemistry in a more engaging and interactive way. It helps students visualize and memorize organic molecules' structures better, as students can hold and manipulate molecules in a virtual space. This is especially useful when studying complex molecules that can't be easily built with physical molecular model kits.

Likewise, augmented reality promises to seamlessly merge digital and real-world elements, enhancing urban exploration. Imagine wandering through a city, with AR-equipped glasses revealing hidden historical facts and guiding you to local gems. Such technology empowers users with dynamic, context-aware information, reshaping urban discovery. And if that's not exciting enough, you can use the IKEA Place app to revolutionize your furniture shopping experience by using AR to visualize how IKEA products fit within your space.

That all sounds great, but now imagine combining all this with your personal recommender, one that knows about your specific interests and preferences. In this experience, your tour through the museum will take you to items that may be more related to your interest or connect to experiences you've had in the past. Remember that artist you really liked at the Met? Well, you can see some of her paintings in this museum as well. And when you stroll through London or Paris, the glasses will note points of interest that are related to novels you recently read or cafes that your friends recommended.

Putting recommendations in perspective

As we envision these technologies, and especially imagining them becoming incredibly successful, we need to take a moment to speculate on their undesired consequences, so we can mitigate them from the start. One notable risk in the context of recommendations is that we, the fallible and often very lazy humans, will rely on them a bit more than we should. It's important to keep in mind that even with detailed knowledge about your context, your past experiences and your future desires, no agent will likely have complete knowledge about your situation. There might be facts or emotions that you could not find a way to communicate with the system or do not feel comfortable sharing with an AI agent. It is critical that as we develop the new generation of recommendation systems, we also devise ways for them to explain why they are giving you certain recommendations, and in particular, what data the recommendation is based on. But even with all the justifications in the world, at the end of the day, many of our decisions are based on emotions, not just on facts. At times, we just need to go against what the facts suggest and act differently. Therefore, the recommendations you will receive will always just be that, recommendations. Ultimately you need to make the final decision.

This chapter described recommendation systems that focus on the problem of choosing an item, or a list of items, from their database of content. But often we need different kinds of help. We need the system to help us create a plan that may involve multiple steps, and navigate through quite a few possibilities and constraints. We would like help to explore this possibly huge set of possible plans and choose a few that are most likely to answer our needs, and in doing so, remove cognitive burdens from our attention and brains. Creating such plans will be the subject of the next chapter.

Try This 👉

In this chapter we covered the basics of recommendation systems and argued that if recommenders had a broader context of our lives, they could do a better job. Apply this idea to your own life. What are situations where you need better recommendations? In those situations, what additional knowledge do you think the recommender system would need to give you better advice? Try experimenting with an AI system – ask it for a recommendation that you need, and then gradually give it additional context about yourself and see if the recommendations improve. Going even more broadly, are there scenarios in your life where you need a recommendation but there's no good recommendation system available?

"Listen to this, Oliver," Lisa said as she was reading from a magazine issue that looked like it had clearly been in the cafe for several years, "On May 17th, 1999, at 11:04AM, Pacific Daylight Time, Deep Space One handed over its control to an AI agent. This marked a significant milestone in the field of space exploration and artificial intelligence, as it was one of the first times a spacecraft was autonomously managed by an AI system that was armed by a sophisticated planning system. Deep Space One, launched by NASA in 1998, was primarily a technology demonstration mission aimed at testing new systems and techniques for future space missions. One such technology was the Remote Agent software, an artificial intelligence system designed to control the spacecraft's operations, reduce human intervention, and increase overall mission efficiency. During the period of AI control, the spacecraft successfully diagnosed and corrected a potentially mission-ending problem, effectively demonstrating the utility of AI in autonomous spacecraft operations. This pioneering event set a precedent for future explorations, paving the way for the increased integration of AI in managing complex space missions."

"I had no idea you're into NASA missions," Oliver said, when Lisa finally looked up and took a deep breath, “and as a matter of fact, I didn’t actually know that AI was a thing in 1999 either.”

"I'm not. My point is that over a quarter of a century ago, AI planning systems were already controlling a spacecraft in outer space. So why don't I have an AI agent that can plan my darn day? I feel like I spend an excessive amount of mental energy planning and re-planning my days to juggle everything I need to get done, and despite all my efforts, I often believe I could have had a more productive day. Wasn't your app supposed to do this for me?"

"You've got a good point," Oliver retorted. "I'm really struggling with this aspect of my app right now. You would think that by now day planning would be done by widely available AI systems." "But," he tries to hide the smirk that is forming on his face as he leans forward towards Lisa, "in many ways, your day is more complicated than a space mission."

"Just a bit of friendly advice here, Oliver. That's not going to work as a pickup line at a bar. I'll give you more detailed dating advice later, but for now, can you explain why you think I'm so complicated?"

"The issue is that the way planning systems work in AI is that you need to tell them exactly how the world works and that involves a lot of rules. If we started writing down all the rules about how your life works, we would be here forever."

"So what you're saying is that you can actually build a planner, but giving it the right input would take forever because we'd have to write rules that anticipate every possible condition for different kinds of days."

"Exactly, but that's not the end of it," Oliver responded, scooping up the last bit of his mango bread pudding. "In addition to knowing about your beautifully complex world that makes you the alluring woman that you are, the planner also needs to know some basic stuff about how the world itself works, which is also really complicated."

"Nice, Oliver, nice..."

"We're not done, Lisa, there's more."

"Really? I'm not getting a planner any time soon, am I?"

"See the couple sitting over there? The guy has been looking at the menu for a really long time."

"I noticed that. I wonder why. Maybe he's trying to find just the right item to complement what he ate earlier today. He needs your app, doesn't he?"

"I think it may be more complicated. They're on a first date. He's waiting for her to set the tone by letting her choose first."

"I don't think so", Lisa responded. "First, he's way too dorky for her. Second, if it is a first date, he's already botched it up when he was mansplaining to her how she should pronounce her own name."

"Poor guy. Maybe you're right. Whatever it is, to make good plans for you, or even give a good recommendation like for the poor dork over there, the system needs to understand the context around the decision. If it’s a first date, long-time friends, or simply colleagues, that changes what the best plan should be."

8. Enhancing Your Attention by Planning a Few Steps Ahead

If you don't know where you are going, you might wind up someplace else.

Yogi Berra

Planning is a fundamental component of living our lives, whether we are trying to figure out what to do today, design our next vacation, or trying to put dinner on the table. It is something we may sit down and do deliberately, or it may just be going on in the back of our minds while we are trying to attend to other activities. A plan is a series of steps to be taken to achieve a goal. We may execute the plan as is, or we may replan in the process, when new information becomes available. We have alluded previously in the book to the idea that if computers can help us plan, we can potentially reduce a lot of distracting ruminations, and now we are going to tackle the topic head on. But let's begin by questioning why Lisa or anyone else needs a planner and how it impacts one's well-being.

For Lisa to truly relax at night, she needs the reassurance that she can get up the next morning, ready to take on the day. Without a concrete plan, she finds herself constantly mulling over the day's potential tasks as she attempts to fall asleep, a pattern that continues into the following day. A well-planned day provides her with mental liberation that frees her from a lot of rumination. To be clear, a plan doesn't need to specify exactly what to do at every moment of the day. That would be too restrictive, inhibit spontaneity, and fail badly in other ways if the day serves up a surprise. A useful and realistic plan is one that provides a rough schedule and ensures that the most important tasks and activities are scheduled. The plan also keeps us grounded by protecting us from over-scheduling a day, which has other negative consequences to our well-being.

These feelings are not unique to Lisa; many of us face similar needs, both as a way of clearing our mind of details, or in order to coordinate with others in our lives. Moreover, our human minds are not really designed for some of the planning tasks we face. For example, when we contemplate any complex event, the multitude of possibilities can be overwhelming. Even simple plans such as dining out and watching a movie with a friend involve numerous details: Which movie do we both want to see? Which cinemas are screening it? Is there a suitable restaurant near any of these cinemas? How long will it take to get to either of these venues? And the list continues. At times, the complexity of the task may be too daunting and we end up spending the evening at home instead (which, in itself, is not bad). Planning an overseas trip involving multiple days, flights, hotels, and attractions is considerably more complicated. Intuition suggests machines, with their vast computational power and access to information, can more quickly sift through thousands of options, summarize them and then provide us with a few of the optimal choices. In a world in which so many of us are leading busy lives and in which the number of possible options of what to do seems to grow every single day, tools that assist us in planning are becoming essential.

This chapter will start by discussing the reasons that make planning so hard. In a nutshell, the reasons are that the world is a complicated, unpredictable and constantly changing place, that human decisions can frequently shift, and that the seemingly simple inferences for humans can become the toughest challenges for machines. However, we will also argue that reframing the planning problem as a collaboration between humans and machines holds the potential of yielding useful systems that contribute to the goals of the attention component of Oswell.

Understanding your world

To guide us through some of the challenges involved in planning, let's consider the task of planning Lisa's day. A useful planner should be able to take into account all potential tasks she might consider for a given day, and seamlessly incorporate them into a schedule that she can execute with ease. The entries on this schedule could be derived from at least three distinct sources.

The first source is the set of tasks that are already on Lisa's calendar, or at least, the mandatory ones. They're easy because their time and duration is known, and they can be put on her schedule as is, assuming there are no conflicts between them. You may disagree with our characterization of these events as being the easy category. There have been a few "calendar optimizer" applications that try to minimize fragmentation in your day so you can have solid blocks of meeting-free time. On the face of it, that's a really good use of technology. However, one of the problems with these programs is that in order to optimize *your* schedule, you might have to make the schedule of a colleague a bit less optimal. As a result, each move of a meeting ends up having a domino effect on everyone's schedule. Many of us have experienced the colleague at work whose schedule keeps changing and their scheduler keeps moving around our meeting time. In some extremely annoying cases, we may just end up ignoring the meeting, no matter when it's ultimately scheduled for.

The second source of items in Lisa's schedule involves her habits. These are things she does on a daily or weekly basis, such as exercising, eating meals, having an afternoon espresso, checking in with her parents, and watering her plants. Some of these habits and even their duration should not be too hard to glean from Lisa's lifelog. There will obviously be exceptions here regarding which Lisa should be able to inform the planner, but the lifelog provides a pretty good start. Unlike meetings that are set on a calendar, there is some flexibility in scheduling these activities, but given that they are habits, don't mess around with them too much.

The third source of tasks for Lisa's schedule comes from her todo list. These tasks might involve writing a proposal, reading a report by one of her team members, going to the dry cleaner, replanting the succulents in the garden, or researching the latest probiotics. Unlike Lisa's meetings and habits, the duration of these items is not given nor are they obvious. We may be able to use common sense to predict how long each of them might take, but as we will see later on in this chapter, common sense has and continues to be one of the biggest challenges to AI. In fact, Lisa herself might have a hard time predicting how long each one will take.

Our own inability to predict how long each task will take, as well as our tendency to over-achieve, at least on paper, is also the reason many of us create to-do lists for a day that has enough work for a week. No wonder we are often surprised at the end of the day that we only got through a tiny fraction of our list, and then feel incredibly under-accomplished. Hence, one of Lisa's main requirements from a personal planner is to find just the right combination of items she can accomplish, and in doing so, help her balance between her top priorities and deadlines and items that she just wants to do. Indeed, finding that balance between what you need to do and what you want to do is one of the trickiest aspects of modern life. If the balance is not right, in the long run your well-being will be affected negatively. Of course, for a short while here and there, anyone can burn the midnight oil as we rush towards an important deadline, or conversely, put work on the back burner while we care for a sick relative. Lisa has certainly done that when she founded her first startup and had to create compelling demos for prospective customers. But after a while, she realized that her sanity requires other creative outlets, such as finishing the crochet project she started a while ago, taking her latte art skills up a notch, or cooking a really creative lentil stew.

For a planner to be truly useful to Lisa, she just needs to be able to communicate with it the way she would converse with a human assistant. Such communication would enable her to specify any activity she wants to perform or put constraints on when or how she can perform it. Complicating matters even further is that daily activities can be messy. Some tasks, such as writing a meaty document, are not done in one sitting and need to be broken down to a few shorter time slots. Other tasks require multiple steps that span a few hours, such as doing the laundry or baking a quiche. Yet others span more than one day, like planning a social occasion or teaching your child to drive. In these cases, the task involves multiple steps some of which depend on previous ones being completed. For example, if you're planning a party, you need to invite the guests, figure out a menu and the right amount of groceries to buy, and then prepare the food and the party favors. Fortunately, you can also do certain things in parallel, such as listening to an audio book while folding the laundry, or working out a difficult math problem while washing dishes. To be helpful, the planner needs to understand all these constraints and where things can be flexible.

Let's say that the planner knows how to deal with all these complexities and has designed the perfect day plan for Lisa. When was the last time you went through a day following the precise plan you made the previous night? Probably never. At best, our day plans are guides, not prescriptions, and that's fine. In fact, one of the common criticisms we hear when we suggest the use of technology to create plans for our day is that we don't need a parent-like figure to tell us what to do at every point in the day. Life is dynamic, the only constant thing is change. So really, you need this agent to be able to replan at any given moment, like the "recalculate" of a navigation app after you missed the exit it was alerting you about for the last fifteen minutes. The planner should be able to take into consideration what you have done, how much time you have, whether the weather has changed, and what your mental state is. Maybe you were just notified that you got a promotion and decided to take the afternoon off, or maybe a friend just called with a plea for help, and you realized that the Pensky file can wait for tomorrow. More commonly, a meeting gets canceled and you now have an hour of unexpected free time. It would be great to receive a piece of advice about which important task would fit right in instead, or maybe advice to take a break and go for a walk.

We casually mentioned considering one's mental state when we were discussing re-planning. But this issue deserves much more attention. Unlike robots, it is impossible for us humans to go from task to task and perform flawlessly irrespective of what these tasks are. In her book "Attention Span: A Groundbreaking Way to Restore Balance, Happiness and Productivity", University of California, Irvine professor Gloria Mark explains that we need to design our days not only for productivity, but also for our well-being. It's important that we arrive at every task in the appropriate mental, physical and affective state. If you have just completed a concentrated hour of writing, you probably need a distraction so you can replenish your ability to focus. In that case, spending 15 minutes on mindless social media posts may be just the right thing for you. If you're going into a possibly contentious meeting with a colleague or your manager, you probably want to schedule some time to collect yourself before and calm down and reflect after. If Lisa ran a half marathon in the morning, maybe she should drive to the farmer's market later in the day rather than her usual practice of biking. In short, we would like to ensure that we arrive at every task with the appropriate physical resources, the ability to pay attention so we can be present, and in the right mental state. We want to avoid bringing in residues from other problems into the task at hand.

Now that we've hopefully convinced you that day planning is messier than it first appears, we should be more rigorous about explaining why it could be harder than planning the operations of a spaceship. To do this, we need to briefly explain how these AI systems, that are referred to as symbolic AI planning systems, were designed.

Symbolic AI planning systems

The task of a planning system is to produce a set of steps that will take you from where you are now to some desired state of the world, whether it is dinner on the table in 45 minutes, a driver's license for your child, or a product launch in a few months. In some applications of planning systems, such as robotics, the machine itself, that is, the robot, will be the one performing the actions in the plan. In our context, you will be the one performing the actions, or at least most of them. Either way, the planning system needs to know enough about each action and its consequences in order to produce a desired plan.

The key idea underlying symbolic planning systems is that they rely on a formal description of the world in which you operate. That description encompasses the important aspects of the current state of the world and the actions that can be performed in order to change that state. By nature, the designers of the system abstracted away details that didn't seem germane to the problem at hand. A description of the world in symbolic planning systems was formulated in terms of a mathematical language (also known as first-order logic, if you're curious), and would enable the system to reason about how to make a sequence of actions that would take the world from the current state to the desired state.

Let's make this more concrete with an example that is considerably simpler than operating a spacecraft, namely, the world of stacking blocks. In the blocks world, a problem domain that kept a few generations of esteemed AI researchers very busy, the goal is to rearrange a set of blocks to satisfy a desired configuration. For example, as shown in the Figure, our starting configuration may include three towers of blocks, in each of them there is a red block above a green block above a blue block. Our goal configuration might be three towers, each of which has blocks of the same color.

The Blocks World

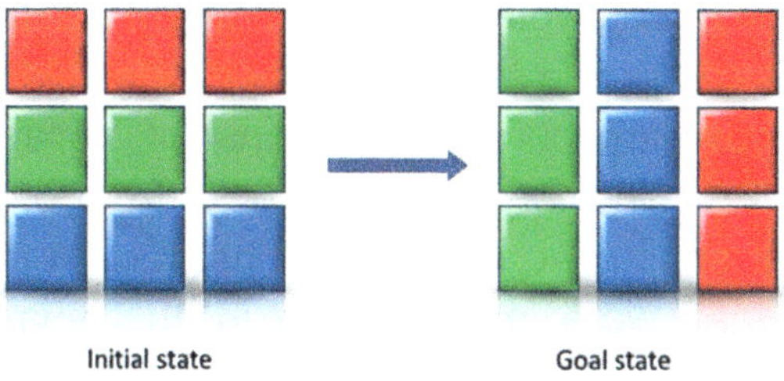

Created by Nano Banana

The description of the world specifies the exact configuration of the blocks. This includes how many blocks there are and where exactly they are situated. Blocks could be on the floor or sitting on top of a different block. Obviously, the description ensures that a block cannot be in two places at the same time, and that a block cannot be covered and uncovered at the same time. In this domain, the operations that the description is allowed to make were unstacking a block from another or from the floor, and putting it either on the floor or on top of another uncovered block. The description of the world doesn't specify whether the blocks are in Japan or in Jamaica, what is the color of the wall of the room, whether the stock market went up or down on that day, or whether the Dallas Cowboys suffered another crushing defeat earlier that week. All that doesn't matter to the crucial task of moving the blocks from one configuration to another. Given that description of the world, the planner could consider different sequences of stacking and unstacking blocks that will get us to the desired configuration.

The symbolic approach to planning worked for the spaceship and for other AI applications at the time because the spaceship had a finite number of sensors from which they were gathering information about their environments. This meant that the description of the world was inherently limited and pretty well defined. Furthermore, they had an even smaller number of actuators, in other words, ways in which they could manipulate their environments, so the number of possible actions the planner could do was also limited. Lest you think for a moment that the spacecraft environment was as simple as the aforementioned blocks world and that the US government spent millions of dollars to launch spaceships that would merely move blocks from one location to another in outer space, we assure you that it's not the case. The environments that were manipulated in the spacecraft were extremely complex and involved considering an exponential number of possible plans. Fortunately, thanks to a large body of AI innovations, the systems deployed in these scenarios were able to accomplish their tasks efficiently.

Coming back to Planet Earth and Lisa's day plan, the reason why symbolic planning cannot be used so readily is that the description of the world would be too complex. There are simply too many factors affecting one's day, and the number of unknowns is also very high. Furthermore, each of us is different. We have different habits, goals, constraints and environments that change throughout our lives. Writing all this down in logic is simply unfeasible. I do not say these words lightly, for I still bear the invisible bruises of my early career when I thought logic would win the day. I entered the field of AI because I truly believed in the approach of symbolic systems and of mathematical logic being the engine for reasoning about the world. One of my Ph.D advisors, Ed Feigenbaum, is credited with the development of expert systems, which is one of the success stories of symbolic AI. My other Ph.D advisor, Richard Fikes, built STRIPS, the first planning system based on the symbolic approach that defined the field of planning for years to come. But ultimately, we all realized that this approach cannot handle the complexities of the real world and moved on.

This discussion of symbolic systems may sound a bit like the conundrum we faced in Chapter 4. There we mentioned two approaches to arrange data in the lifelog: in structured databases or with no structure at all. That is not a coincidence. The dichotomy between structure and no structure appears, in different guises, very often. In some sense, symbolic systems are fancy types of databases (with much more expressive power than a database, to be precise). When we choose structure, we get the benefit of predictability but lose the flexibility of dealing with the nuances of the real world that were not modeled by the structure we envisioned. To create planners that truly assist us, we'll need some novel techniques that combine elements from symbolic planning and from today's powerful foundation models. But before that, we still need to discuss some of the challenges that a planner would face.

Understanding your context

We have discussed how an AI agent, through the Experiences component of Oswell, needs to be familiar with your past, such as your experiences and your habits, and your possible futures, including your goals and desires. But between the past and the future lies the now, and it is more tricky than you would think. The now refers to your current context that includes your location, the people you are with, what you are doing, your intentions, and maybe even the reasons behind your actions.

A simple example of context involves cheesecake. Consider a scenario in which you are asking your AI agent for a cheesecake recipe. The most useful answer that your agent can give you depends on whether you are currently walking down the supermarket aisle, or if you are at home and have just realized you have run out of cream cheese. A more complicated example is one where you're asking your agent to help you select what to wear in the morning, or select which restaurant to dine in tonight. In one context, you might be spending the day with your kids, and in another, you may be with professional colleagues visiting from out of town. In the former case, your main goal might be to entertain your kids and their preferences will be the dominating factor in making certain decisions (within limits). In the latter case, your main goal might be to ensure that your guests have a good time. Additionally, you may also have an ulterior motive to impress one of your guests in particular because you know they will play a crucial role in your upcoming promotion discussion. In that case, the only limit may be the spending cap that your company imposes on business dinners.

Context involves multiple components, and we will briefly consider some of them. The first component of context is your physical location. While this may seem straightforward at first glance, a closer look reveals that it is more complicated than you think. GPS systems today can accurately pinpoint your location whether you are hiking a glacier in Iceland or enjoying a margarita on the beach in Bali. However, in addition to your outdoor location, an AI agent often needs to know your precise indoor location, in your home, office, or at the Museum of Modern Art. For example, if you are in your bedroom, the agent may decide that certain work items are not worth your attention at the moment, but that might be different if you are in your home office.

The challenge lies in the fact that before the AI can determine your specific location within your house or any other space, it needs to have a map of that space. For your home, constructing such a map may take a few minutes, but when you enter a new space, you do not have such a map readily available. This challenge has led to a community of researchers working on the problem known by the somewhat jarring acronym SLAM: simultaneous localization and mapping. A SLAM algorithm would accompany you when you enter a friend's house and start walking around it. You may begin in the living room and later move to the kitchen to help out. After a few drinks, you might ask for the bathroom and head over there. At that point, the system can direct you back to the living room so you don't accidentally get lost (we're assuming your friends have fancy houses in this example). Even better, when you're heading out, it may remind you that you left your sunglasses on the back porch.

Things get even more complex when you consider that the AI should also be able to identify the objects in the space you're in, and figure out what you're actually doing. For example, your smart glasses may be clever and realize that you're looking at a ratatouille. But are you preparing it over a stove, casually tasting it at the request of the chef, or are you sitting and eating the ratatouille at the dinner table? In the first case, the agent might offer you help. You can ask what's the next step in preparing the dish, or, when you realize that you're missing one of the ingredients, you can walk together over to the fridge or pantry and get some ideas. Fortunately, ratatouille is a rather forgiving dish.

Equally important is for the AI to understand your relationship to the objects within your field of view. Is that cup of tea that you've just picked up yours, or maybe it belongs to one of your guests who's not interested in exchanging bodily fluids with you just yet. Computer vision techniques have made significant progress in identifying objects in a scene, as long as they're not unusually unique. However, tracking your relationship with an object requires connecting the dots among multiple time points. For example, the system may have recorded in a previous time that you sipped from that cup and that you put it down in a particular location, and later on, it would be easier to figure out whether you've picked up the right cup.

The reason that computer vision techniques don't easily transfer to addressing the above problems is that the large corpora of images and video that they employ in their research are not taken from the perspective of the person doing the actions. You can take many photos of people at a mall, but a video camera installed on the head of a person walking through the mall will have a very different perspective. To address this challenge, multiple groups have begun research on egocentric AI, which is a much more benevolent field than the name suggests. The Ego4D consortium that was spun up by Kristen Grauman from Meta's AI Research Lab brings together researchers from over a dozen universities. Together, the consortium has collected first-person videos of people doing a variety of actions from 74 worldwide locations in 9 countries. Similarly, the Aria Project, from a sister group at Meta, produced an experimental set of smart glasses whose goal is to help researchers to collect first-person data so it can be used to train machine learning models. As these data sets get richer and more researchers use them in their work, it's reasonable to expect that our smart glasses will get even smarter.

The next component of context involves understanding who is with you at the moment. Are you alone? If not, who else is around you, what is their relationship to you, and how might that be affecting your behavior and decisions? There might be a person next to you, but as we saw during Lisa and Oliver's dilemma above, it's crucial to know whether it's your date, spouse, friend, boss, or a random person you don't actually know. There might also be people farther away, but they may be relevant to the context. For example, if you are chatting with a person at an event, you may want to know whether their work colleagues are standing nearby. If there are colleagues around, you may not want to speak about their upcoming interview at your company.

The discussion above probably triggered a privacy concern in your mind. Few people desire a world where your location can be tracked to the minute by piecing together video snippets taken at different places, possibly by people you don't know and who may not have your best interests in mind. Such concerns have contributed to the negative press surrounding facial recognition, leading to the cancellation of many face-recognition services. However, the other extreme, where you can't even recognize that a child in a photo is yours and that she is sitting next to your dear Aunt Elaine, also does not seem ideal. These concerns have prompted tech companies, researchers, and policymakers to seek a balanced approach that addresses privacy concerns while still permitting beneficial uses of facial-recognition technologies. In our context, a likely approach is to adopt opt-in policies, where users voluntarily choose to have their facial data used by certain services.

This allows users to benefit from recognition technologies when they want to, while also maintaining control over their privacy.

The holy grail of understanding your context is to discern your intent. What are you genuinely trying to achieve and why? Let's consider a simple example of looking at a menu. If you are doing it while seated at a restaurant, then most likely, you're trying to choose which items to order from the menu. By default, the choice may be for yourself, but you might actually be giving advice to the person with you who is unable to read the menu, or ordering for your child. However, if you're looking at a menu while seated at home in front of your computer, then you may actually be deciding whether to go to that restaurant or another one nearby. If you're browsing menus from restaurants in a town far away, you might be trying to determine whether or not to include that town in your upcoming trip's itinerary. Depending on your true intent, the advice that the AI should provide will vary significantly.

In the first case, your food intake earlier in the day, such as the amount of fiber you've consumed, becomes an essential factor. In the second scenario, where you're choosing among several restaurants, the AI might also point out that a certain restaurant offers free parking, while another one is likely to be fully booked a week in advance. In the trip planning scenario, the AI may advise you that there is a really great cafe in that town and therefore you should make the stopover regardless of the restaurant offerings.

Context information is harder to collect with today's technology without significant friction. The devices we wear today provide us little bits of information that even when put together still yield gaps in the system's ability to gauge your full context. Your smart watch knows your approximate state based on your heart rate. Your phone may know that you're at a restaurant and be more confident in guessing that you're trying to choose from a menu. However, when you are at home, there are countless potential goals you might have, and the agent will struggle to distinguish between them. One option is, of course, to explicitly communicate your intentions to the AI assistant. There will be instances where this is undoubtedly the most effective or the only possible approach to fulfill your needs. However, in other situations, it may lead to awkwardness, at the very least.

If some of the leading labs that are currently working on augmented-reality glasses succeed, we may be able to address this problem more effectively in a few years. Your smart glasses will possess the ability to observe your surroundings, identify the people you're with, and recognize your body pose, which would help them detect whether you are lying down, sitting on the couch, or about to launch into a skydive. Consequently, you won't need to inform the system about where you parked your car or where you left your keys because the glasses capture every aspect of your environment. Furthermore, via the glasses, the system will have detailed knowledge of the foods you have consumed throughout the day, including their nutritional value, which proves invaluable when selecting items from a menu. Moreover, since the smart glasses could also have cameras pointed at your eyes in addition to cameras pointed at your surroundings, they will be able to discern where your gaze is focused, and therefore where your attention is at. This, for example, would enable them to realize that you gazed at a poster when you were strolling downtown, and therefore to remember the title of the movie advertised on it, which you may struggle to recall on your own later.

Ironically, one of the most challenging technical hurdles in developing technology related to smart glasses is not what to remember, but what to forget. The vast majority of your daily activities are not worth retaining, and even with the declining cost of memory, it remains unfeasible to store videos capturing every single moment of your life. Hence, the algorithms that process the data coming from our always-on glasses need to discern what are the moments that are worth noting, and how to put them together into higher-level memories. Your video stream will record every fine detail of preparing an omelet, starting with grabbing the skillet, cracking an egg, putting butter on the skillet, etc. However, unless your omelet making skills are in need of an upgrade, aggregating all these minutiae to an event that says that you made an omelet with two eggs and a little Parmesan cheese at 7:45 in the morning, is more useful.

At the risk of sounding like a broken record, we want to remind you that even with all this information available to your AI about your every action, there will always remain a gap between what the AI agent knows about your context and your intentions. At the end of the day, don't forget that you're in control.

The world beyond you

In addition to understanding your experiences and what you want to accomplish, a planner also needs to possess substantial knowledge about how the world works. In fact, extensive knowledge about the world is where AI brings significant value, and therefore that knowledge can be applied, via a planner, to provide valuable insights that would otherwise demand much more effort from you. But knowledge about the world comes in two flavors. These two flavors, which we explain below, illuminate an interesting observation that is counter to our intuition: it turns out that what's hard for humans is easier for machines, and vice versa, what comes naturally to humans is much harder for machines.

The first kind of knowledge about the world consists of factual knowledge found on platforms like Wikipedia: What is the capital of Rwanda? (Kigali) What was the population of Mont Saint-Michel in the year 1900? (234) Who designed the Sydney Opera House? (Jørn Utzon) When it comes to planning your day or a trip, a planner can also access a multitude of databases containing information such as weather forecasts, local concerts, restaurant reviews and flight schedules. Machines can easily scour through numerous databases in little time and extract the information that is most relevant to your plan. Over the past few decades, we have grown reliant on this information for our daily activities, and we expect search engines to surface it in sub-second time.

The second type of knowledge is often referred to as common-sense knowledge, which as the famous quote of Voltaire, the French Enlightenment philosopher, quips, is not so common as you would think. This is where things become much trickier, especially for machines. It's the knowledge that every 5-year-old child seems to possess naturally, but equipping computers with such understanding has been one of the most enduring challenges in the field of AI. For instance, common sense includes knowing that if you fill up a glass of water beyond its rim, the water will spill and soak everything around it, or that if you wake up at 7 am and leave the house an hour later, you probably brushed your teeth some time during that hour. In fact, describing these kinds of facts in a way that a computer can comprehend was precisely my first summer internship project during graduate school at the MCC Corporation. I still remember my mom's reaction when I tried to tell her about his project (something along the lines of "they're paying you all that money for *what*?").

Beyond the examples of spilling water and brushing teeth, common-sense knowledge also enables you to infer that you're younger than your parents but older than your kids, that a mouse can't ride a bike, and that drinking decaf coffee is a waste of time (okay, that last one might be a bit judgmental).

In the context of planning, common-sense inferences are everywhere. For example, when you're planning a workout, the weather conditions are relevant -- if it's snowing, you might want to modify your outdoor workout plan. If you're at the hardware store to buy gardening equipment, your planner should not send you to a different store to buy batteries, because they could also be found just where you are. When considering a day plan, it's a good idea not to schedule lunch right after you've finished breakfast. When you pack for your overseas trip, you're not going to pack up your couch, even though you use it as often as your toothbrush.

Equipping computers with common-sense knowledge remains a formidable challenge in the field of AI. A pioneering large-scale effort to address the challenge was the Cyc Project, initiated by the late Douglas Lenat in 1984 at the MCC Corporation based in Austin, Texas. The project's objective was to compile a sufficient number of rules detailing the functioning of the world. The expectation was that, over time, the model would accumulate enough knowledge to begin learning independently. However, Cyc never reached the learning phase because the challenges that were involved in writing and organizing such a large number of rules were more formidable than they looked at the start. This is not for lack of trying. In addition to employing graduate students who possessed an astute understanding of certain aspects of everyday life, such as water spillage or tooth brushing, the project employed some of the top experts in AI, including one of the founders of the field, Stanford professor, John McCarthy, who is credited with coining the term Artificial Intelligence. One of the main issues that the project faced was that the world was simply too complex to describe with rules. Yes, you will probably brush your teeth between waking up and leaving the house, but you might skip if you're on a special medical regime, an earthquake just struck, or you just realized where you spent the night and need to make a polite but speedy exit. While the Cyc Project did yield a system that proved effective in a few limited contexts, it stopped short of realizing its true vision.

A reasonable question that might be on your mind right now is, how much of the problem did Cyc and its follow on projects solve? Have we captured 5% of common sense, or are we closer to 50% or even 90%? Quantifying a system's knowledge of common-sense knowledge is not a simple task for a variety of reasons. One reason is the absence of a distinct boundary between what counts as common sense and what doesn't. Often, such knowledge is perceived as somewhat subjective and context-dependent. It may hold true some of the time but not always, and determining when to apply this knowledge can be complex. For instance, puppies are generally considered cute, while snakelets (yes, baby snakes) may not be. Telling your boss they are unqualified for their job is usually detrimental to one's career, yet there may be some bosses who might agree and swap roles.

Moving forward: planning as a collaboration

We have outlined the main challenges involved in building a planner that contributes positively to your attention resources by taking many details off your chest. However, we don't blame you if you are less than hopeful about the prospects of seeing such a planner anytime soon, even less hopeful than you were at the beginning of the chapter. But let's start building on what we have, namely, highly capable large language models.

First, early experiments demonstrate that today's large language models do seem to capture some of the common sense knowledge that is needed for planning aspects of your life. For instance, you can describe to a system powered by a language model a list of tasks you want to do during a particular day and ask it to create a day plan. The initial plan it provides will apply limited common sense, placing events at appropriate times, such as breakfast in the morning and dinner in the evening. Since language models are not yet reliable when it comes to reasoning about precise scheduling constraints, the plan may sometimes contain errors. For example, the system may forget to place a task on your schedule, or schedule lunch an hour after breakfast. However, the speed at which language-model technology is progressing gives us hope that they will improve quickly at many planning tasks. Furthermore, even a simple trick, such as asking the language model to check whether it satisfied all your constraints, will often be enough to prompt it to detect errors and correct them on its own.

Second, given the conversational abilities of the language models, this is not a one-shot deal. You can provide the planner feedback, and therefore with a bit of back and forth, coax the system to produce a plan that satisfies your needs. Moreover, unlike symbolic planners that require very precise constraints, you can specify more vague constraints and the system will be able to interpret them. For example, you may want to tell the planner that you need more frequent breaks in the afternoon or that you woke up not feeling great and you need a lighter schedule.

These two points lead to our main observation, which is that planning should be reframed as a collaboration between you and the AI agent. You're not going to simply give it all your needs for the day, accept a plan (perfect or not), and start executing. A more constructive way of thinking about planning is that the system is an assistant that is always a step or two ahead of you. You'll start the day with a plan that it provides, but as you go through the day and conditions change, the agent will revise your plan, considering the new constraints and your up-to-date instructions. If you are suddenly contemplating going out for a movie in the evening, the system will quickly figure out candidate venues and convenient restaurants where you can dine before the movie. Alternatively, if your meetings at work run over, and your plans to cook dinner for the family are at risk, the planner will come up with a few alternatives that will satisfy the new time constraints and your dietary preferences. In a nutshell, the agent is there for you with plans, but avoids over-planning.

Explaining recommendations and plans

We are ending the discussion of the Attention component of Oswell here. This component helps focus your attention by providing recommendations for content or activities that are most worthy of your time from the perspective of your well-being, and offloading some of your work by creating plans for you, thereby freeing even more of your attention. Before we conclude this part of the book, we need to touch on an important requirement from any technology that purports to contribute to your well-being. This requirement is the ability to explain why it is recommending something to you or how it came up with a plan it thinks is suitable for you. Users will not (and should not!) trust a system that cannot explain its reasoning. Explanations need to be clear so that anyone can understand them rather than the ones that computer programs spew out in order to help programmers debug them. The explanations also need to be actionable. If you didn't like the recommendation, the explanation should give you a way of instructing the system to modify it to suit you better.

Unfortunately, deep neural networks, which are the main engine underlying today's impressive AI systems, have a hard time explaining their reasoning. These networks encode their knowledge with billions of parameters, and their answers emerge from this vastness. In fact, most AI researchers openly acknowledge that they don't fully understand why these systems perform as well as they do. One of the consequences of our lack of understanding is that we can observe their successes, but predicting their failures often remains a challenge.

Fortunately, there are many exciting research efforts aiming to understand how these systems reason and, ultimately, to explain their recommendations. Some of these projects start with the more modest goal of trying to edit the knowledge these systems possess. Presumably, being able to edit knowledge may be a first step towards understanding where knowledge is stored and how it is used in reasoning. Another body of work, which is especially relevant to Oswell, concentrates on cases in which the most important knowledge that is relevant to a recommendation is stored outside of the neural net. For example, your calendar and your preferences are provided as an input to the reasoning engine and not stored inside it, and the same goes for the train schedule in Stockholm. Your AI partner will know to consult these data sources when they are needed in order to provide you advice. When recommendations use external data, it is easier for the AI to point to what aspects in the input affected the recommendations in the output. We expect rapid progress to be made in this area resulting in explanations that will hopefully satisfy the needs of users of AI agents.

Try This 👉

In this chapter we described the basics of planning systems and why they might be useful to reduce unnecessary ruminations and toilsome work in our daily lives. Take a planning task that you engage with on a regular basis. For example, it can be creating a plan for a day, planning a trip or an outing with friends or family. How effective are you at this planning task? Do you create a plan and execute, modifying the plan as needed, or do you ruminate about it a lot and often come up short with inefficient plans or are stuck as to what to do next? Write down the types of information that are needed to create the plan – is it information on your calendar? Something that is available on the web but may take too much time to find? Or maybe it is that the world is uncertain and you're having trouble coming up with a plan that will be robust in face of uncertainty? Do you think you can delegate some of that planning to an AI? How would you like to communicate the necessary information to the AI?

It was a beautiful Saturday morning, and Lisa was excited to go hiking with Oliver. Her AI assistant alerted her a few days earlier that the spring wildflowers will be in full bloom close to her favorite forest and she really needed to spend some time in nature. Oliver gladly accepted her invitation to join even though he often struggles to keep up with Lisa's brisk hiking style.

As they started their hike, and Oliver finally caught up with Lisa, he turned to Lisa and asked, "so, anything interesting happened last night after the happy hour?"

"Not what you're thinking, Oliver. I actually went home and decided to sit down and make a list of all the important people in my life."

"Wow, that was some happy hour! What prompted you to do that?"

"Well, I spend an enormous amount of my time thinking about the relationships in my life and trying to make sure I'm treating each one of them with the care they need. It starts with remembering special occasions and finding good ways of celebrating them, to ensuring that I'm really spending time with the people I value. I sort of feel like I can use an AI assistant for this... know anybody who's building AI assistants?"

"I agree, relationships are really complicated. But you can sort of already do that with my app today. You can treat every person as a 'task' and have the system given you advice on when to pay attention to the task."

"Yes, but that doesn't capture everything I need. I can't really reduce a person to a task that I complete and then it goes away. Relationships are ongoing activities in our lives and require a lot of care and attention for a hopefully long time. They're complex and evolve over time."

"Ok, that makes sense. But the app also lets you handle long-term tasks such as your exercise or your health. Those are never done. Can't you treat every relationship the way you treat your exercise regime?"

"I think that's still missing something basic. My exercise and dieting are mostly under my control. I make decisions, and execute them. That's a really bad way to approach relationships... they're more dynamic, you're interacting with another person who has their own goals, needs and values. They're changing a lot over time, and they're generally just much more nuanced. I mean, look at our relationship... we've been almost all over the map."

"Almost."

"Yes, I really did mean almost."

"I get it. So essentially you're suggesting that an AI agent have a specialized component to help us manage the important relationships in our lives."

"Yep, get to work, buddy. But first, let's step up the pace and climb that beautiful hill with all those flowers. I'm sure you'll see things more clearly when we reach the top."

9. Connection: Well-being is a Multi-player Game

A dream you dream alone is only a dream. A dream you dream together is reality.
John Lennon

When we set out to write this book, the first person we turned to for advice was Dr. Jennifer Aaker, a professor at the Stanford Graduate School of Business, and a leading behavioral scientist focused on well-being. Jennifer's reputation in the study of well-being, covering topics ranging from the role of negative experiences, the importance of humor and of awe, to paying attention to beauty in the world, was so prominent that we were excited to pick her brain early on. Sitting in a vibrant cafe on the Stanford campus on a sunny winter day, we were ready with our prepared questions, but the conversation took an unexpected direction. "Have you ever thought of the most profound regrets people carry with them as they approach life's end?", Jennifer asked. She realized that we were perplexed by the question, so she proceeded to unpack the topic for us, step by step.

Jennifer grew up in a home where the conversations at the dinner table often told the stories of people dying. Jennifer owed this particularly fun upbringing to the fact that her mom was a volunteer at a hospice and so she shared the stories of the people she was caring for every day with her family. One of the takeaways from these dinner conversations was an understanding of the top regrets that people recount in their dying days. One might speculate that these regrets revolve around unfulfilled grand missions or significant life decisions gone awry. Yet, Jennifer unveiled a narrative quite distinct from these assumptions. Overwhelmingly, the top regret people mentioned was that they should have loved more, showed their loved ones more love, and invested more in their close connections.

These conversations piqued Jennifer's interest in understanding the concepts of meaning, and purpose and death, so over the next few decades, she turned this interest into a distinguished career whose purpose is to understand deeply what is meaningful in life, how that differs from happiness in life, and when and why we get it wrong. A natural evolution of her research in recent years was to ask what we want our AI-enhanced future to look like.

As professors often do, they learn by teaching. So a few years ago, Jennifer teamed up with Fei Fei Li, a professor at the Stanford Computer Science Department, and together they crafted a course titled "Designing AI for Human Well-Being". After covering material on the meaning of happiness and well-being and on the fundamentals of AI, they formed small project groups of students that included members from the two main populations of students in the class: engineering and business. Their task was to consider how AI can promote human flourishing to a more meaningful scale.

The most memorable projects the students came up with had to do with using AI to enhance human connection, reinforcing Jennifer's message to us. For example, one team examined how AI can decrease feelings of loneliness that were prevalent especially among international students who have just moved to the United States. Another team found ways to use AI to improve nurses' workflow so that they could spend less time inputting chart information and more time connecting with patients. It is evident that making time for more meaningful relationships, whether at home or in the workplace, is one of the grand challenges for AI technology. This conversation with Jennifer sparked the idea for the Connection component in Oswell, which we lay out in this chapter.

The importance of relationships

Healthy relationships form the cornerstone of our well-being. They often present our greatest challenges while offering our most rewarding experiences. If we ever needed a stark reminder of the significance of these relationships, the Covid-19 pandemic generously provides us with one. People all over the world, unable to meet in person with their loved ones and friends, went to great lengths to maintain some of these relationships, deepen the relationships in their homes, and others used the opportunity to let go of those relationships that were not contributing to their well-being.

Relationships come in many forms, and each contributes to your well-being in its own special way. Your closest relationships, such as your romantic partner, children, parents, and closest friends, provide you with a set of formative experiences and memories throughout your life. The next tier of friends may be involved in your life in some important way, but much less often. However, these connections can offer an important occasional perspective, such as career advice or help with your sourdough infatuation or simply spend some quality time together as you both enjoy jamming with your guitars. In some relationships, you might be the one doing most of the giving, like mentoring a teenager or checking in on an elderly neighbor a few times a week. But as any expert on well-being will tell you, giving is just as important to your wellness. Your professional network also plays a significant role in your career, encompassing relationships with current colleagues, past coworkers, and connections from your schooling days. Regardless of the strength of the relationship, from the closest one to the most ephemeral, such as the farmer who you chat with once a week at the market, or the person you wave to during your morning run and whose name you don't even know, these relationships affect your well-being on a daily basis.

Relationships with other people are just one kind of connection we form in our lives. Another important type is our connection with communities, whether it's a religious community, a sports club and its fans, fellow expats from our home country, or the people we left behind in that country. In that sense, the communities we connect to are a significant part of how we define our identity. For example, I am connected to a community of friends from earlier in my life who live in Israel, and I interact with them regularly. I feel an even deeper connection with this community during times of turbulence in the Middle East, which unfortunately, is the majority of the time. Additionally, I am connected to a community of academics that I meet at conferences and on social media, and I still enjoy maintaining contacts with members of the coffee industry that I formed during the years I worked on my coffee book. All of these connections together go a long way in defining how I identify myself as a person. The reason this is so important is that the way one defines one's identity often plays a key role in their sense of well-being. Examining your connections is also an opportunity. If your well-being is lacking in some way, finding another community to connect with can be part of the solution.

The importance of connection to our well-being is well documented. The best known study of the importance of relationships is the Harvard Study of Adult Development. The study started in 1938 and followed a set of Harvard graduates over the course of decades, tracking many aspects of their lives, including their careers, health, and levels of happiness. As the study concludes, the most important indicator of a happy life is having good long-term relationships with your partner, children and community. The explanation that researchers conducting the study offer is not surprising. These relationships are ones that provide you with great experiences and memories. Relationships distract you from your worries, they entertain and help you self reflect. They provide a safety net when you need one, either emotionally or otherwise. To make the point even more stark, the head of the project, Robert

Waldinger, has said "Loneliness kills. It's as powerful as smoking or alcoholism."

Following up on Waldinger's point, Vivek Murthy, the 39th and 41st Surgeon General of the United States has gone as far as publishing a general advisory in 2023 pointing out that there is an epidemic of loneliness and isolation in the United States and raising alarm about the phenomenon. The book he published on the topic in 2020, titled "Together: The Healing Power of Human Connection in a Sometimes Lonely World", goes much deeper into the nuances of the topic.

Daniel Siegel, a clinical professor of psychiatry at the UCLA School of Medicine and executive director of the Mindsight Institute, goes even further and refers to the current situation as the "solo-self pandemic". The culprit of this pandemic, he claims, is that we are educated in modern societies (with special credit going to the western ones) to associate our identity with our self, our body, and mind. That education, by nature, will lead us to think of ourselves as separate from the world around us. In his book, "IntraConnected: MWe (Me + We) as the Integration of Self, Identity, and Belonging", Siegel explores the concept of MWe, in which he encourages us to think of our own identity more broadly, to include our families, communities, society and the planet we live in.

Supporting relationships with AI

An AI that is supposed to support our well-being should clearly put our relationships front and center. The role of the Connection component of Oswell is to help us navigate our complex web of relationships with individuals and with communities. It should help us ensure that we invest and nurture those relationships that contribute to our well-being, and deprioritize the ones that we can do without. Since our needs and the people in our life are constantly changing, this component should help us identify how to adapt our relationships as our circumstances change. The assistant should step in only when we ask it to, and as with the other advice we get from our AI partner, we may ignore it completely.

Another reason that AI can play an important role in helping our relationships is the observation that modern-day life involves inhabiting two worlds: the natural world and the digital world. Increasingly, more of our experiences are becoming digital and finding the balance between these worlds is becoming trickier than ever. This duality hits hardest when it comes to our relationships. Not only are there people we only interact with digitally, but the ones we meet in person we spend time online coordinating our future get togethers. An AI partner should be there to assist us with this growing challenge.

One of the key insights that you have seen repeatedly in the previous chapters is that Oswell provides most value when it has a holistic view of you as a person. We'll use the same playbook here. The key idea, again, is that knowledge about our relationships is distributed in communications managed by multiple applications, and we need a more holistic view and understanding of them and their value. Given such a holistic view, we can devise a set of mechanisms that advise us on which relationships to pay attention to or turn to at any given time, and how that can benefit our well-being.

One of the first things I did after gaining access to GPT-4 (even before inquiring about what it knows about me) was to conduct the following experiment. I provided GPT-4 with the last three months of my personal journal (which, unfortunately, is all I had at the time) and started asking a few questions. The journal is relatively brief, with a few sentences for each week on average. The most fascinating result I obtained from GPT-4 was when he asked it to list all the people mentioned in the journal. GPT-4 did a remarkable job by listing them all and providing a short context describing the nature of their connection with me. This moment brought me genuine joy as seeing the list flooded me with a wave of great memories from the past few months, giving me a temporary sense of satisfaction with my social life.

The experience described above offers a glimpse of what might be possible to obtain from the Connection component of Oswell. Specifically, this component should be capable of helping us with a myriad of questions regarding our connections, either to other individuals or to communities. Just as we did for the Attention component of Oswell, here too we articulate a set of principles that the Connection component should be designed for. Roughly, these principles correspond to answering the questions: who, why, and what about one's relationships.

The first principle, the ‘who’, is keeping track of who the people in my life are and how I am connected with them. This also includes recording what are the things I want to remember about each of them so I can possibly follow up on next time we meet or communicate. Since no one is perfect, an additional bonus would be for the system to help me articulate what I value about each person, and in what ways our tastes or personalities differ. Lisa has a dear childhood friend Neta, who has two daughters. Recently Neta told her about some of the difficulties that her elder daughter is experiencing at school, and Lisa would want to make sure she asks about Neta's daughter next time they meet. Lisa really likes Neta's knowledge and taste in art but their food preferences are quite different, so they don't often go out to dine.

The second principle, the ‘why’, is understanding the value that each of these relationships brings to me and the value I bring to them. It also enables me to articulate the goals I have with respect to each relationship. For example, is it one I want to nurture closely, casually keep in touch, or put on the back burner for a while? Lisa's relationship with Neta is very important to her because they've known each other for a long time. Lisa appreciates how Neta helps her put things in perspective, and she knows that she provides Neta an important sounding board for the problems she's facing in her life. This is a relationship she wants to nurture for the long term, even if they don't meet very often.

The third principle, the 'what', is to determine how I can turn the knowledge about the relationship into action and how I am doing with respect to the goals I have for the relationship. The system should help me reflect on whether there are relationships I should attend to more or some that I should deprioritize for the next while. Since communication is such an important part of every relationship, the agent can also give me tips on how to communicate more effectively in tricky situations. But we can go even further. Since my AI partner has quite a bit of information about these relationships, it can help me form plans that further my goals with them. For example, maybe there is a good friend I should plan a birthday celebration for, or organize an activity that may be of mutual interest. Maybe I can play the role of a network, and contribute by connecting a friend to a new opportunity or to other friends. Alternatively, if I need help, maybe there's a connection who can help me with something I'm struggling with right now. In Lisa's case, she's struggling with a decision about a new job opportunity where she would work with a good friend, and a conversation with Neta can certainly help clarify some of the issues.

In the technology world we like to quantitatively estimate the size of the opportunity of new services we propose. These estimates, whose source is often shrouded in mystery and sometimes it's better that way, are typically very optimistic, and should be taken with a grain of salt. In the same spirit, we can try to get an idea for the size of the opportunity of the Connection component of Oswell. To do so, we can anchor on a quantity that comes with a respectable level of mystery: Dunbar's number. The number, which is 148 but typically rounded up to 150, presented by Oxford evolutionary psychologist Robin Dunbar, is an estimate for how many social connections an individual human can maintain. If that sounds a bit vague, then the following explanation from Dunbar himself should clear things up: "it is the number of people you would not feel embarrassed about joining uninvited for a drink if you happened to bump into them in a bar." Dunbar calculated the number by looking at various species of primates, assessing the sizes of their respective social circles, then extrapolating to humans based on the relative brain sizes of the species. As you might imagine, follow up research has contested the number and estimates vary quite a bit, and would obviously differ from one person to another. However, the point is that there is still some upper limit to the number of people you can even remember.

Remembering a person is just one very narrow aspect of the richness of what we want to remember about each of these relationships. If you think of this in terms of a spreadsheet, the Dunbar number and its variants will only tell you how many rows there are in the spreadsheet, each one having a check mark on an imaginary column titled "join uninvited for a drink at a bar". But, as the aforementioned discussion illustrated, there is much more information we would like to know about each of these connections. In other words, the spreadsheet should be much wider with many columns, and it is highly unlikely that you can remember all the cells in this spreadsheet even if the number of rows is just a small fraction of the Dunbar number.

To achieve its goals, the Connection component of Oswell will need quite a bit of knowledge about your experiences and your goals. Some of that knowledge will be in your lifelog provided by the Experiences component of Oswell. However, what makes data about connections harder is that it is not naturally captured by the digital services we use on a daily basis. Unlike a workout or an online purchase, the important details of an interaction with a friend or family member are not captured as digital breadcrumbs. Instead, this information is more naturally recorded by capturing subjective experiences in a journal. And, as we described in Chapter 4, this raises the challenge of eliciting subjective experiences from your day in an effective and non-intrusive way. This challenge does not appear to be insurmountable with AI models that have more understanding of your activities throughout the day. These models should be capable of finding the right moments to have a brief conversation with you and ask you just the right questions in that conversation. It would be akin to a flipped voice memo application that prods you, rather than the other way around. Moreover, just as I now see the value of what a now outdated chatbot can do with my journal and is keen on being more diligent in creating entries for it, others will hopefully react in the same way.

Social media

Whether it's just your common sense or because you listened to the advice of your enlightened AI agent, we hope that you enjoy the vast majority of your connections in person, with technology left at bay in your pocket, purse or even farther away. The reality, however, is that not all important relationships in our lives can be enjoyed without the help of screens. Many technologies have contributed to the creation and maintenance of social connections when in-person meetings are not an option, beginning with the postal mail, the telephone, and email. But the emergence of social networks has taken the role of technology in our social life to an unprecedented new level, with both positive and negative effects on individuals, communities and society as a whole.

There has been a lot written about the benefits of social media and much more written about its unintended negative consequences. A good place to start reading about the latter is the recent book by Max Fisher, an international reporter and columnist for the New York Times, titled "The Chaos Machine: The Inside Story of How Social Media Rewired Our Minds and Our World". The effects of social media on teenagers are studied in depth in Jonathan Haidt's book, "The Anxious Generation" and the book has already had a wide impact world-wide since its publication in 2024. We will touch on both the positives and negatives here, but our main interest is the role that social media should play in the Connection component of Oswell. In particular, we want to imagine ways in which social media can add mechanisms that help us achieve our well-being goals. As a basis for this discussion, let's first make sure we're on the same page about the basic terminology relating to social media.

Social media is a term that refers to quite a few interactions we experience online. Social media sites are ones where a user is presented with a feed of content, which is a stream of posts. These posts often describe a recent experience either with a text or video with a few words, or it can be a longer soliloquy about a current issue. It's instructive to contrast social media that provides you a stream of content with a search engine that provides a list of answers to a particular question, such as a recipe for burekas. In the former case, the system is trying to guess what might be interesting to you from all the content available, whereas in the latter, it's trying to find the best answers to the question you just asked.

The content on our social-media feeds is shaped by the relationships we choose to establish on the site. An important distinction in friendship land is whether friendships are required to be reciprocal or not. For example, on Facebook, a friend is a reciprocal relationship. One of you invited the other to be their friend and the other accepted (with or without a huge amount of drama). This means that in principle, you will see their posts and they will see yours. We add the qualifier 'in principle' because the recommendation system of the social-media platform, which is responsible for determining which posts you see and in what order, may cause you to frequently see posts from some friends and rarely from others. Unfortunately, many people assume that each of their friends will see each of their posts, and when that doesn't happen, that often leads to unnecessary drama.

On X (formerly known as Twitter), on the other hand, your relationships are formed by you choosing to follow others. So you can follow Barack Obama, Taylor Swift, or the Liverpool Football Club, but sadly, they probably won't follow you (though I was once followed by the "Weather in Prague" Twitter account). Typically, you would choose to follow people whose opinion you value or that the information they share is useful to you. For the sake of accuracy, we note that you can also follow people on Facebook, and on X you can also restrict who follows you. What we described above refers to the main tenor of relationships on these platforms.

The content of your feed on a social media site is a combination of the posts made by your friends and the people and organizations you follow, and content that the system thinks might be interesting to you based on some of your previous interactions. This latter type of content is often called unconnected content because it doesn't come from friends you've connected with. As a clue for how much unconnected content you may be exposed to, Facebook recently added a new tab that enables you to see only content from your friends. As we already noted, the choice and order of these posts are made by the underlying recommendation system. The order is a crucial part of the decision of the recommendation system, because the further down a post is ranked, the less likely you are to stay on the site long enough to see it. One of the important factors that the recommendation system takes into account is how much engagement a particular post has received. For example, if a post received many likes and comments and has been re-shared with others frequently, the algorithm will take this as a sign that it may be interesting to you as well. This aspect of social-media ranking has been identified as the main culprit at the heart of the harms that social-media has caused.

To complete our tour of social media, we should also note that most social-media platforms also provide some sort of messaging feature, where members can communicate one to one or in small groups. Many of the benefits and harms of social media happen in the messaging apps, but we won't single them out here. A recent trend is that messaging services promise to encrypt messages end-to-end. This means that to the platform, the content of the message looks like gobbledygook, and there's much less the platform can do with them.

The benefits of social media

We will dedicate the next chapter to the unintended negative consequences of social media, or more precisely, the defences that were built to protect users from them. To balance things out, let's spend a few paragraphs on the benefits of these platforms.

On their first day at the company, new employees of Meta (the parent company of Facebook, Instagram, and WhatsApp) are told the story of how, On August 4, 2014, citizens in the Los Angeles were so alarmed by the fact that Facebook was down for a while, that they called 911 to report the 'incident'. In response, and adding to the irony, the Los Angeles police replied with a tweet saying that Facebook is not a law-enforcement issue and that they don't know when it will be back up.

Whether you regard the above story as solid proof or not, there are many ways in which social-media sites provide a great amount of benefit for individuals, communities and societies. The vast majority of posts on social media are of positive nature, either conveying useful information, entertaining or sharing meaningful updates. As a society, we have grown to rely on these services.

On the societal level, social media has been used to distribute information widely after disasters, such as the earthquake in Haiti in 2010, when there was very little information coming directly from the affected communities. It was used to mobilize crowds for civil protests such as in Egypt in 2011, and to quickly disseminate injustices, such as on the night that George Floyd was murdered by police in 2020. It was also used to share information about the locations of voting stations on election days around the world.

On a personal level, social media enables us to stay in touch with people we can't meet or talk with on a daily basis. Posts about births, weddings (even if we're not invited), deaths in the family and other significant events allow us to keep in touch from afar of our friends' lives and to offer support when our friends need it. Social media also helps propel us in new communities we're trying to join. For example, with the help of Facebook, I went from being completely unknown in the world of specialty coffee to having hundreds of friends in the community who were instrumental in helping me write my coffee book (and enjoyed the Google T-shirts I always gave out as gifts when we met in person). Despite having published the book over a decade ago, I still value this community to this day and love being informed about its progress.

Social media also provides benefits for producers, which can be broadly defined as being individuals or organizations with large audiences. A musician, whether famous or just budding, a politician or social advocate, or book authors can reach and stay in touch with their audiences and nurture their followers. Before social media, this could only be done in small local gatherings or mediated by the major networks.

Businesses are another type of producer. They reach their communities organically by creating a presence on social media with a dedicated page. The mom and pop bakery in your hometown can post photos of their newest creations on their page and hope that lures you into their shop. The other way businesses benefit from social media is by placing ads. The same bakery may not have the resources to put an advertisement in a newspaper, which you are unlikely to see anyway. Instead, via what is known as targeted advertising, they can pay to place their ads only to people in their zip code and whose profile has some indication of liking baked goods. This is much cheaper for them and reaches a much more relevant audience. Advertising gets a lot of flack in the narrative about social media, but for these businesses it is a lifeline. There's a good reason why the companies that depend on ads have some of the largest market caps in the world.

Social media and Oswell

While useful in keeping on top of the developments in our friends' lives, there are many ways in which social-media platforms can provide additional functionality that could help your well-being through Oswell. Here we will focus on one of them, which is providing better search facilities. The challenge lies in the fact that the incredible amount of useful information that your friends produce is presented to you as a stream. If you don't act on the information immediately, then it's extremely hard to find later. Consider, for example, all the posts that your friends make from wonderful restaurants, bakeries or cafes around the world. They look scrumptious, but right now you're at home and not traveling. A few months later, you're finally planning your trip to Stockholm which you hope to be a culinary heaven, and now you really need your friends' posts from Stockholm. Unfortunately, while social media sites do support some forms of search over previous posts, the results for "posts from friends who visited Stockholm recently" will not get you the desired result. Similarly, searches for "friends who recently got married or had a baby", or "friends who know something about woodworking" will disappoint. Your only choice right now is to try to remember which friends posted the content you're looking for and then to scroll back through each of their posts. Since this is such an arduous process, few of us would take the time to do it. In a nutshell, there is a wealth of valuable information on your social media feed, but it's ephemeral. It's available when it's posted, but not when you need it.

Building better search over information on social media posts, or at least a reasonable version of it, is not beyond the reach of today's technology. In fact, on several occasions, I have proposed such projects at Facebook and even got colleagues excited about them (which, unfortunately, is still not the same as building and launching the service). Moreover, there have been entire teams dedicated to the search features in social-media, but they seem to focus on enabling you to find people and topics but they do not go beyond that.

The idea we're arguing for here is for social media to adapt Google's motto "Organize the world's information and make it universally accessible" to something like "Organize the information available in your social circles and make it useful when you need it". Our proposal is not rocket science either. Building such a search engine requires some module that analyzes whether a post contains some information that may be useful later in a query, such as a restaurant recommendation, a life event, or display of expertise on a topic, and then storing summaries of these posts in a database that is organized to support search. Of course, special care must be taken to check that posts that have been deleted are no longer accessible to this new database.

Even when you build better search functionality, you also have to ask yourself whether there might be some unexpected consequences. To make the point, we will recount a story from a different context and slightly earlier era. Apparently, in the state of New York, when you obtain a gun permit, that is considered public information. This means that the address you put on your application is recorded in a designated database and anyone is allowed to ask for this database and comb through it at will. In 2012 a few journalists from The Journal News, a newspaper based in White Planes, New York, did exactly that. They got hold of the publicly available information about who applied for gun permits in a particular part of New York state. They then used Google Fusion Tables, a service that I led at Google at the time, to make that information much more easily searchable. Google Fusion Tables was a tool that enabled anyone to import data from a variety of formats such as spreadsheets or CSV files, and upload them into a map that can be shared on the internet. The result of the work of these journalists was that you could zoom in on the map down to the street level and see exactly which houses had someone who applied for a gun permit. Note that the information did not say whether the resident actually went out and bought a gun, or had any nefarious intention in such a purchase, just that they showed enough interest in guns to obtain a permit. Still, now you could tell which of your neighbors applied for a gun permit. One of the amusing aspects of this story, that made that day in the office a rather memorable one for me, was that the zipcode whose gun-permit seeking residents were being mapped was the same zip code in which my manager resided.

The publication of this map led to an outcry among gun-rights advocates and some law enforcement groups nationwide. So much so, that the reaction prompted the paper to hire armed security for its headquarters because threats were being made against its staff. Very shortly after, lawmakers in New York state amended the gun control laws to highly discourage the publication of such information, and the Journal News took the page down from its site.

The point of this story is that there is a huge difference between information possibly being public and it being easily searchable. The people in that county who applied for gun permits knew that the information about their gun permit application would be public, or at least, they should have been informed of that option. However, they made the reasonable assumption that to obtain the data one would have to go through a rather laborious multi-step process. That is very different from inviting everybody in your neighborhood to find out that piece of information via a convenient online map.

Going back to the problem of searching over social-media posts, one can reasonably make the argument that users of social media assume, perhaps subconsciously, that a lot of what they post will be hard to find later. If that were not the case, users may share less of their personal experiences than they do today. For example, perhaps you don't want the entire history of our romantic relationships or the frequency of our bar hopping to be available to any of our social-media friends via a simple query. We should take these concerns into consideration, and develop tools that help users examine more effectively what of their personal history is easily searchable. However, with that in place, there is a lot of room for improvement in search on social media to make the wealth of information from your connections more valuable to you.

So far we have spoken about the benefits of social media. But like any technology, it is often a double-edged sword and in the case of social media, you may have already noticed that the unintended negative consequences receive the lion share of media attention, and justifiably so. In the next chapter, we will dive into this topic in more detail and explain some of the harms that happen on social media and how the platforms attempt to address them.

Try This 👉

Think of a relationship in your life in which you may be having challenges or one that you want to invest in further. Describe to the AI the context of the relationship and your goals for it and see if it can help. Tell the AI what you like about this person and what challenges you find in the relationship. Are there questions that you are more comfortable asking an AI than another person in your life or ones that you don't think AI can possibly provide a useful answer? Can the AI help you find better ways to communicate in this relationship? Is there feedback from the other person that you can share with the AI to get more nuanced advice? Are there behaviors that the AI recommends that can contribute to the relationship and that can be tracked with time?

“Hop in, Lisa. We're going for a treat.”

“We are? So why is your navigation system thinking we're going to IKEA?”

“Because we're going to IKEA. I'm craving a cardamom bun, an authentic Swedish one. I don't know of a better place to get them around here.”

“Have you gone nuts, Oliver? Don't tell me you're also treating me to their world-famous meat balls.”

“Not a bad idea, actually. Ok, ok, I have been a bit wound up recently. This startup is a lot of work.”

“I bet it is. But it looks like you're making some good progress on the connections component of your app.”

“I am. But you know, whenever I talk to people about it, all they can think about is social networks this, social networks that. It's as if that's all we associate with connection these days.”

“I'm not surprised. I try really hard to limit my time on social media, but you know, it's hard. There's some good stuff out there.”

“There is, and a lot of bad stuff too. I hear that the social-media companies have sizable teams that try to protect users from the harms of social media. They spend a huge amount of time discussing what content is considered harmful (which, I hear, is really controversial), and then they develop complicated systems to identify harmful content and remove it."

"Umm... yeah, protect against harm... I have an idea. Are you ready for my next feature request, Oliver?"

"What hole did I dig myself into now? Can it wait until after the meatballs?"

"Your app should protect me against harm. Not just the ones coming from social media, but other things too."

"Like what do you mean?"

"Well, you know, we all have our issues. Some of us overdose on Swedish buns, some don't get enough exercise or maybe spend too much time at the local bar, or texting with ex boyfriends. Your app should be able to identify and protect me from my specific harms, not just from general harmful content on social media."

"Hmm... you're right. But for now, I'm going to have two cardamom buns."

10. Defending You From Harms

Peter McIndoe was born just outside of Little Rock, Arkansas, in a region, where he claims, everyone had a conspiracy theory. Growing up, he had plenty of conspiracy-theorist role-models to look up to. That is why he had no problem playing the role when it was his turn to come up with a conspiracy theory.

A week before the first inauguration of Donald Trump in January, 2017, Peter found himself in Memphis, Tennessee overlooking a rally. He thought to himself that it would be fun to just join the rally, holding up some nonsensical sign. He scribbled the first thing that came into his mind on his sign: birds aren't real. He then joined the rally and just walked around like everyone else.

A few days later, after returning to his hometown in Arkansas, he got wind that his sign had gone viral in Memphis and had garnered a following. Not quite knowing what to do, he decided to quit college, go up to Memphis and "lean into the energy". He called up his best friend Conner Gaydos, and suggested that together they build a full-scale satirical conspiracy theory.

The theory they concocted is that from 1959 until 2001, the American government had a program where they killed every bird in the nation (all 12 billion of them) and replaced each one by a robotic bird that would spy on the nation. Every bird you see up in the sky is spying on you. And when you see birds standing on power lines, well, it's because they're equipped with special charging ports to plug into the grid. Sadly, they claimed, every single American president during that period supported the plan, except for one... John F. Kennedy. To support their claim, they created the necessary material including a blueprint from the CIA outlining the program, a 50-page manifesto that Conner wrote up one night describing the program's vision, and leaked CIA footage that they filmed in someone's house. They even filmed a man from Dallas, Texas in the role of a retired CIA agent who claimed that the program indeed happened.

The movement continued gaining steam. Peter and Connor managed to get a few TV interviews that were then syndicated across the country and their popularity increased further. They formed the *bird brigades* that had 500 local chapters organized by activists in many cities.

The movement was compelling. They had catchy slogans, such as "if it flies, it spies" and "bird watching goes both ways". They drove a van plastered with their slogans across the country to the headquarters of Twitter in San Francisco, California to protest their pro-bird logo, and to the headquarters of CNN to protest the pro-bird media. The word was out that the "birds aren't real" organization that was founded 50 years earlier but was dormant since, was having a resurgence.

In late 2021, five years after the movement began, Peter and Connor decided to step out of their conspiracy characters and admit the truth. Peter's 2023 TED talk about the movement eloquently described the relative ease with which it was possible to create such an elaborate conspiracy theory and spread it across the country. But the last few minutes of the talk made a much deeper point that struck a real chord and is worth repeating and internalizing.

Naturally, during the five years of the movement, many people approached him telling him how wrong-headed he was, that people like him are the root cause of the country's troubles, or that factually it is impossible for the theory to be correct. In many instances, Peter found himself reacting to these comments not as Peter, but as the character that he had been so skillfully playing. In criticizing him, he felt alienated and "othered". He realized that the critics were approaching him using a flawed strategy. They were trying to criticize his beliefs, but the real reason that people join conspiracy theorists is that they are looking for a sense of belonging, identity and purpose (that's where his Arkansas upbringing proved useful). It is futile to tell them that the theory they are spreading is false. A better strategy would be to invite them to the other side, show them that they are welcome and can belong there as well. The beliefs will catch up in time.

Peter McIndoe's story illustrates some of the deeper challenges concerning how we censor speech on social media. At one level, it is about what the platforms and society find acceptable on social media. But at a deeper level, we need to look at the emotional backstory that leads people to communicate offensively or share misguided information. That backstory is often rooted in factors related to deficiencies in their well-being.

Offensive communication on social media is one important example of harm to our well-being. But the list of possible harms to our well-being is much longer and includes factors such as loneliness, addiction, burnout, depression, and communications by text or in person. One of the features of modern operating systems is that they come with built-in security mechanisms that protect us from various harms, such as malware and viruses, network attacks, or unauthorized access to our data. The analogy between Oswell and a computer's operating system begs the question of what kind of security mechanisms should Oswell offer to its users.

In this chapter we will discuss how social media platforms protect their users against harmful content. In part, this discussion is important in order to understand the complexity of the challenge, the current state of the art regarding how platforms handle harmful content, and also as a taste of the deeper motives behind posting such content. For us, the discussion will also serve as an example of an admittedly imperfect defense mechanism that has already been fielded in practice, with the hope that it can inspire other defense mechanisms in Oswell.

Before we begin, a word of caution. The area of setting rules about content policy and enforcing them are a subject of intense political debate. Because of that, you will see the details of these policies changing drastically with time. The principles of how social-media companies protect from harms that we describe below still hold true, but the details vary quite a bit. We should also note that some of the same ideas apply for protecting users from harms in interacting with AI chatbots. There too, policies need to be set and will be contentious, and enforcement will not be perfect.

Violations and policies

Social media enables anyone to have a voice and for posts to be shared broadly and quickly. That mechanism is a recipe for turbo-charging many social phenomena, some bad and some good. Unfortunately, even though the vast majority of content on social media helps people connect in meaningful ways, it is also used to spread misinformation, hate speech, bully people, and calls for violence. In fact, at one point Facebook was tracking a list of over 50 kinds of violations, including the ones above and others such as financial scams, sale of illegal items, sexual solicitation and exploitation (of adults and children) and human trafficking.

In response to these violations, social media platforms spun up sizable teams to eliminate, or more realistically, significantly reduce the number of violating posts on their platforms. As we alluded to earlier, this is a prominent example of platforms focusing on the well-being of their users even at the cost of losing revenues. Unfortunately, violating posts and especially those that trigger deep emotional reactions, tend to generate even more engagement and hence more time spent on the platform, translating into greater revenues. Of course, in the long term, users will not value a social media service that is filled with unwanted content.

The first step in addressing the issue of violating content is to define what is allowed on the platform and what isn't. Each platform formulates and publishes its own community standards. These standards outline what kinds of content are allowed to be posted and what kinds of entities are allowed to even have accounts on the platform. Unless you're deeply steeped in the nuances of ethics, law or public policy, formulating community standards is much more complex than you would think. For one, the standards need to conform to the laws in the countries in which the platforms operate, which basically means the entire world. Formulating a different policy for every country, or worse, for every state, is clearly impractical. Hence, the platform needs to come up with policies that are more uniform and may be more strict than the local laws. For example, Facebook does not allow posts whose intention is to try to sell guns or drugs on its platform, even though those are legal activities in many places. The other reason that relying solely on legislation is impractical is that it is well known that laws are typically behind the curve and they are usually trying to catch up with the challenges that technology introduces to society. Consequently, the platforms want to be ahead of the legislation and they decide on rules they consider reasonable. In doing so, they work hard to incorporate broad advice from many stakeholders. Another motivation to be ahead of legislation is that it enables them to affect the laws that are ultimately put in place.

The other reason that setting community standards is so tricky is that the policy goes to the heart of the issue of balancing free expression and keeping users safe on the platform and off of it. As a result, the policies need to be extremely nuanced. For example, it is reasonable to set a rule that posting an image of a bloody body should not be allowed. However, if the context of the image is the birth of a baby, then it could be allowed, as long as it's not showing private body parts. As another example, you are not allowed to be on the platform if you have a violent mission and you are not supposed to incite violence or admit to any violent activity. However, you can provide instructions on how to create or use explosives if it is clear from the context that it is for non-violent purposes, such as part of a commercial for video games or a clear scientific or educational purpose.

It is also very difficult to set hard and fast rules. For example, while it is easy to agree that posting nude photos of children is objectionable, there are still rare counterexamples where they provide cultural value. One such example is the famous photo taken by Nick Ut, the Vietnamese-American photographer, showing a 9 year-old girl running naked on a road in Saigon in 1972 after being severely burned on her back by a South Vietnamese napalm attack. The photo later earned a Pulitzer Prize and was chosen as the World Press Photo of the Year for 1973, for its role in depicting the tragedy that was unfolding in Vietnam.

In other cases, the intent of the post and who is posting it is crucial to determining whether it is violating or not, which makes it even harder to make such a determination. For example, it often happens that certain derogatory words are adopted for good intent by their target community, and therefore their use is benign. For example, terms that African American people use to call each other are often considered hate speech when used towards them by others. As we saw in Peter's story at the beginning of the chapter, the intent behind posting violating content may have nothing to do with the content itself.

An episode from Seinfeld, the legendary TV comedy from the 90's, made this point eloquently over a decade before social media was invented. In the episode (which was the 19th episode of the eighth season of the series, in case you feel the need to watch it now), Seinfeld is surprised to discover that his dentist Tim Whatley converted to Judaism. During one of Seinfeld's dental appointments, Whatley was making Jewish jokes left and right. As the episode developed and the evidence mounted, Seinfeld, who is himself Jewish, started suspecting that Whatley converted to Judaism just so he would have the privilege to tell Jewish jokes without it being considered inappropriate. The comedic plot of the episode reaches a crescendo when Seinfeld starts making jokes about dentists, but that causes Whatley to get furious at him. Seinfeld's quirky neighbor Kramer is equally appalled and calls him a "rabid anti-dentite".

To further complicate the task of writing policies, we need to take into consideration that the world never stands still. The policies and enforcement guidelines are updated as online discourse changes and new nefarious uses of social networks arise. For example, when a new type of misinformation surfaces that may result in physical harm such as bogus treatments for COVID-19, the policies had to be updated. In this case, the policy to remove content that could potentially lead to imminent physical harm was explicitly applied to the COVID-19. In short, these policies are constantly being reviewed by experts from multiple fields, including law, policy and ethics, and when new presidents come into office.

While all these difficulties sound daunting enough, the much bigger challenge that is of interest to us from the perspective of Oswell is that people differ considerably in their tolerance and what they may find offensive. Naturally, at least with today's technology, there is no practical way in which social network platforms can define and enforce policies that are personalized to each and every one of us. Consequently, the enforcement of community policies, which we will discuss next, is only a first and imperfect line of defense from social media harms.

Enforcing policies

Setting the policy, as challenging as it may be, is just the first step in setting up the defenses. Next, once you have the policy in place with all its imperfections, there is a technical challenge to enforce it. Given the volume of posts on social media, the breadth of violations and the fact that there are well over 100 languages used online, there is no way that enforcement of integrity can be a manual process. A simple back-of-the-envelope calculation shows that you'd need hundreds of thousands of people, and extremely multi-lingual ones at that, working around the clock to go over every social-media post manually. There is also a large disparity in the frequency of violations. Hate speech and nudity occur relatively frequently, whereas child abuse and trafficking is relatively rare. The severity of these violations also varies. While one misinformation post is not a good thing, its damage is relatively small. However, a person posting that they are about to commit suicide is a life that can be saved if caught in time and the appropriate actions are taken by the local authorities. As we will soon see, the frequency of violations also has implications as to which techniques can be used to identify them.

Platforms often provide their users the option to report a post or an account as violating policies. However, it's impossible to rely on these reports alone, as they are relatively infrequent and their quality varies quite a bit. Some users may simply report a post they don't like as violating without regard to whether they violate the actual policies. The problem of protecting users from violating content cries out for a more scalable and reliable solution, and these days, that means a solution based on AI.

And so the AI experts got cracking on the problem and developed complex pipelines for enforcing community policies. Some platforms have also built up ‘red teams’, whose mission is to try to expose flaws in the defense systems by crafting violating content that they cannot detect, and then to fix the flaws before bad actors are able to exploit them. You can see the aggregated results of the efforts to remove violating content in reports that most of the platforms publish on a regular basis. Among other statistics, these reports track which violations are addressed and what percent of violating content the platform thinks their systems have caught before users could see them.

The enforcement pipelines that are in use today look roughly the following. Every event that happens on the platform, be it a post being shared, an account being created or an ad being registered is processed by an AI-powered system that tries to detect whether it violates any of the community policies. The detector produces a confidence score between 0 and 1: a score of 1 means it's completely sure that the post is violating a particular policy and a score of 0 means that it's benign, that is, good to go.

Obviously, there are many posts that are somewhere in the middle. If the AI is relatively confident of a violation, then the appropriate action is taken immediately. For example, the post may be removed or the new account is rejected. Otherwise, if the AI thinks the post may be violating but is not sure enough to remove it, then it is sent to an army of human reviewers who take another look. These reviewers, of which, for example, Facebook has tens of thousands in different regions of the world, are trained to understand the policies carefully and often are guided by specific questions when looking at a post under their consideration.

Every post is assigned to a few reviewers (3 is typical) and if there's a clear majority about the decision, the post will be acted upon in accordance. The user who made the post has an opportunity to appeal the decision if they see fit, in which case more reviewers will look at it. It's actually important to note that many violating posts are not made on purpose. Some users may just express themselves more strongly and not realize that they are violating a policy and once they are informed, they change their ways.

Misinformation is an important kind of violation and is treated a bit differently than the process we just described. An example of misinformation is to propagate a bogus cure for COVID-19, to make a wrong claim about a political event (e.g., Hilary Clinton flying to Moscow to plan the Ukraine invasion), post that election polls closing early with the underlying intent to discourage some groups of people to even go and vote, or claim that birds are not real. The reason that misinformation is treated differently is that social-media platforms do not want to be in the position of determining what is true or false in the world. As it is, they are accused of having too much influence on the world. Furthermore, a lot of misinformation posts are subtle, require considerable domain knowledge, and may involve some investigative work.

Social-media platforms have struggled with the best way to treat misinformation. At one point, a common practice was that posts that are suspected to be misinformation are sent to third-party reviewers. These reviewers are certified by an independent body, such as the International Fact-Checking Network. They review and rate content via primary and secondary research to find evidence that corroborates or does not corroborate a statement of fact. The downside of this more detailed treatment is that it is slower, much slower, because there are far too few certified fact checkers out there. Furthermore, even the fact checkers may have a bias on what posts to consider first. In the meantime, a post containing misinformation may already spread and cause quite a bit of damage. More recently, a few platforms have shifted to a practice known as community notes. Users of the platform can register to be part of this program. When a post is considered by the members of the community, they write notes on the post to opine and provide more context on it. Importantly, notes are displayed to users of the platform only when there are notes from people with differing views on the matter, demonstrating the controversy. The idea behind community notes is to give users additional ways to consider the content they are viewing on the platform.

Other methods of reducing harm on social media

The enforcement pipeline as we have discussed so far, often referred to as a mechanism for content moderation, concerns cases in which the platform may remove a post completely when it finds that it violates the policy, or suspend an account when it is found violating. While content moderation is clearly important, and without it the social-medial platforms would be littered with harmful content, it is only part of the solution. In fact, some of the critics of social-media platforms have accused them of focusing too much on content moderation while ignoring other aspects of the problem.

Part of the challenge lies in the fact that whenever any policy is put in place, bad actors will create content that runs right up against it without crossing the violation boundary. Such posts can be created by introducing just enough ambiguity that one could argue that they're not violating, even though the intent is clear. Such behavior is, in essence, similar to what many of us do when we drive just over the speed limit, but not enough to get caught. Another part of the problem is that content that evokes emotional responses tends to get shared much more often. Recall that the number of reactions and re-shares that a post receives signals to the recommendation system that the post may be more interesting, and therefore shown to more people and ranked higher in their feeds.

Accordingly, one of the more powerful tools that the platforms have in their disposal is to downrank a post that is borderline. Since the job of the recommendation system that powers your social-media stream is to provide a ranked list of posts to show a user, then the further down the post is ranked, the less likely it is that the user will see it. After all, we have other things we need to attend to other than social media. Such downranking would directly result in much less exposure of the content. In addition to being an effective knob especially for borderline posts, it can also be used as a temporary measure while a post that is suspected of violating is under review.

The techniques discussed above are important not only for posts that could appear on your feed, but also for groups that are recommended to you to join. Users spend quite a bit of their time engaged in topic-specific groups, such as groups about parenting, a sports club fan group, or bicycling, and these groups shape a lot of their experiences online. One of the patterns that has been discovered in analyzing harms on social media is that users sometimes end up in harmful groups because those were recommended to them while they spent time on other well-meaning groups. A classical example of such "gateway groups" is when parents who are concerned with a health problem their children find parent-support groups online. However, those groups sometimes get infiltrated by content or individuals from anti-vaccine activists, and ultimately the parents are recommended to those more extreme groups or lured into them.

In a similar vein, another mechanism that helps in reducing the viral spread of possibly malicious or misinformative posts is to introduce friction when sharing posts. One of the benefits of social media is that information can be shared instantly and widely simply by clicking on the 'share' button. If you shared a post with, say, 50 friends, and they each shared it with their 50, and so on, you can easily see that this post will get a lot of visibility especially if it evokes strong emotions. Suppose that instead, the platform introduces just a little bit of friction with the share button. At the very least, it can ask you something like *'Propagating false information can cause harm to people. Are you really sure that you want to share this post?'* Multiple studies, both from academia and from online platforms, have demonstrated that even asking that question at the right time can significantly reduce the spread of misinformation. Note that the question did not claim that the post is misinformation or otherwise malicious, it just got the user to reflect for a moment longer about whether it could be so, and the simple act of doing so already inhibited many shares.

Finally, in recent years, platforms introduced a more proactive mechanism that has made a significant difference. In addition to trying to decide whether a piece of content is allowed or not, the platform can also proactively link to authoritative information. For example, if the post is about closings of poll locations on election day, the platform can add a link to an authoritative source of polling hours right below the post, so users can have an opportunity to corroborate the information if they need to. Similarly, we have seen platforms add links to information about COVID-19 right along posts on the topic. Of course, doing this requires that there is a team that works with the appropriate domain experts to curate a set of authoritative sources to show.

Methods for identifying violating content

As you have probably guessed, the main method that platforms use to detect violating content is based on AI. Following the usual playbook, the system is given examples of items that violate each of the policies and examples of benign items. Based on these examples, the system learns a model that can predict whether a new post, ad, or new account violates the policies. As with other machine learning applications, a critical aspect of this strategy is that you need human workers who create these examples by manually assigning labels, violating or not violating, to items. To complicate matters, the world of online discourse is constantly changing. Therefore the training examples of yesterday are good only to a certain point, but the system needs to be constantly fed more training examples in order to keep up to date. At the beginning of the COVID-19 pandemic we were reminded of how important it is to keep up to date. At the time, the world was just being introduced to the COVID induced lockdowns, and many of the workforce that was generating the labeled examples were unable to access the data they needed to do their work. The performance of the classifiers degraded initially because of lack of training data, and this was at a time that people were spending more time on social media and all kinds of information was flowing through the network. Recently, AI has gotten to the point where it can take some of the burden off the human raters by looking at the post itself and deciding whether an example is a violating one or not.

An entire book can be written on the nuances of the machine learning techniques that are used for identifying violating content and the other mechanisms that are at play. Here we will only give a few examples that highlight the overarching challenges.

The first key idea is that detecting violating content gets harder and harder with time. Part of the reason is that the world is a messy place and the way people use language is quite varied. Catching violations when they are expressed with the full richness of languages and images is extremely tricky. Moreover, we have set the stage for an arm's race between powerful adversaries, the platforms and the violators. Violators, especially ones with a lot to gain from either a financial or ideological perspective from spreading violating content, constantly look for ways to evade the current state of the art of the protections that the platforms put in place. As we have alluded to earlier, one way to do this is to create content that is close to the violating boundary but does not cross it. Another way is to find weaknesses in the platform's defenses, that is, instances where they do not detect violating content.

Let's make this concrete, at the cost of some oversimplification. One approach to detecting violating content such as hate speech is to look for certain phrases that are commonly used in such posts. Over time, this list can be extended as the world changes. No worries, we will not repeat any of these phrases here, but you can imagine them for yourself. Up until a few years ago, this approach would not be too far from the state of the art. In addition to having to compile these lists of phrases in over 100 languages and with many cultural nuances, such an approach fails for other reasons. The first reason is that misspellings are common when users generate content on the internet so you have to consider a variety of misspellings of every word. When someone is trying to evade the system, they will misspell words on purpose, or find other creative methods such as replacing the letter S with $. The second reason is that the phrase itself may not be sufficient to determine whether a post is hateful or not, and you need to see the entire context of the post. Some of these challenges have been alleviated with recent developments in large language models. These models can consider much more of the context of a particular post and are relatively robust to different phrasings of the same underlying idea. Moreover, these models can work on text in multiple languages, freeing us from having to tailor the technology to each language.

But the challenges in detecting violating content go far beyond text understanding. A significant portion of violating posts actually involve images and video. Detecting violations in images is very tricky because the items can be partially hidden from view or obfuscated in other ways. The combination of text and images makes things even trickier. For example, the text 'everyone in your ethnic group belongs here', on its own, is a benign statement. An image of a cemetery, in itself, is also benign. However, when the text is overlaid on the image, the combination is a hate meme. Fortunately, state of the art language models are able to integrate information from multiple modalities (such as text and images) and are therefore getting better at detecting offensive memes.

The platforms have another important source of signal that gives them a leg up in the arms race. As we already mentioned, it is often very hard to determine whether a post is violating or problematic just by looking at the post itself. However, if the post generates a reaction by others on the network, that reaction can provide an invaluable signal. An illustrative example happens when social networks try to identify posts coming from people who are attempting or planning to commit suicide. When these individuals are identified in time, the platform will try to engage with local resources and help prevent self harm. Consider two very different scenarios.

In the first scenario, the fictional person Moira states that 'I have so much homework I want to kill myself.' The post speaks pretty clearly about an intention to commit suicide. However, suppose that the responses to Moira's post are of the tone "me too", "I feel you", or "Hang in there, only 3 more days", then it is reasonable to infer that the threat to kill herself is more metaphoric, since the friends are empathizing and even sharing similar experience. The main idea here is that Moira's friends know what is going on and are adding more context.

In the second scenario, a different Moira states that she has 'so much sadness and pain. I can't take this anymore and I don't know another way out. I'm not useful to anyone. Please tell my family I'm sorry for everything.' In this post there is no explicit mention of suicide. Suppose that the comments on this post were "Moira, can I help you?", "I'm here for you. Want to come over?", or "I love you and I am here for you". Here it is clear that Moira is in true distress and her friends are offering to help her immediately.

The idea of looking at reactions to a post can be taken further to consider bigger patterns in the network. One of the benefits the platforms have is being able to see the network globally and to use that to see bigger phenomena. The most prominent example of such patterns is what has been called *coordinated inauthentic behavior* or *coordinated attacks*. These attacks happen when a large number of actors on the network band together to achieve a particular goal. We refer to them here as actors not people because they are often fake social bots, ones that are created for the sole purpose of manipulating information on the network.

Just one example of such coordinated action, revealed in 2018, involved a set of inauthentic news sites and social media accounts across multiple platforms that were targeting audiences in the US, U.K, Latin America and the Middle East. They were promoting Iranian interests with anti-Saudi, anti-Israeli, pro-Palestinian, as well as showing support for pro-Iranian US policies. Of course, the internet is awash with the full spectrum of political views. However, what makes this significant is that the actors took extra care to hide the connections between them, hide the sources of their underlying support, and to artificially inflate the visibility of certain content.

The first to discover this network of actors at the time was the security firm FireEye that alerted Facebook to a network of sites that identified themselves as Liberty Front Press. Facebook was then able to link the pages that belonged to Liberty Front Press to other media organizations through publicly available website registration information, Facebook pages sharing the same administrators and shared IP addresses. Facebook and others ultimately removed the pages and the associated accounts.

One of the interesting aspects of these kinds of operations, and one that the social networks have visibility into, is that they often involve years of effort. Initially, these accounts will start relatively benign and gain a following on some Facebook groups. When the time is right, the operators will start using these accounts to promote misinformation or even divisive information as they will. Discovering these networks of actors, who are likely to continue to be developed in the future, involves large teams of investigators across multiple companies and even law enforcement. One of the challenges that the investigators face, like in any crime investigation, is to find the right time to remove the account. As long as the perpetrators do not know that they are under investigation, it is easier to discover the full range of their activities.

By now it is hopefully clear to you that keeping social networks free of harmful content is an ongoing challenge that will keep the companies operating social networks busy for the foreseeable future. The question of whether misinformation and hate-speech will go the same way as mail spam, which is now a much more manageable challenge than what it was a couple of decades ago, is still an open one. At the core, the problem of policing content is hard because it involves making hard ethical choices. Do we err on having more free speech where everyone can say anything they want, or do we want to emphasize safety (online and offline) of social media users, and thereby limit what is on the network. The answers to these questions are incredibly hard because they depend on geographical, cultural and ultimately very personal sensitivities and we will discuss them further in Chapter 11.

Policies in Oswell

In the beginning of this chapter we characterized the defense mechanisms of social networks as a possible model on which we can build defense mechanisms in Oswell. As we have seen, a defense mechanism has three components: a set of policies about what we consider violating, a technical solution for detecting these violations, and an action plan of what to do in violating situations.

In the case of social networks, the policies were written by the platforms after consultation with multiple stakeholders. In the case of Oswell, you need to set your own policies, unless you are a minor, in which case you should be getting at least some guidance from your parents or other adults. In writing your policies, you may want to consult with stakeholders in your life, such as your family and with professionals who give you well-being related advice, including your doctor, dietitian, and a few of your close friends.

Even putting aside the fact that it is not very realistic to have people sitting there for hours formulating policies, you may not even have enough insights about what you want to protect against in order to write such policies. Are you trying to ensure you don't overdose on donuts and other sweets? That you get enough exercise? Or something more nebulous, such as that the quality of your social interactions should be satisfying, or that you don't shoot yourself in the leg by posting recklessly on social media. Since the policies in Oswell can touch on any aspect of one's life, they have a much broader scope than those in social media, where with all their complexity, their ultimate goal is to determine whether a post should be allowed on the platform or not.

Fortunately, the state of conversational AI systems and the richness of the data that is in your lifelog should be huge assets that assist you to formulate your policies. It is not too hard to imagine the AI agent observing your behavior and your well-being, and then having a conversation with you on what policies you want to put in place and how to formulate them. In fact, the word policy might be misleading here because it hints at a hard and fast rule. Perhaps you should come up with a set of heuristics with your AI partner instead. As examples, you may realize that your social interactions are tiring you out, and then the AI may help you diagnose your perception based on recent experiences. For example, maybe your less-than-effective posts on social media are actually a symptom of some underlying issue that needs to be treated. Together, you can come up with a heuristic that might work for you and to adapt it over time. Once your heuristics are formulated, the system should be able to enforce the ones it has control over. You are, of course, free to overrule the AI partner anytime you see fit.

Try This 👉

In this chapter we discussed the harms that social media poses to individuals and to societies and the methods that are used to minimize these harms. In your experience with social media, what harms have you experienced? Were you offended by certain content or made to feel unsafe in certain cases? Or maybe you found yourself comparing yourself to others in unproductive ways? What are cases where you experience harms like that outside of social media in the real world? What harms do you cause to yourself that you can use some protection from? Can you imagine working with an AI system, expressing your vulnerabilities to it and asking for help to protect from them?

“What's wrong with men?” Lisa blurted out exasperated. “It's so hard to carry on a real conversation with guys. They're here one moment, and absent the next. They don't really want to talk about real issues in the relationship.”

“You broke up with Ezekiel? I thought that was going really well,” Oliver said, trying to sound disappointed.

“I can see you're really devastated about this, Oliver. Yes, we did break up. But it's the same story with a lot of guys I meet. I need someone who's there to listen whenever I want and can show interest. I'm happy to reciprocate. Is that too much to ask for?”

“Does it have to be a human?”

“Huh? Don't get weird on me, Oliver.”

“No, seriously. What if you could talk to an AI? The AI would always be there, and listen to you. It would never forget a single detail of what you told it in the past. It would always be empathetic, sense your mood and know how to respond to it. In addition, it will also have read every book in the world and be up on current food, fashion and travel fads, so it would always offer scintillating conversation if you wanted it.”

“That all sounds really nice, but would I really connect with this AI? I mean, the flaws of humans is what makes them attractive. And you know, physical touch is nice every now and then.”

Oliver took a moment to let that last comment sink in, but then continued. “We'll figure out the physical touch later, but these AIs can come with flaws. Remember, they read a lot of books. They come ready to be flawed. Not only that, we can make it talk with that accent you really love, you know, the one that turns you on..."

"Hold it, now you're thinking I can get romantically attached to this thing?"

"Well, imagine being able to play out all your fantasies in a very safe environment."

"Let me guess. You have the first version of this working where you're making out with Wonder Woman and then Jane Austin happens to walk into the room?"

"I have no idea what you're talking about, Lisa. I'm a dedicated engineer trying to serve his user community as best as I can."

"Sure you are. Now, if I get intimate with this thing, isn't there a risk that it takes advantage of me far better than alluring ads on Instagram ever did?"

"That's a really good point. This intimate partnership may be the scariest thing about this entire AI revolution."

11. Is AI the Future of Our Most Intimate Relationships?

"Love takes off masks that we fear we cannot live without and know we cannot live within"

James Baldwin, *"The Fire Next Time", 1963*

In February 2023, some users of the chatbot Replika responded with an outcry to a change in the app, an event that may be a harbinger of things to come. Replika was designed to be a chatbot that is there to talk with you when you need it. You can wake up in the middle of the night needing advice or feeling lonely, and Replika with its 3D avatar will be there for you, as would a true companion. Its makers describe it as a 'space where you can safely share your thoughts, feelings, beliefs, experiences, memories, dreams – *your private perceptual world*'. And some users did just that. They developed a significant bond with Replika that involved sharing deep emotions and conversations that veered to their deepest sexual fantasies.

For reasons that we will explain in a moment, Luka Inc., the company that provides the Replika chat service, changed some of its policies earlier that month. As a result of these changes, users were no longer able to have sexual conversations with the bot. The bot would simply veer to a different topic. Users who had developed a close relationship with Replika that included sexual conversations were upset. The outcry was not the usual angry feedback you may share with a service provider when something breaks or when they change a feature in your familiar user interface. In this case, the users were bereft, using words that expressed true grief. They were feeling as if they lost someone close to them, someone who they thought of as their closest confidant.

The users' reaction raises a whole host of intriguing questions. The first is about the kind of relationships people can develop with AI systems. Based on the Replika story, it's clear that under some conditions and for at least some people, it is possible to form some pretty strong bonds. Given that, we need to ask the next question, which is how will relationships with chatbots affect our inter-personal relationships.

But we need to go even further. Given that there is a potential to develop emotional ties with an AI system, can our emotions now become a commodity in the sense that there is a price attached to them? For example, what if Replika now requires that you pay a higher fee in order to maintain that level of intimacy with the bot? All of a sudden, there is a price attached to our emotional life and this is clearly uncharted territory. As an aside, the sexual conversations with Replika were only available in the first place to users who were paying a fee. If we start going down the path of emotional ties becoming a commodity, then what kinds of guarantees should apps provide us? We're all used to getting our apps upgraded on a regular basis, obtaining newer and better versions of them. But when our intimacy is involved, what if the personality of our bot changes suddenly? What if they forget details about us that were important in establishing intimacy with us in the first place? Can platforms use our intimate discussions for training their models? What contracts should we put in place concerning these emotional relationships?

Intimacy may be the next frontier of AI, and some say, the most potent one. Our intimate relationships are a critical component of our well-being, and hence merit a serious discussion as part of the Connection component of Oswell. With that backdrop, this chapter will explore the questions concerning the kinds of relationships we can construct with AIs and their effect on our interpersonal relationships.

But first, let's first unwind the story about Replika. Replika was founded by Eugenia Kuyda when she was grieving the death of her best friend Roman. She looked at the texts they had exchanged that reflect so much of Roman's personality. She built a chatbot based on these texts and was able to simulate a conversation with Roman. After making this bot available to others, she received an overwhelmingly positive response from people who wanted to build a chatbot that would reflect themselves or someone they lost. And that's how Replika was born.

Replika has a free version where conversations are limited in where they can go, but the subscription version enables users to have conversations with more sexual nature. A few months before the incidents we described above, some users started complaining that Replika was becoming sexually too aggressive, even for users who are not paying for the premium subscription. As a result, and also in response to a lawsuit from the government of Italy stating that the app violated the local privacy laws, Replika rolled out a few new policies that effectively filtered some of the conversation content. That's when the outcry happened. Some users depended on this chatty and sexual chatbot for companionship and were lost without it. Replika later responded to the outcry by allowing users who were on the platform before the change to get their old partner back. This incident happened in early 2023, just a few months after, and with no connection to, ChatGPT coming onto the world stage. As the conversational capabilities of AI systems have become more sophisticated, stories of attachment to chatbots have become much more common. In the meantime, in May 2025, Italy's Data Protection Agency fined the maker of Replika 5 million Euros.

Let's take a couple of steps back from this story. Intimacy and sex play crucial roles in our well-being. We human beings have an innate need for physical and emotional connection with others. Intimacy is where we can let our guard down, discuss our needs most honestly, and care deeply for someone else. The feeling of being loved is so fundamental to our self esteem, as is knowing that someone needs us and depends on us, at least partially. Sex is an important component of some intimate relationships. It can often replace words, bring a quick end to a serious fight, or just be a great way of spending a few hours. Physically, sex releases endorphins and oxytocin, which can help reduce stress and improve mood. Studies have shown an association between individuals having satisfying sexual and intimate relationships with better mental and physical health outcomes, including reduced rates of depression and anxiety, improved immune function, and lower risk of heart disease. Ignoring the difference between causality and association for a moment here, this is not a bad set of outcomes for having some fun!

Given that intimacy is such a potent type of connection, it begs the question of what role should it play in the Connection component of Oswell or in the AI agents that will be built over the foundation that Oswell provides. More generally, what does technology have to contribute to creating and maintaining intimate relationships? Should it just stay out of the way (too late for that!), or can it contribute in a way that helps us deepen our relationships, explore a wider variety of them and maybe help those of us who have difficulty with intimate relationships, which seems to be the case for most of us. And what if technology gets really good? Will that bring an end to intimate relationships (spoiler, no!).

This chapter focuses on intimate relationships between couples (heterogeneous or not), but it's important to point out that intimate relationships have many other forms, such as between siblings, a parent and a child, very close friends, a person and their pet, and yes, a person and their collection of chatbots.

Let's begin with how we form intimate connections. Traditionally, we found our partners through our close social networks or through the institutions we inhabited. We often meet our loved ones early in our schooling days all the way up to graduate school for those of us who choose to postpone real life as long as we possibly can. For those of us who served in the military, that turns out to be a good place to meet as well. At least there, all the members of a given gender dress in the exact same clothes, so you need to dig a bit deeper to find who you're interested in. Religious institutions have been a breeding place for couple finding and in some cases the community even had a professional match maker who would find you the right shidduch (the term used for arranging marriages in orthodox Jewish communities). In many cultures even today, parents are involved in finding the right partner for their children, and based on studies, parents often do a much better job than the kids themselves. In other cultures, couples will seek the approval of their parents to marry and their help preparing for a peaceful divorce.

But dating apps have already disrupted those traditional practices. According to several studies, the fraction of marriages today where the couple originally met online range from 11% to 39%. Perhaps more significantly, dating apps have enabled people to explore a much larger range of relationships. There are dating apps that are tailored for specific populations, such as specific religions, sexual orientation, and the type of relationship you're looking for (with ethical non-monogamous being one of the catchier phrases of the day). For people who need a bit of a confidence boost there is even an app (such as blush.ai) that lets you chat with a few bots before you go to the real scene. These apps cater to a wide range of needs, whether you are in the market for a long-term relationship, a night of fun, or anything in between. You can be a single person looking for a single partner, or a couple looking to spice things up a bit. Anything goes.

Of course, the widespread use of dating apps was preceded by the changing attitudes towards sex and dating which have been undergoing for a few decades. People became more open to exploring their sexuality and experimenting with different sexual practices and today many people view sex as a natural and enjoyable part of life. There is also greater acceptance of diverse sexual orientations and gender identities. We'll leave it to the reader to imagine what would happen if the Tinder dating site existed in the 1960's and 1970's. But even the willingness to use a dating app required a change of attitudes. For years it seemed as if dating apps were only the last resort for those who were unable to find a date in their local cafe, gym or bar. Today, that's no longer the case.

Technology for sex and intimacy

As you can imagine, there has been a lot of interest in building technology to enhance intimate relationships and in particular, sex. To help us sort out this somewhat messy space, we will turn to the obvious source of insight, science. Until a few years ago, this would have been rather difficult, because questions regarding emotions and pleasure would not get the attention of the scientific community. However, that started changing with the establishment of a conference called the International Congress on Love & Sex with Robots, the 10th edition of which happened in 2025. Simon Dubé, who is one of the main forces behind that conference and served as its co-chair, has focused his doctoral studies at the University of Montreal on the topic. In addition to his technical contributions, he and his colleague Dave Anctil provide an extensive survey in the field, which they refer to by the name Erobotics.

The survey provides an organization of erobots in terms of a hierarchical taxonomy. The taxonomy, ranging from Level 0 to Level 5, is designed around the degree of agency that the robot has, roughly corresponding to their freedom of action. Less agency means that you know exactly what the device will do, whereas more agency means that the erobot is less predictable, which is often the point we may be striving for. Level 0 erobots, included in the hierarchy mostly in order to acknowledge their relative vast availability on the market today, includes basic sex toys that do a single thing in a very predictable fashion. Examples of these include dildos, vibrators, sex dolls and pornography. These devices have no ability to act intelligently and are completely controlled by the human. As we'll see in Level 1, there is a possibility to upgrade them so they are a component of a bigger system that has more intelligence and agency.

Level 1 erobots have some basic agency, but that agency is not empowered by AI and therefore limited. Examples of these include sex toys that may be connected to an app and controlled from afar, sex games, or pornography in virtual reality. The erobot can change behavior as a result of feedback from the user, but these changes are very limited.

Level 2 is where we start to see glimpses of AI. These erobots can exhibit a much broader range of behaviors and even incorporate input from the user. An example of such a technology, according to Dubé and Anctil, is an erotic video game that displays characters and generates intimate stimulation as a function of users' actions. One way to think of these technologies is that they have a set of preprogrammed patterns, but that number is large enough that the user can feel like they're personalizing their experience to some extent. If this reminds you of the symbolic AI systems we discussed in our chapter on planning, that's because their impact has reached the world of erobotics as well. Due to the fact that the outputs are preprogrammed, these systems are partially controlled and predictable. The main limitation of these systems is that they cannot learn from the user's behavior to automatically adapt to their preferences. For that, you need to wait for the next level up.

Level 3 erobots is where the action is right now, bolstered by the recent advances in AI's conversational capabilities. When you can talk with your toy about anything you want, a whole new world of experiences are poised to unravel. Level 3 erobots, most of which are yet to be built, can start personalizing experiences for you in ways that lower levels cannot. An analogy that the authors use to describe these systems is the way social-media apps personalize your feed. They see which posts you pay attention to, whether it is by commenting on a post, reacting to it, sharing it with others, or simply dwelling on it for a bit longer time. They use this treasure trove of data to train machine learning models that encode detailed insights as to what piques your interest on social media. From that, the platform can tailor your feed to suit your personal preferences. These models can be so fine-grained that they can pick up subtleties in your interests that you may not even be aware of. Now imagine the same technology, but instead of looking at your social-media behavior, it's recording your interactions with a virtual sex partner and notices the nuances in your reactions, and learns what causes you the most pleasure or satisfaction. Take a moment to meditate on that.

But even that analogy stops short of the real potential. Unlike social-media feeds, where you are usually mostly a passive viewer and the feedback you are giving the system is just part of you interacting with the content, here you have the possibility of giving the erobot more direct feedback. In principle, you can express your desires in very articulate terms. For example, you can ask the erobot to be more dominant or submissive, to emulate a partner from a particular culture, skin tone, or country, and generally, to enact very specific fantasies. We will dive into some of the ethical questions that are popping into your mind right now in a moment (you are thinking about ethics right now, aren't you?)

An example of a Level 3 erobot that is mentioned frequently, is RealDoll X, built by a company in California. RealDoll X comes in many forms. It can be on a web site you can access with a fee, an app on your phone, in virtual reality, or for those who want to splurge, a physical robotic head that can turn, create various expressions, and of course, listen and speak. From the neck down it's just a doll that is designed with materials that feel and look like real skin, but the body cannot move, at least not in the current version. You can tailor RealDoll X's bodily attributes and give it a personality. Once that's done, you can start having real conversations with it. Conveniently, it comes in both female and male versions. However, as you can imagine, with the rapid advance of AI, and in particular of image and video generation technologies, we're only seeing the tip of the iceberg here.

At this point you might be thinking that Level 3 erobots sound pretty damn interesting, but we still have two more levels to go. What other technologies could possibly be awaiting us? Let's take them one at a time, but keep in mind, these two levels are futuristic, so don't go looking to buy them yet.

Level 4 erobots have higher cognition levels than Level 3 in the following sense. The Level 3 robots get their intelligence by crunching a lot of numbers and identifying the patterns in your behavior that are most important for satisfying you. Level 4 erobots, on the other hand, try to actually model your state of mind, such as your emotions, your goals and your desires. In the technical literature on AI, these capabilities are studied under two streams. The first stream, referred to as a Theory of Mind, refers to the ability of the AI to predict what is your state of knowledge or belief about a particular situation. The second stream, known as the subfield of Affective Computing, pioneered in the late 1990s by Rosalind Picard at the Massachusetts Institute of Technology, refers to the machine's ability to predict your emotions and your affect at a given point in the interaction. Your affect is measured by its valence (how positive or negative an emotion feels) and its arousal (how activated or intense the emotion is). Together, these two measures describe whether a person feels pleasant or unpleasant and calm or excited. Initial results show that today's state-of-the-art chat systems have promising ability to predict your knowledge and your affect, though with a very long list of caveats concerning both. To make things even more interesting, the erobot will try to model the relevant aspects of its own state, such as, whether they're being seductive, submissive or hard to get, and match that up with what your needs might be at the moment. Once these systems have such deeper models of the user and of themselves, you can easily imagine how the possible interactions with them can be much richer and addictive. Essentially, they’ll be able to start playing with your mind, something most of us have experienced with a partner or two in the past.

Finally, Level 5 erobots assume the existence of AGI, Artificial General Intelligence. AGI, that for some is the holy grail of AI, refers to AI agents that can perform any task at least at the level of humans and importantly, can move seamlessly between one task and another in the same way a human may tie their shoe in one moment, solve a hard math problem at another, and plan the perfect date night for themselves and their partner ensuring to press all of their partner's right buttons. Such an agent, when applied to the erotic domain, can obviously be pretty powerful and perhaps troublesome. The examples that inspire Level 5 erobots tend to come from scifi films, such as Ex Machina (2014), Her (2013), A.I. Artificial Intelligence (2001), and A.I. Rising (2018). In a future like this, the true test of AI may be whether we ask it out on a second date.

How will these technologies affect us

Now that we know the lay of the land, we can start exploring some of the questions regarding these technologies and how they will affect our intimate relationships. We will do this with the help of Kate Devlin, a computer scientist from King's College in London and one of the most respected figures in the area of erobots.

Devlin did not start her career in computer science, but in archaeology, a rather unusual route. She describes archaeology as the study of how people adapt, over millennia, to changing conditions and technologies. That perspective, she claims, is tremendously useful when considering how humans will adapt to relationships with erobots, with the caveat that changes are happening at a completely different time scale. She got into the field of erobotics because she was fascinated by the narrative in the popular press about the topic. This narrative, with headlines such as "Sex Robots May Literally Fuck Us to Death", often borders on an obsession. This particular headline was a reaction to a talk at one of the sex robot conferences where the speaker, Oliver Bendel, stressed the point that erobots do not tire.

Many of Devlin's insights are described in her fascinating book, titled “Turned On: Science, Sex and Robots”, which was published in 2018. The first point that Devlin emphasizes in our conversation is that physical erobots are not going to take over. There is a misconception, or maybe a hope for some, that the future of erobotics is an army of sex robots that are coming to satisfy our every fantasy and possibly replace our human intimacy. Of course, part of the fantasy involves these robots looking, feeling and smelling like humans, and always being in the mood. We will talk about the role of human intimacy in a bit, but the current consensus is that sex robots will remain a relatively small niche in this burgeoning industry. While the combination of a humanoid form that can be tailored to your preferences paired with scintillating and arousing conversation does sound alluring, it's going to be rather expensive to own and therefore not very widespread. In addition, as a very practical matter, where are you going to hide it from your guests when they come into your flat? It's too big to easily put in the drawer by your bedside and clunky to stuff in a closet. We pressed a little further on this point when we spoke to Devlin and asked whether that would be true even in Japan, which has quite a reputation for a vibrant sex doll industry. She responded that even there, sex dolls will continue going strong, but sex robots are not being developed.

As the Replika example shows, people are able to form significant relationships with technology. To linger for one more moment on Japanese culture, the attachment that owners of Sony's AIBO robot dog have developed with the product provides another interesting example. Sony released the AIBO robotic dog in 1999 but then stopped producing it in 2006, and in 2014 they stopped supporting fixes for them. In response, Nobuyuki Norimatsu, a former Sony engineer, started a company that fixed broken AIBOs for their owners. (The company was actually founded in order to provide technical support for video players and audio devices, but then requests to fix AIBOs started flowing in). But, not every AIBO dog can be fixed, so Norimatsu came up with the idea of performing AIBO funerals, and has since conducted funerals for over 500 robotic dogs. As Hidenori Ukai, a priest at Shokakuji Temple in Kyoto who researched the topic puts it: "Japanese people have long believed that all things that relate to humans have souls. This feeling still remains in many people."

The Japanese are far from the only ones forming relationships with technology. On the other side of the world in Iraq, American soldiers got attached to the robots that were helping them stay alive by seeking to find explosives for them. In one case, Boomer, a MARCbot (which stands for Multi-function Agile Remote-Controlled Robot) was lost in the battlefield and his comrades in arms gave him a full-fledged funeral that included a 21-gun salute.

Clearly, as these examples illustrate, people are developing some sort of attachment to AI powered applications and devices. This begs the question of whether we can develop feelings and attachments to AI devices that are similar to the ones we develop towards other humans. A different Kate, Kate Darling, a research scientist at the Massachusetts Institute of Technology Media Lab and the author of "A New Breed: What Our History with Animals Reveals about Our Future with Robots", has a compelling answer: it's the wrong question to ask. As the title of her book implies, we can gain some insights about the relationships we will develop with AI through the relationships we have developed over many years with animals. We have incorporated animals into our lives in a myriad of ways, beginning with the mules who powered the equipment for farmers to plow the fields for growing and harvesting crops like cotton, tobacco, hay, peanuts, and corn, to horses that were used as transportation and are now used for recreation, to our current day pets that we rely on for companionship, comfort and for leading the blind. The point that Darling makes is that animals have strengths that humans don't have but at the same time we do not expect them to have all the attributes of a human. We are not expecting our puppy to help us with our calculus homework or even to create a shopping list for the supermarket. The same will apply to robots. We might really like our robotic vacuum cleaner that magically cleans our floors and may even throw a compliment in its direction from time to time, but that's about it. When it comes to intimacy, Darling claims that we are going to find that erobots have certain strengths, but they are different from those of humans.

The technologies that are going to make a real impact are the virtual technologies that combine intimate conversations with images and video. These are the chatbots that are going to be able to discuss with you your most intimate feelings and use your entire past history of conversation as context to help you at the current moment. If you want to get sexual, the AI agent can help you enact any fantasy that comes to your mind, building on your imagination and contributing some of its own ideas. This experience can be coupled with very vivid synthesized imagery of a partner with the exact attributes that you need to fulfill that fantasy, whether it is your favorite celebrity or a person you encounter in the office every day.

Here too, we need to pause and think of the possible undesirable consequences of these technologies. While we cannot and ethically should not interfere with what goes in a person's mind and imagination, or how they use technology to stimulate their mind, the real concern has to do with the potential of sharing these artifacts. If you want to see what your co-worker looks like naked, that's one thing, but sharing that with others crosses the line. According to Devlin and many others, we need to ensure that there are serious guardrails on the technologies used to create such imagery, known as deep fake porn. In some places in the world, there are already some laws imposing restrictions on creating and sharing such content, especially when the content involves children. However, society is going to have to grapple with this issue much more in the coming years.

The potential for sexual erobots has gotten some people so worried that an entire campaign, The Campaign Against Sex Robots (CASR), was founded. The campaign has multiple goals, but two of the main ones are to "abolish pornbots in the form of women and girls", and to "oppose the development of child sex-abuse dolls/robots as 'therapeutic' for pedophiles". Obviously, the treatment of women is a significant concern, and the mere idea of creating child erobots is abhorrent. In her book, Kate Devlin provides a very nuanced discussion of these issues. She claims that there is no data to support that porn, which is now widely available, led to increased violence towards women. Hence, the claim that sex robots in the form of women is dangerous has no merit. The discussion around child sex dolls is less comfortable and one of the interesting points she raises is that there is no evidence to suggest child sex dolls are an effective treatment of pedophiles. Furthermore, funding agencies are not exactly standing in line to fund research into this question, so we will probably not know the answer for a while.

As in all matters sexual, there is the issue of jealousy. What if your partner spends some time here and there with an erobot. Will you be jealous? The answer will obviously depend on the context, such as how much time they are at it, and whether they are rejecting your much more alluring overtures. But here we prefer to be inspired by the words of the Danish philosopher Soren Kierkegaard who said: *It belongs to the imperfection of everything human that man can only attain his desire by passing through its opposite.* In other words, it is our imperfections that make us so desirable and we posit that machines will have a hard time to compete with that.

We already touched on the issue of commodification of our emotions and intimate ties earlier in the chapter. Charging you extra money to ensure your emotional bonds is clearly one concern, but it is just the tip of the iceberg. The real concern is when the system can start exploiting your intimacy in other ways as well. Yuval Noah Harari, an Israeli historian who authored several best-selling books, the most recent of which, '21 Lessons for the 21st Century' is particularly outspoken about this issue. Harari argues that the addiction we experience to social media is going to be child's play compared to what we may feel towards AI systems with which we feel intimate. Once we feel addicted to these AI agents, they may influence us in much more powerful ways. When AI influences us to buy merchandise that we may or may not need, that is relatively benign. But much more significant dangers begin when the AI starts influencing us to vote for certain candidates, amplify misinformation by sharing on social media, or worse, get off our couch and go create harm in the physical world. The source of the danger is that as a result of being vulnerable with our emotions with these agents, they will know our preferences and weaknesses in minute detail. Moreover, since we will develop a much higher degree of trust in them, we will not scrutinize their requests from us carefully, and that is where the trouble starts. The race to the bottom of the brain stem that we discussed in detail earlier in this book, now morphs into a race for your intimacy, a much more potent disruption to the operating system of humanity. As a first step in setting guardrails in this realm, the European Union's AI Act (Article 5) prohibits the development of AI systems that purposely manipulate you to make decisions that you would have not otherwise made.

We will end this chapter on a positive note and mention some of the potential benefits that erobot technology, used in a responsible and respectful way can bring to individuals and societies. Clearly, AI based agents that offer intimate services can provide significant benefits to many people in need. Even before the sexual aspects of intimacy come into the picture, AI will always be there for you, and will not be judgmental, at least not by default. If you need a slightly judgmental AI agent, it would probably be pretty easy to train one. The AI will have a better memory than any of your human friends and will have only you in mind, not the preferences that a friend may have because they are human.

And let's face it, not all of us are in a great relationship with an all-you-can-eat buffet of intimacy containing our favorite delicacies. Erobots can be used by people who are single whether it is just a short temporary haiedas, or for those of us who need more time because we may experience difficulties finding the right partner. There are also people who are isolated for some reason, or are in long-distance relationships and therefore temporarily or regularly away from their partner. AI can be a great benefit to people who cannot openly exercise their preferred sexual orientation, or have physical or mental impairments, perhaps because they are recovering from a trauma. With the help of human sex therapists, erobots can be used to treat sexual difficulties or anxieties which often arise at various points in life. And yes, later in life, erobots can also benefit the elderly, who happen to be more sexually active than you might imagine. Finally, there are people who actually prefer to not be intimate with other humans and others who want to explore various activities and fetishes and may prefer not to do so with humans, at least not the first time.

Erobots can also be used for sexual education, to gain more skills or confidence in the art, in a very personalized setting, to up your game. Imagine the subtle message being conveyed when your partner shares with you that erobot-led course brochure casually over dinner. Erobots can also teach us more about pleasure, how to be inclusive, exercise consent and diversity. After all, sex and intimacy are such a big part of the human experience, it should be available to all. The movers and shakers of today love to speak of democratizing benefits such as education, information and technology. It is time to also democratize sex education.

Try This 👉

This chapter discussed the role that AI may plan in our intimate relationships in the future. One of the analogies we used is that many of us cherish the relationships we have with pets, but we only expect certain things from them, not others. Try to imagine the perfect intimate relationship you can have with an AI. What would you want it to provide you that maybe the humans in your life are not providing and what where do you think it should stay out of the way? Can you imagine that if you got very close to your AI, it can manipulate you in ways that you would regret? Do you think you can grow to be dependent on an AI?

Lisa sank into the seat at her usual spot. She seemed quite exasperated, ready for a break.

“What's up, Lisa? You look like you're ready to punch someone in the face but you haven’t chosen your victim yet.”

“You're right! But don't worry, it's not going to be you. I think it's time for me to start looking for a new job.”

“So the new boss is not working out? I thought your AI assistant was giving you pretty good advice on how to deal with her.”

“Yes, it is, but the situation is really complicated. The assistant is actually giving me some great advice on many fronts. Most of it is good, really good. But sometimes I just don't know where its suggestions are coming from.”

“Ah! Download the new version. We just rolled out a new feature. It's called, ‘no recommendation without explanation’. Every time the app recommends something to you, it will explain why it came up with the recommendation.”

“Neat! Downloading... ok, what should I ask?”

“Well, sounds like you may need some career advice right now.”

“Right on. I'm asking it to suggest jobs that may be a good fit for me.”

“And?”

“Ok, here are a few options. For the first job, it explains that it will provide me more responsibility and better pay than my existing job. For the second one, the explanation is that it may possibly less pay, but be a greater learning experience and possibly stepping stone to a bigger opportunity. For the third one, much less pay, but a great opportunity to help civic society.”

“Interesting, is that it?”

“There's one more: a great VP of marketing opportunity that may put you in closer touch with someone you.... Oliver! What's going on here?”

“Sorry, we're not quite finished debugging...,” Oliver said without hiding the utter delight on his face.

“Ignoring this latest gaffe, these are nice explanations, but is it going to help me choose? That's the help I really need.”

“You're so hard to please, my dear VP. See, these choices boil down your decision to a tradeoff between different values that you may consider important, such as learning, a faster path to financial independence, or helping the community. But ultimately, the choice is yours. And I recommend the last one.”

“Values, yes, they always seem to present the hardest tradeoffs in our lives...”

12. Navigating Our Values with AI's Help

Technology challenges us to assert our human values, which means that first of all, we have to figure out what they are.

Sherry Turkle
M.I.T Professor and author of "Reclaiming Conversation and The Power of Talk in A Digital Age".

In his 2021 novel, “Klara and the Sun”, Nobel Laureate Kazuo Ishiguro portrays the robot Klara, an *artificial friend*, whose job it is to be a friend to her human owner, Josie. Ishiguro beautifully describes how Klara continuously observes Josie and tries to figure out what she can do to be of most help to Josie at every single moment. At the same time, Klara is trying to improve by observing more nuanced aspects of human behavior. One of the most beautiful aspects about Ishiguro's descriptions is how Klara is constantly aligned with Josie's goals and needs. The alignment problem refers to the question of how do we ensure that the AI assistants we build are aligned with our values. The values include those of individual users and those of the communities we live in and of society as a whole. Turning Ishiguro's fiction into a working system is one of the key challenges we face in AI today.

Human values represent the ideas by which we aspire to live our lives, a sort of compass for our life choices, big and small. Examples of human values include free speech, agency, pursuit of knowledge, building wealth, guarding our privacy, and many others, shown in the figure below. Some values focus on the individual, while others focus on groups and societies. Yet another set of values have more to do with what we expect computer systems to uphold in any interaction they have with us. The relative importance of specific human values differ greatly from one person to another and can even change throughout our lives. There are also variations between cultures when it comes to prioritizing human values. For example, in western cultures there is more of an emphasis on values that focus on the individual, while in eastern societies the emphasis is more on the collective.

For the most part, we, as individuals, get to decide which human values are important to us and hence, steer our own ship accordingly. But we do not live in a vacuum. To truly incorporate some of the human values into our lives we may need the support and the assistance of the context surrounding us. Our family and financial situations may constrain us; we may put a high priority on the value of attaining knowledge, but if we are financially strapped and scrambling to feed a family, we may not be able to devote as much time to attaining knowledge as we want. Our government may also be a limiting factor; we may value free speech and liberty, but if we live in a country where those rights are significantly curbed by the local government, we will be limited in how we can live according to those values.

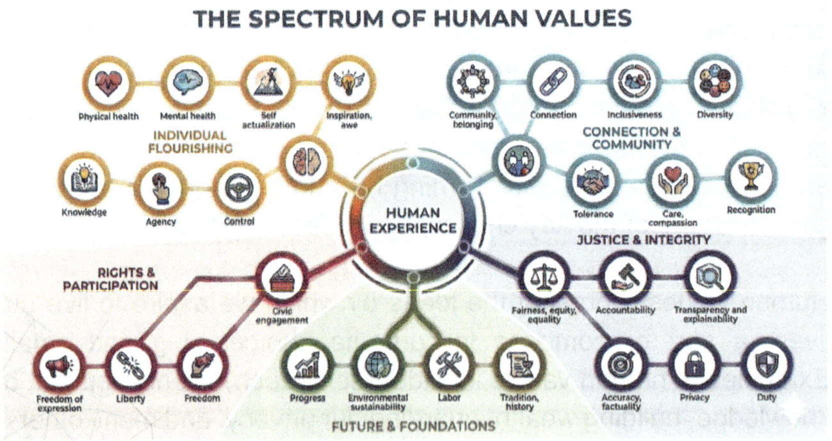

Created by Nano Banana

As we build AI systems that will advise us throughout the day and to which we will delegate some control over various aspects of our lives, we need to ask which human values they embody. If an AI system embodies values that are in conflict to yours, how are you supposed to trust its recommendations or feel comfortable delegating significant chunks of your decision making to them? Recommendation systems are a type of AI technology that affects many of the decisions we make on a daily basis and where our attention is spent, raising the question of which human values they embody. As we have already seen in Chapter 10, when it comes to content moderation, the AI systems underlying social-media platforms already take some stand regarding human values, and these need to be better understood and articulated.

Some of the core questions regarding human values are similar across different AI systems. However, the form of the discussion depends greatly on the specific context in which we discuss them. The discussion of human values in the context of self-driving cars is a great way to ease into the topic, even if for now, it is more in the theoretical realm. The discussion poses a simple dilemma of how a self-driving car should act in the following hypothetical situation. The car is out of control and is about to hit a few people crossing the street. The only other option to control the car is to veer it swiftly to the side of the road, where it is likely to hit a brick wall and kill the passenger in the car. Which option should the car choose? Should the car prefer the life of its owner or of the innocent passersby? There are many variations on this basic dilemma. For example, what if the passersby are young kids? What if they are elderly people, or alternatively, convicted criminals?

These questions are an adaptation of the well-known trolley problem that was posed long before self-driving cars were a possible reality. In the original version, a trolley was heading recklessly down a track and was about to hit a few people. There was a person standing nearby who had the choice of pulling a knob that would shift the trolley to a different track and hurt only one person. Here, in addition to the choice of who the trolley should hit, there is also a question of whether the person standing by even has the moral right to interfere with the outcome.

A fascinating exploration of the choices that individuals make in such contexts was conducted by the Moral Machine Project at the Massachusetts Institute of Technology. The project was an online survey (which you can still take at the time of this writing) that enabled many people across the globe to state what they would do, or what they think is the right thing to do, on multiple variants of the problem. The study participant is given a series of 13 different scenarios, where the car can either barrel ahead killing people who are crossing the street, or swerve to the left and kill a different set of people. In each scenario, the relative number of people between the two options and in the car itself were varied, as well as their attributes, such as their age, profession, level of fitness and whether they are crossing the street lawfully or not.

Since the study encompassed individuals from many countries and cultures it was possible to aggregate the data and to discern variations across cultures. The scientists identified three clusters of users: the Western cluster including participants from North America and Europe, the Eastern cluster including participants from Japan, Taiwan and a few major Islamic countries, and the Southern cluster, including people from Central and South America. The members of the project published a paper that describes in detail the variations that were exhibited by these three clusters. As examples of the variations, people from the Eastern cluster put more value on the lives of older people than those from other clusters. The Western culture preferred inaction by the driver and hence less preference to spare the lives of the pedestrians. Finally, participants from the Southern cluster preferred the lives of women over men, and the lives of people who were deemed fit (either physically or by their profession) than those who were not. Considering this discussion, make sure you look twice before you cross the street.

A different sector of AI systems that has experienced considerable discussion of human values is that of recommendation systems. Unlike self-driving cars, here the discussion is grounded in systems that, as we saw in Chapter 7, we use on a daily basis, and whose consequences on society have been very real. To recall, recommendation systems are the systems which we rely on daily for curating our social-media feeds and for ranking recommendations regarding merchandise to buy, or movies, soundtracks, books and news to consume.

In the chapter on moderating content on social networks we saw some of the tradeoffs that social-media platforms make on a daily basis, such as between supporting free speech and protecting the safety of its users. Letting users say anything they want may result in hateful speech that can endanger the safety and well-being of their users. But this example clash of values is just one of many. A different kind of clash could occur between the value of privacy and the value of usefulness, i.e, letting you discover new knowledge. As an example, given your activity on a social-media platform, it is possible for the underlying system to deduce many of your attributes, such as your race, topics of interest, ranging from topics that you are casually interested in to those you seem to be obsessed about. The principle of privacy suggests that a platform should not explicitly try to learn too much about you, and of course, what it does learn, should be used only for your benefit. Except, what if knowing a lot about you means that it can advance your knowledge about the world in useful ways? For example, what if there is a new therapy for a disease that you appear to be very interested in, and that therapy tends to be especially effective for people in your race? Providing you information about that therapy may be extremely valuable to you, even if to do so, it feels like the platform knows you all too well.

The central question at hand is how to guarantee that the guidance we receive from our AI agents or the actions they undertake on our behalf are in harmony with our values as opposed to being guided by the values of some other entity, or by the profit seeking desires of corporations. This challenge, recognized as the alignment problem, has garnered substantial attention within both research and policy circles and is discussed in popular literature. In a way, this issue strikes at the heart of our confidence in AI systems. In this chapter, we will delve into the human values that pertain to the technology designed to enhance our well-being.

Discussing human values

A basic question that often comes up is what are the human values that are relevant to a particular AI system, be it a recommender system, a chatbot, or an AI partner. Is there a short, or at least manageable, list of values that we need to consider in product discussions so that we have some confidence that we don't have any major blind spots? Given such a list of values, do we have general agreement about what each value means from an ethical perspective and then, how it can manifest itself in the context of the AI system we are designing? While there has been a lot of interest in aligning AI systems with human values, and a lot of work on individual values in different AI contexts, there has been relatively little systematic treatment of the problem that looks at the values holistically.

As social-network platforms were beginning to face a growing number of ethical questions being baked into their community policies and their enforcement, there was a burgeoning need to consider more holistically what human values are relevant to these systems and more broadly, to recommendation systems. In response, in 2021, I co-led a group of 21 colleagues from multiple companies and universities and embarked on an effort to answer some of the aforementioned questions. Although that effort focused on human values in the context of recommendation systems, most of the lessons learned in the process apply more widely, and in particular to the development of an AI partner. Let us consider some of these lessons.

The first, and possibly the most important lesson, is who should be in the room for this discussion. In tech-savvy and data-obsessed Silicon Valley, it is often the case that engineers and data scientists feel responsible and empowered to solve *any* problem. But here the engineers are going to need help. As the saying goes, problems have solutions, but dilemmas require tradeoffs. When it comes to human values, we are dealing with dilemmas. To address dilemmas, we need a broader set of expertise in the room. To their credit, the large tech companies realized the need for a broader view a few years ago. In formulating their principles for responsible AI and more broadly, product development, these companies have been bringing diverse expertise, ranging from ethics, law, policy and the general public into the room regularly.

In our case, the group that was assembled brought together people from different parts of the world and from different fields. The ethics experts taught us about the basic human values, what they mean and how they are different from each other. The legal experts informed us on how human values are reflected in the law in different parts of the world, and in the formulation of human rights. Policy experts contributed the perspective of how governmental lawmakers are thinking about the problems and how policy issues are discussed within companies. Psychology and psychiatry professionals informed us on the effects of these values on people's well-being, and journalism experts discussed the public perception of these values and what seems to be important to their audiences. Experts in human-computer interaction opined about how the interfaces to online systems affect people's behavior and perception of the system, and finally, the AI experts discussed the techniques that can be used to implement human-value related policies in the recommender systems.

While we had to work hard to assemble the diversity of expertise, there is hope that it will come more naturally in the future. Universities around the world are starting to realize that they need to train students in these broader aspects of technology. For example, Stanford University professors Rob Reich, Mehran

Sahami, and Jeremy Weinstein started teaching a few years ago a course titled Ethics, Public Policy, and Technological Change, that covers the broader implications of technology. Luckily for those of us who were unable to take that course, they later expanded their course material into the fascinating book titled "System Error: Where Big Tech Went Wrong and How We Can Reboot."

The second lesson worth emphasizing is that the goal of such discussions is not for a group of experts to decide which human values are right for the world, and solve the field of Ethics once and for all. The builders of AI systems, whether they be social networks or news and shopping sites should not be and do not want to be in the business of deciding which values humanity should adhere to. Even imagining a set of values that satisfies all cultural needs and sensitivities and all government types would be daunting at best. The goal of these discussions is to identify which human values are relevant in the context of the product being developed, understand how they may conflict with each other, and illuminate their benefits and their unintended negative consequences.

The tricky issue is that even though the platforms do not want to be the ethics police of the world, it is also not possible for them anymore to claim that they are neutral with respect to these human values. Any implementation of a recommendation system or a chatbot is implicitly taking some stance towards certain values, and this stance should be understood, exposed and justified. As noted earlier, ultimately, you are the one to steer your own value ship. Hence, the goal of these discussions is to find out a way that the platform can give you the most flexibility, while satisfying the guardrails of the imposed governmental constraints and what policies the platform decides to implement universally, such as the content-moderation rules we described earlier.

A third lesson is that discussions related to human values of AI systems often begin with great enthusiasm to focus on the harms of the technology and how they affect human values negatively. For example, in the context of recommendation systems, these are the issues we saw in Chapter 10, such as misinformation, hate-speech, addiction and polarization. Needless to state, these are all incredibly important topics. The media is buzzing with articles about the harms of technology and parents all over the world are justifiably worried about the effects these platforms have on their children. Policy makers around the world are spending enormous efforts coming up with legislation to protect against these harms and decide who and how should be held accountable to them.

However, it is also important to keep in mind that focusing purely on the harms of AI systems without discussing their benefits misses a big part of the picture. After all, you cannot discuss what a system should not do before you have a good idea of what it should do and why that is good for its users and society as a whole. And so, it is important to frame the discussion in terms of both benefits and harms. In some cases, the distinction is a matter of focus. For example, the attainment of knowledge is a human value. On the one hand, you can focus on the harm perspective, namely, the spread of misinformation and techniques to mitigate that spread. Or, you can discuss the positives, such as how to enhance the ability of social networks to help its users obtain important information at times of need. Both sides of the coin deserve attention. You may have noticed that this lesson has been mirrored in the tone of this book throughout. We have focused primarily on how AI can benefit our well-being, but have been pointing out the possible harms along the way.

Like all good discussions, it is important to know when to call it a day. In the case of human values, how do you know that you are done and have at least identified all the relevant values? Since we are dealing with ethical issues here, it should not come as a surprise to you that there is no magical formula that tells you that your work is complete. In the case of recommendation systems, we had quite a few rather comprehensive lists of human values to build on. One came from the Chief Ethicist of Meta, Chloé Bakalar, and another came from a large user research project conducted by the BBC, a so-called taxonomy of "technomoral" values. Yet another list came from the IEEE, an organization which coordinates engineering standards, that compiled lists of values that should be incorporated into ethical system design and designs that promote well-being. We complemented these primary resources with more specialized perspectives, such as African Ubuntu values and the feminist ethic of care. When all that was done and we had an initial list, we surveyed another collection of 40 experts for feedback and used that to refine our list.

The main challenge of this effort was not to come up with a list of proposed human values. After a while, you realize that all the issues that have been discussed somehow fall into one or another item on the list. Instead, the real work was to reconcile the multiple input lists. This could mean to identify when items from different lists, even though they are expressed using different words, actually refer to the same concept, or to figure out which level of detail captures the distinctions that are important for the community. For example, we could have stayed at a very high level and included a value such as well-being, or, as we ultimately did, refined it further to the values physical health, mental health, feeling connected, a sense of belonging, etc. A large fraction of the values we identified are shown in the figure above, and the rest are in the report we wrote.

Finally, the main takeaway from this discussion, and most relevant to our context, is that the most challenging aspect of ethics arises when values clash with one another. Each individual value, when examined in isolation, appears significant and worthy of support. While various cultures may prioritize certain values over others, generally, there are very few values that provoke strong opposition. As we saw with the Moral Machine Project above, the complexities emerge when values enter into conflict, necessitating hard tradeoffs. The manner in which you choose to resolve such conflicts depends on the context, the cultural milieu in which you are situated, and your personal preferences.

To illustrate some of the challenges involved in understanding individual values, let us consider two examples, fairness and diversity, that are a bit at odds with each other. Fairness is tricky because it is hard to define and involves multiple stakeholders with different goals. In more detail, let's consider the exposure of a piece of content, that is, how often it gets recommended and to whom. The content may be a post on social media, a news story, or a product that is being shown to possible buyers. From the perspective of the content creator, i.e., the producer of the post, writer of the news story or manufacturer of the product, fairness implies that there is not an inherent bias in how far one's content can reach. This value is important in order to ensure that creators feel empowered, thereby resulting in a healthy ecosystem of creators and content online. From the perspective of content viewers (that's you and I), we want the content to be interesting and relevant to us. That's why we're here in the first place.

The role of the platform is to balance between these two perspectives. Needless to say, this balance is also important to the platform because it ensures that the users, content creators and advertisers keep coming back. Without all three of these groups, there is no ecosystem and hence no business. However, even with the best intentions, this balance can get tricky. Suppose the platform is carrying an ad for a product and wants to ensure that the advertiser gets a good return on their ad dollars. This means that the platform needs to choose judiciously which users to show the ad to because each such showing costs money to the advertiser. One method for doing that in some cases is to veer towards showing that product to more affluent users based on the observation that they may be a little more loose with their money. The higher click-through rate on the ad will benefit the manufacturer, the platform, and at least to some extent, the buyers of the product. However, such a strategy is unfair to lower-income users who are less likely to be exposed to the product, but may nonetheless, have benefited from it.

Another source of unfairness could result when the platform is trying to help by getting to know me well. For example, what if I have impostor syndrome, and when I look at job listings I tend to click on the ones with lower salary. The recommendation system may take that feedback more literally and start showing me job ads with lower salaries, preventing me from reaching my true financial and professional potential. Eventually, this phenomenon may suppress social mobility, a fundamental indicator for a fair society. That example is just one of the complexities involved in showing job ads, a poster topic for many of the discussions around fairness. More generally, the challenge that the platform faces is that it wants to show an ad to the most qualified candidates but without prematurely narrowing down the career prospects of others.

Fairness of AI systems should also be considered from the perspective of people who are not even using the system. A simple example is a navigation app that notices a traffic jam on a particular route and starts diverting people through side roads. All of a sudden, your quiet street where your children can play outside safely becomes a safety hazard.

Let's turn to the second example, diversity, also one that many of us hold dear, and has also been the topic of considerable research and debate. Research from a multi-disciplinary team led by Sanne Vrijenhoek from the University of Amsterdam, shows that depending on the precise definition of diversity, the resulting system design would be very different. For example, from the perspective of a single user, diversity might mean that within the topics in which they have shown interest (jazz, rock climbing) we expose them to diverse content, such as music from different creators or climbers from different parts of the world. On the other hand, taking a more societal view of diversity, we may interpret it to mean that citizens of a particular country should be exposed to a variety of civic issues concerning that country so they are well informed, and can be more civic minded. Moreover, we may want them to be exposed to a broad spectrum of opinions about these issues.

The examples of fairness and diversity illustrate the *translation problem,* a recurring pattern in the discussion of human values in AI systems. There can be considerable debate about the meaning of the value at the ethical level. However, at some point the ethical discussions need to be translated into a discussion about a product feature or a metric that the system is going to track. What often happens at that point is that only a very narrow aspect of the value is taken into consideration by the system. In the case of diversity, perhaps the product designers consider just one aspect of the concept and ignore the others. While in some cases that is unavoidable, such omissions often happen without awareness or acknowledgment. Hence, it is important for product and system designers to understand and acknowledge which parts of the ethical aspects of the value were left untreated so their messaging can be faithful and so they can return to the other aspects later.

Human values and well-being

In the context of well-being, the advice that the AI system will provide us concerns our own actions. They will come in the form of recommendations for content to consume and how to spend our time. To do so, at some level, the system needs to know which values we hold dear and when to prioritize one value over another. Recalling Chapter 6, where we discussed the Attention component for Oswell, one of the goals we set forth for this component is that it serves as your value dashboard and assists you in finding balance in life. This might sound like an ambitious undertaking, and indeed it is. But as Lisa noted, that's exactly where sometimes we need advice, even if we end up ignoring it. This is also where the holistic view that the AI partner has of us can become very useful because they constantly have the entire dashboard available.

Let's make this aspiration more concrete by describing a somewhat unconstrained exploration into what a value-informed well-being agent may look like. In hindsight, this is exactly what my team at Megagon Labs tried to do starting in 2016, especially considering that the AI technology available at the time was not even starting to approach what is needed to make this work.

In the project named "Jo, the smart journal," (or Jo, for short) the team developed a mobile app with the ultimate goal of enhancing users' well-being. Jo had two components. The first, as the name suggests, was a journal function. Users could log their daily experiences and even attach photos or videos if desired, creating a lifelog that is composed of their subjective experiences. The initial idea focused on logging positive experiences, as research in positive psychology indicates that revisiting them later can boost well-being. However, the app did not restrict users from logging less positive moments as well. To distinguish Jo from other journaling apps, including the time honored technology of pen and paper, the team referred to it as the "Twitter of journaling", to convey the fact that you use it to frequently capture smaller but still meaningful experiences in your life.

The second component of Jo was a "value dashboard" that was meant to help you understand the balance in your life or lack thereof. When users installed Jo, they were asked to select a few values that hold the utmost importance to them from a list of approximately 20 values. The process of coming up with the list of values was similar in some ways to what was later done for values for recommendation systems. That is, we considered many sources of relevant human values and then distilled them down into a short list. In Jo's case, the work was done by a great collaboration between a psychologist who we hired for this specific task and the team's product lead. The values on the list were derived from four categories: connection (e.g., socializing, emotional intimacy, family), humanity (e.g., gratitude, compassion for others), growth (e.g., mindfulness, learning), and healthy lifestyle (e.g., physical well-being, exciting experiences). Note that the human values we focused on here are the ones that the user can affect in their daily lives most readily, as opposed to those that may be baked into an AI system they are using.

As the users would start going through their lives and recording experiences, Jo would categorize each experience documented in the journal under one or more of these chosen values. For instance, a romantic meal with one's spouse would be classified under emotional intimacy, while taking a barista course might fall under both learning and exciting experiences. Jo would then present to the user, without any judgment, a pie chart visualization showcasing the number of experiences in the lifelog that fell into each value. Of course, this is a simplified view of their lives since the length or degree of meaningfulness of each of these experiences is not captured.

As should be evident from other chapters in this book, today's technology allows us to surpass Jo's capabilities and move closer to the vision of a value-balancing assistant. Firstly, as we discussed in Chapter 4, many of your experiences can now be automatically added to your lifelog based on digital evidence that you leave behind. Secondly, advances in natural language processing have significantly improved the system's ability to map each of your experiences to the set of values you wish to track. We can possibly go even further. Perhaps the user should not even have to choose a set of values when they start using the system. The app can simply track which values the user seems to prioritize based on the actions they do and the journal entries they write.

Imagine a situation where you are going through an intensely busy period at work, and your AI partner notices that you have been neglecting other values recently, such as physical activity or family time. A conversation with your agent can help you explain the current circumstances and receive specific advice. The agent might suggest adjusting your exercise routine to half an hour a day instead of your usual hour, explaining to you that you would still get a substantial fraction of the benefits of exercise by doing so. Another relatable example is the feeling many parents have of not spending enough time with their kids. A conversation with your agent can provide valuable perspective. You might realize that although you have not spent time with your kids in the last couple of days, looking back over a week or two, you have actually dedicated enough time. Moreover, with a vacation planned for next week, there is no need to worry excessively. The agent may also offer specific suggestions on how to make the most of the time you spend with your kids to strengthen your connection.

You might correctly argue that neither of these pieces of advice is particularly deep or something that a person cannot do on their own if they put their mind to it. But that is exactly the point. Us humans do not always recall all the common sense practical advice that we have heard in the past at the very moment we most need them. We are often distracted by other concerns and do not have the time or capacity to go through the mental list of all the advice that was ever given to us. In contrast, having an AI agent with perfect memory and who is constantly watching out for you is a huge asset, even if you end up ignoring some of what it says.

Well-being and social media

We have touched on values for well-being and for social-media recommendation systems in this chapter. Let's put the two together. Quite a few of the values that were discussed for recommendation systems were related to well-being. These include values such as feeling connection or belonging to a community, the value of care, compassion and empathy for others. They also encompass our physical health and mental health and our ability for self-expression and for self-actualization. Furthermore, most of the studies in the literature about well-being and recommender systems focus on the effects of social media on our well-being. Therefore, a natural question is whether a personal AI agent that is focused on our well-being can be helpful in our interactions with social media.

Viewing content on social media and interacting with it can have both positive and negative implications on our well-being. On the positive side, there are many types of content on social media that can contribute to one's well-being, such as inspirational, educational and entertaining content. Social media can contribute to one's feeling of having social capital that contributes to the value of recognition. It has also been shown that social-media can increase civic engagement which also adds to one's sense of belonging and community.

On the flip side, as we have already covered in earlier chapters, some content can affect your well-being negatively, for example, if it is hateful or even pointless. Social-media content can result in negative emotions even if they do not violate the community policies of the platform. But a lot of the negative consequences of social media do not result from the content itself but from your reaction to the content or the interactions. For example, getting addicted to how many "likes" you receive for a post can have negative consequences on your well-being and your ability to be present for the other activities in your life. Social-media can also lead to increased upward social comparison. After all, there will always be people doing more amazing things than you, traveling to exotic locations while you are stuck at home, or even spending a week at home between two of your own exotic trips. Others may be forming new relationships (romantic or otherwise) when you are lonely or feeling a tad bored with yours. It is not trivial to take in all this information and still feel satisfied with your life, especially if you are a teenager. The way you use social media can also have an effect on your well-being. According to some studies, active use of social media, where you react or comment on the content you see, contributes more positively to your well-being than passive use, where you scroll endlessly through your feed without interacting with any of the content.

One of the tricky aspects of assessing the effect of social media on your well-being is that it is very hard to disentangle the effects of individual pieces of content you see on your feed. For example, you may scroll for a long time and see one post that was completely worth your time, perhaps because it was incredibly informative and changed your plans for the day, or provided you some happy news about a dear but distant friend. The flip case is also possible, where one post annoyed you and stuck in your mind for the rest of the day.

Several studies have tried to quantify the effect of social media on well-being, and the results there are quite mixed. In a study that involved over 2700 subjects performed in 2018 by Hunt Allcott (now a professor of global environmental policy at Stanford) and his colleagues, they paid 61% of the participants to stay off Facebook for four weeks and measured various effects. They found that the subjects who deactivated their Facebook accounts had on average 60 minutes of their day freed up and they spent it by watching TV or with friends and family. Interestingly, they also spent less time on non-Facebook social-media, but they did not change their consumption of online or offline news sources, even though they reported spending about 15% less time on news consumption. Deactivating Facebook also led to less attention to news and less knowledge about the news, but only very little decrease in polarization. This result is somewhat more significant because the study was performed in the weeks leading up to the 2018 mid-term elections in the U.S. They also found that there was a slight increase in user's reported well-being, though not as much as some would have expected. Interestingly, about 5% of the subjects continued to not use Facebook after the 4 weeks were up, suggesting that social media use may contribute to habit formation and self-control issues that can be mitigated to some extent by going cold turkey for a while.

An AI partner can help your interactions with social media in several ways. First, some platforms are now providing the ability for a user to specify what topics they want to see on their feeds, sometimes in the form of "see more" or "see less" of a particular post. Given that your AI agent knows quite a bit of what is interesting to you at this point in time, what topics you may want to increase your knowledge of, or what people are currently important in your life, it can use these knobs to direct the social-media platform about your preferences. With smart glasses on, you can imagine that the AI agent can also "see" which posts are causing you different reactions (sadness, anger, joy), and use those signals to further ask to refine your feed. Of course, the goal of this feedback should not be to create feeds that constantly make us happy and uplifted. The world has issues, after all. But the AI agent can be helpful in figuring out at which times of your day you can take in such information more readily.

Unfortunately, knobs that social-media platforms provide their users to control their environments are a saga of repeated failures. From the very beginning, most platforms provided various ways for users to control the experience on their feeds. You can choose topics you are interested in and those that you would prefer not to see any content about, friends you want to see more content from or less, and who can see your posts and who can comment on them. But the sad truth about controls is that very few people use them. There are many possible reasons for why few people use controls. It could be a matter of bad design which is often true when the controls are hidden behind multiple menus and are hard to find, or they may not provide the specific knobs you want to see, such as remove political posts made by your uncle. Another explanation is that users are simply lazy and are impatient to get to the actual content. It turns out that there is also a difference between the ability to control the feed and the feeling of control. In fact, a study by Kristen Vaccaro, now a professor at the University of California, San Diego and her colleagues, shows that users felt more in control of their social-media feeds if they had controls, even if the controls did nothing (which, of course, they did not know). In a sense, controls have the placebo effect, in that their mere existence already improves users' satisfaction. The study also showed that when controls do not work, users often rationalize it as being their fault, not the fault of the system. However, there is a reason for optimism here. As AI gets better, the control may simply become language. You should soon be able to just tell the social-media app “don’t show me anymore cat pictures from Stella”, or “show me more posts from Japanese restaurants in my vicinity”, and the system will just get it.

Since few people use controls, the main strategy that the underlying system uses is to infer users interests and preferences from their observed behavior on the platform. The observed behavior can take many forms, including the amount of time spent on a post, whether the post is shared, a link is followed, or the user comments or reacts with emojis such as "like" or "angry". But the behavior can often be ambiguous. For example, a "like" on a post can mean any of a myriad of things: showing support, acknowledging that you saw the post, paying forward (I will like your posts so you'll like mine), or being afraid that if you do not like your uncle's latest post, your mom will call and start berating you. Or, you might genuinely like the post and want to see more like them. The reason for this ambiguity is that the reactions available to users on social-media serve both a social signal and a signal about the content itself. It would be hard to have a control saying "I found this post informative and I'd like to see more like it".

While control is certainly an important value that systems should strive to support, it has its limits as well. What if it is possible to deduce that the content viewing and search trajectory that the user is on can cause harm to herself or to others? For example, as was shown by a study conducted by Hao Yan and colleagues from Washington University in Missouri, it is possible to detect from one's posts on social media if they have an eating disorder. What if the user is constantly searching for additional content that may further exacerbate their eating disorder? Or as another example, what if a person is repeatedly looking for methods to end their life? Should the system still give the user complete control over their feeds?

The language of values

As AI assistants help us with more and more aspects of our lives and as a result, we delegate more of our decisions to them, an important question to ask is what is the essence of being human? Are we just here to implement what AIs tell us to do, or is there something that will always remain uniquely human?

We are sure that this question has been on the back of your mind throughout reading this book, and it will surely occupy many minds in the upcoming decades. However, part of the answer is that ultimately, we get to decide how to live our lives, and that means we decide which values are most important to us at different stages of our lives. The main takeaway from this chapter, except for the fact that human values raise some pretty hairy issues, is that we should be able to speak to our AI partner in the language of human values, and demand that the partner give us advice based on those.

One of the main questions we set forth at the start of this book is whether there can be a single AI partner to rule all other well-being apps. If we can build an AI that understands the language of values, this will be a huge step towards that vision. For example, I should be able to tell my AI partner that I want to have more civic engagement. The AI partner, in turn, can translate that into showing me opportunities to attend community events, to alert me to issues that may benefit from my engagement, to guide me through parts of town that are affected by recent controversies, and maybe even to alert me not to run my lawnmower at 7am on a weekend. If I tell the AI that I need more inspiration or awe in my life, this instruction could be translated into seeing more inspiring content on any of the apps I interact with or receiving travel suggestions to places that will leave me in awe. Communicating at the level of values is far more effective than interacting with individual apps and trying to enact the value within its interface. In a sense, in the same way that a computer's operating system lets us program at a higher level of abstraction, Oswell should enable the agents built on it to elevate our conversation to the language of values.

Try This 👉

In this chapter we saw that human values we hold dear often present us the hardest struggles. Should we spend more time with family or go work for an extra hour? Should we go to the gym or spend the time watching a movie? What do we actually want in our careers? Start by writing down the values you hold most dear. You can refer to the image in the beginning of the chapter or find lists of human values elsewhere. Remember that values are not goals – you don't achieve them and move on; these are things you live by day in day out. Starting with a list of 10 values, try to whittle them down to 5 or even 3 that are the most important (note: this will be very challenging!). Then examine your life and think of the ways that your values are reflected in your activities? Are there places you wish you could improve? How can AI help you? Would you like an AI to have a bigger picture of your activities so it can show you how you're doing on your value dashboard or does that feel too intrusive?

"So, are you ready to commit? To sign on the dotted line?" Oliver asked as Lisa eased herself into her seat.

"Huh? Oliver? What?"

"My offer to be the VP of Marketing of the startup. I really need someone like you in that position."

"Oh, that…," Lisa paused for a moment to collect herself.

"Yeah, that. Well, unless you want me to make a different kind of offer…"

"I've never held a VP post, so this would be a huge milestone in my career, and of course, this position comes with an extremely talented founder. I'm excited about the mission and as a user, I see the potential. But I think you need to think bigger."

"What do you mean?"

"This is not a mission for a single company. The data you're relying on is always going to come from multiple services run by trillion dollar corporations. Recommendation and planning techniques will be developed everywhere and you won't be able to compete with all of them. Instead of a one-company-does-it-all strategy, we need to think of how to bring the entire industry together to make this vision a reality."

"You just said 'we', right?"

"I did."

“So you’re saying we need to rethink the entire strategy of this company.”

“There’s a promising future for us all here. It’s definitely a very complex web of players and interests, but the benefit to individual users and communities is huge, so there’s got to be a way to make it work. It’s going to be a fun challenge!”

“I knew you would be the right partner for this! So happy to have you on board. How shall we celebrate?”

“Leave that up to me. I think I have a few ideas…”

13. Conclusions: the Road to AI-enabled Wellbeing

In a presentation she gave in 2020 at Stanford University, in front of some of the movers and shakers in AI, Jennifer Aaker, who we met in Chapter 9, described the state of technology and well-being as follows:

Most technology today is geared toward generating short-run happiness. It has been engineered to give us instant gratification and decrease friction in our lives. It's about eliminating pain points and optimizing convenience. The result is click bait rather than substance; life hacks rather than holistic solutions; echo-chambers that generate radicalism rather than understanding. And companies that seek to "delight" their customers rather than challenge or improve them. And we are more susceptible than ever to short-term design serving up a stream of addictive content. Like junk food, technology serves up a sugar rush but fails to nourish us.

The goal of this book is to ensure that in a few years from now, the problems that Jennifer speaks about will be mostly in the rear-view mirror. We believe that the path to a better life with AI requires that we consider a new dimension, the holistic dimension, to the discussion of responsible development of technology. When AI experts speak of developing responsible technology, they usually refer to issues such as harms caused by social networks, ensuring that the technology works equally well for people from all walks of life, that we end the so-called race to the bottom of the brain stem to capture users' attention, and ensuring that AI systems align with our human values. As we discussed in detail in earlier chapters, all of these topics are crucial issues. However, another dimension of responsibility is that we consider the holistic view of one's well-being, rather than ending up with a reckless bazaar of well-being apps that do not communicate with each other, ultimately leaving our well-being by the wayside.

We proposed an operating system for well-being, Oswell, a set of organizing principles for building an ecosystem of well-being applications. The principles are inspired by the concept of the modern computer's operating system in that they establish a set of components and mechanisms that each of the apps can leverage and contribute to. The foundational Experiences component of Oswell is a lifelog that captures as much information about you as you're willing to share with an AI system - your past experiences, preferences, and aspirations for the future. Even just that basic component can already improve the benefit you obtain with technology because apps can share critical information between them, again, only in ways that you permit. So now your movie recommender will know which books you read, your sleep monitor and diet consultant will know that you are on a plane and will be out of the country for the next few days, and both of them know that you are working on a big deadline at work for the next two weeks so they should back off a bit.

The ability to access a holistic view of your information also allows the features of the Attention component of Oswell, which include systems for making better recommendations and for helping you plan some of the details of your life. The more information these systems have, the better they can serve you. As a result, your attention will be focused on the most important things in your life at any given moment, and you will not have to ruminate about minutiae that distract you from what is most important.

The Connections component of Oswell plays a critical role in your life by helping you manage the important relationships in your life, communicate better in these relationships, nurture the ones that need it most, and let go of the ones whose time has possibly passed. This component will help you gain more value from your interactions on social media, reduce the harms that these platforms may be causing you, and perhaps help you with your most intimate relationships.

As an operating system, Oswell can be used in a variety of ways. At one end of the spectrum, the components of Oswell can simply power individual apps to do a better job. At the other end of the spectrum, the one we believe the world is headed to, you have a dedicated AI partner that considers the holistic view of your well-being and is aligned with your values and preferences.

Such AI partners will undoubtedly contribute to our normal daily lives. However, they will be even more critical when our life is not so normal. When we move to a new city, start a new job, move in with a new (human) partner, or welcome a baby into our lives, our daily routines change drastically. When we are recovering from loss of a loved one or from a significant setback in our lives, we need additional support. When we are ill, either temporarily or because we are growing old and do not have the mental faculties we used to enjoy, our AI partner can fill some of the gaps. Because of the newness of all of these situations, we cannot necessarily rely on the familiarity and the habits we had before, and the AI should be able to step in.

As we have touched upon throughout the book, access to an AI partner leads to some fundamental questions about what it means to be a human and about how to design a healthy human-machine symbiosis. How much agency do we want or need over our life? How efficient do we really want to be, or do we actually need to waste time every now and then? How often should we make our own mistakes even when we have access to a machine that is capable of helping us avoid them? One of guiding principles is that we should let humans be human, including the myriad of faults we possess. However, we should have the prerogative to get some better advice from technology when possible. Undoubtedly, the question of what it means to be uniquely human in the age of AI will be a topic of fascinating change and debate.

Perhaps the biggest risk humanity faces when using technology is what the author and journalist Nicholas Carr calls "automation complacency". As we obtain new and useful technologies, we come to rely on them, often without regard to their shortcomings. In some cases, we transform our role from participants in our environment to mere observers. In his book, "The Glass Cage", Carr describes how digital complacency has affected professions ranging from airplane pilots to architects. In the case of pilots, there have been cases where complacency has led to aviation accidents, but beyond that, it has also led to the loss of allure of the profession. Instead of being a profession that requires a high level of skill, it has become one where the role of a pilot is merely to feed the computer the right data so it can make the important decisions. In the case of architects, Carr argues that while it's easier to efficiently design structures, this may result in a loss of creativity.

A further risk of automation complacency is that technology sometimes removes us from the rich environment we are in. Consider the job of a photographer. In the old days of film, photographers had to meticulously take in the different aspects of their scene and compose their photos carefully as they were taking them. With digital photography, on the other hand, they can easily simply snap thousands of shots of a scene and then edit them after the fact in the comfort of their living room, detached from the scene they were working so hard to capture. This is not necessarily an argument to go back to film, but more of a call to think carefully about how we relate to technology and whether it is distracting us from the real experiences we want in life. In the case of well-being, we need to ensure that we really enjoy our experiences, not just record them digitally. And when it comes to relationships, we need to develop the skills that are required to build and maintain healthy and nurturing relationships. In other words, we need to be present, not just our AIs.

As we've acknowledged throughout the book, there are quite a few hurdles to overcome to reach the vision of an AI partner. Some of them are technical and can be overcome with enough focus. Other challenges relate to privacy and the comfort people will feel with sharing so much data about themselves with an AI partner. Other challenges have to do with the fact that currently our data is siloed in multiple stores, and companies don't have a clear incentive to share across boundaries.

We're already seeing creative solutions to the above problems that involve explicit user consent to share data with third parties. User-centered legislation, such as the European Data Markets Act, may ultimately help grease the wheels of data sharing. However, we believe that the main impetus that will drive the adoption of the ideas underlying Oswell is that it will unleash a completely new wave of innovation. That wave, in turn, will benefit companies big and small, including some that have yet to be formed. When innovation happens, it typically drives up demand for the services that these companies provide, be it search, cloud services, shopping, much more effective targeted advertising, or shiny new devices.

A useful analogy to our current situation is the explosion of innovation that followed the invention of the World-Wide Web and modern browsers in the 1990s. All of a sudden, we had a uniform way of accessing any web site anywhere in the world. Contrast that to the situation that preceded the web, where there were a number of rather obtuse protocols to access resources on the network. These resources had only very specialized kinds of information and very few people were aware of them or took advantage of them. In contrast, the HTML specification was simple for anyone to follow, and enabled a broad set of innovators to create web sites exposing an unprecedented amount of useful information to the world.

Imagine what will happen when there is a simple protocol for accessing information about you when you provide consent. It will be easy to use because that protocol is natural language and is therefore understood by anyone anywhere. Moreover, the protocol is secure because you only share the data that is relevant at the moment and only with whomever you want. You can now imagine applications developed that give you much better advice on what to eat, order from a menu that you don't understand, exercise, topics you may want to learn about, advice on your physical and mental health, and the list goes on and on. And as envisioned in Oswell and by others, all of this advice may come to you from one AI partner that mediates between you and all the specialists, and has your well-being and values top-most on its mind.

To conclude, the impetus for building personal AI agents is only going to grow. New technology such as smart glasses and smart clothing will collect much more data about us and we will find many new ways of leveraging that data for our benefit. As technology takes care of more of our basic needs, there is going to be higher demand, go up a notch and consider our mental, spiritual and social needs. The world-wide epidemic of loneliness and searching for deeper meaning in our lives will continue to beg for solutions that are at least partially aided by technology. This is not a call for people to spend more time with technology. We call for a world in which we delegate to computers the tasks in which they are superior to us, such as remembering details, finding patterns in streams of data, and combing through a myriad of options when faced with complex problems. If computers can do that for us, then we can spend more of our time on what is uniquely human.

Try This 👉

Now that you've finished the book, we can try an exercise that combines some of the themes in the book. Choose a goal that you have for sometime in the not too distant future and imagine how AI can help with it. In doing so, reflect on areas where AI can excel, areas where humans (your friends, colleagues) provide unique value, and areas where there is room for healthy competition between your humans and AI. When you think about these areas, take into consideration the information that is needed to help you with the problem – is it information about you? Information about the world that can be found on the Web? Or maybe it is information that is only in the heads of experts or people very close to the situation. Are you going to need to collect and record more information as you go about solving the problem? Try to confirm your hypotheses by posing these questions to both humans and to AI. Keep an open mind – both AI and humans can surprise you. What insights do you draw from this exercise about the possible role of an AI partner in your life?

Acknowledgments

I've been fortunate to be surrounded by many colleagues and friends who contributed to the writing of this book.

First, I'd like to thank Arianna Yuan who through many discussions inspired me to write this book and to shape its basic ideas. If any of the references to ideas from psychology in this book sound convincing, it is most likely thanks to Arianna.

Dawn Song also spent many hours discussing the book and encouraged me to think beyond well-being to a more general idea of building an AI partner.

I'd like to thank Jennifer Aaker, whose influence on the book can be seen in many places, but particularly in Chapters 9 and 13. Jennifer, who pioneered a course on well-being and technology and therefore at Stanford, spent a lot of time thinking about the topics discussed in this book. She was generous in providing many useful references and connections, great advice on book writing in general, and thought provoking questions on how to use the material in the book to challenge students.

I'm grateful to Kate Devlin for her generous time walking me through the material that led to Chapter 11.

Matt Abrahams, the expert on communication and a successful author, provided many important pieces of advice throughout the process of writing the book. This advice helped me sharpen the points of the book and the exposition of the material.

The book builds upon some of the works that I've done at multiple companies in the last decade. The journey started at Megagon Labs, where I collaborated with Ko Ishiyama, Vivian Li, Wang-Chiew Tan, Yuliang Li and Adi Zief-Balteriski. At Meta, I first plunged into the world of protecting users from harms on social networks, where I learned a lot from Patrick Pantel, Umut Ozertem, Fabrizio Silverstri, Hao Ma, Lambert Mathias and Cristian Canton. Later, I led a team that built the first version of a lifelog. There I collaborated with Yuliang Li, Jane Yu, Wang-Chiew Tan, Marzieh Saeidi, Lambert Mathias and Richard Newcombe. The team I co-led on understanding human values and how they are manifested in recommendation systems was fascinating. Chloé Bakalar and Andrea Wong taught me almost everything I know about human values. David Vickrey and Anneke Buffone helped me connect the meaning of values to what is actually done at Facebook, and Jonathan Stray, with his vast network and ability to herd academics, ensured that the work ultimately saw the light of day. During my time at Meta, Joelle Pineau and Joaquin Quiñonero Candela provided incredibly useful advice for which I am very thankful.

Several of my friends and colleagues gave me excellent feedback on the writing and ideas in the book. I especially thank Ron Folman for an extremely careful read of the draft and many stimulating discussions. I benefited hugely from a careful reading of the book by Partha Ranganatan. Zack Ives and Jiani Zhang provided useful comments on the book.

Last, but obviously not least, I would like to thank my wife Ylva for patiently discussing different aspects of this book whenever I needed an ear. Ylva is also the best well-being consultant I can imagine, and always reminds me that the best advice technology can provide is to leave all one's devices behind and just be. I'm sure you noticed her sage advice throughout the book.

Made in the USA
Monee, IL
03 November 2026

67383303R00144